ROGER STEVENSON
JANUARY, 1993

Up the
Financial
Ladder

UP THE FINANCIAL LADDER

in a downwardly mobile society

DALLAS WHITNEY

THE OVERLOOK PRESS

WOODSTOCK · NEW YORK

First published in 1984 by

The Overlook Press
Lewis Hollow Road
Woodstock, New York 12498

Library of Congress Cataloging in Publication Data

Whitney, Dallas C.
Up the financial ladder in a downwardly mobile society.

Includes index.
1. Finance, Personal. I. Title.
HG179.W525   1984   332.024   83-43154
ISBN 0-87951-953-3

BOOK DESIGN BY BERNARD SCHLEIFER

Dedicated to my dear wife, Joan,
whose support and love
made this book possible.

Contents

Introduction

WHAT MAKES MOST financially successful people different? This is probably the most difficult question ever to face financial writers and advisers. Even defining the "financially successful" is difficult, but we can say that they are individuals who are able to control their finances, are able to plan what they will do with their money and do it, are able to understand the opportunities for investing, and use those opportunities to best advantage. Financially successful people are not necessarily rich, but they are always on the way up. This book tells how to join and excel in that group.

Because we all differ in the amount of money we have and the way we handle it, "formula" advice is often worse than none at all, and there is little of that in this book. Instead, each chapter provides the information most people need to round out their own knowledge and to make their own *next* financial decision. It's meant to help you climb to the next rung in your journey up the financial ladder, no matter where you are now.

Throughout years of researching and writing about personal finances for a variety of magazines, I have seen a myriad of changes in the economy and the laws that affect our economic system, but the average person's interest in money management never seems to flag. Finding answers to such questions as, "How can I improve my investments?" "How can I control my money instead of it controlling me?" and "What should I do to ensure a comfortable retirement?" is so important to each individual and family that there is always a need for a guide which can promise the reader a shortcut to financial wisdom. Too often, however, the information we find is so confusing and so biased as to do us no good. *The premise of this book is that you and only you are the one who can decide how to manage your money.*

Before we develop our personal sophistication in money management, we are often forced to sort through mountains of information, avalanches of advertisements, and oceans of paperwork. We're told what we should do by people who don't know our needs, haven't a notion of how we feel, and certainly don't know what our financial troubles are. A seemingly overwhelming task is made even more difficult.

In this book, no assumptions are made about the reader, except that you are expected to be interested and serious. Instead of telling you which bank accounts to open, for instance, the chapter on Banks and Bankers tells you how to judge for yourself which account will serve you best, and also how to get the most service out of your banker, perhaps even more than you realized was possible. The other chapters explain how financially successful people handle their money, relay the distilled advice of hundreds of experts, and lay out ways which you can adapt to a personal financial plan that makes sense for *you*.

The strategy for each chapter is a problem-solving approach which most businesses use, and which is a hallmark of successfully revised financial plans. The steps are as follows:

1. Define your problem
2. Define your goals
   immediate
   short-term
   long-term
3. Devise a workable approach
4. Get support
5. Check your progress
6. Revise your plans

Proof of the validity of this approach is obvious: People who are successful with their finances know what they are doing and they know why they do what they do. Finding out what you need to know is getting easier and easier, while the financial world is getting more and more complicated. When you apply a method to new financial plans, you are much more likely to succeed than the vast majority of Americans out there who are floundering, unsure of what to do next.

Perhaps the most difficult thing about becoming financial-ladder climbers is changing or expanding the way we think about money. Somehow, old habits die hard, even when they are damaging, and developing new habits is psychologically hard. You learned what you already know about managing your wealth, which is probably a lot, and without a doubt, you can improve upon that knowledge with not too great an effort.

One way of finding out what financial winners have in common is to ask those who deal with them every day. I make my living interviewing and talking with bankers, brokers, financiers, and all manner of monetary-service businesspeople, and they frequently cite characteristics of "the ladder climbers." These financial experts repeatedly describe the winners this way:

• They are good listeners and learners
• They are good investigators

- They make decisions for *themselves*
- They are realistic about their finances, and *themselves*
- They are stubborn about succeeding
- They are not deterred by setbacks

A few other characteristics that stand out—they develop credit histories so that when they need to borrow, as we all do at some stage, they are able to get as much as they need, and get good advice to go with it. If they are paid to work eight hours, they work nine or ten. If they are expected to work ten hours, they work eleven or twelve, or they study on the side. When they work for someone, they make their superior's job easier by taking on responsibility that they can make good on. In other words, they get ahead by doing more than the next guy.

If you can identify some of the areas you need to work on, so much the better. If not, you can copy successful money managers in another way, and that is to ask for advice wherever you need it. Perhaps someone close to you can help you identify your personal problem areas and strong points. If not, there are professional counselors, from job and career counselors to personal money managers and analysts, to portfolio managers and investment advisers who can tell you what you have been doing with your finances. With these self-concepts in tow, you are better prepared to avoid bad habits and make better decisions than you would have made yesterday.

A convention of psychologists met in 1980 to discuss why some people succeed in business and others do not. One of their conclusions was that people who win in the business world are simply those who win in life, including life's financial battles. They came up with these suggestions for those of us who want to become winners:

- Be assertive—in a responsible way
- Think bigger—than you did yesterday; be reasonable
- Take risks—that you can afford and yield real rewards
- Set things up—things don't happen unless you do
- Do it right—if you give 50 percent, may as well give 50 percent more
- Learn from mistakes—but don't quit

In every financial goal, these rules apply. You may be more aggressive if you are twenty-five years old and at the threshold of a promising career, while you'll likely take more modest risks if you are alone with your nest egg and are about to retire, but the principles apply to us all. Expanding your goals and universe are natural byproducts of personal and financial growth.

Understanding how to gauge *acceptable* risk is the most difficult thing for most of us. We get stuck in the back alleys of our personalities, entrenched in old habits, and caught in old feelings that are no longer valid. Maybe a fear of math, shared by about 75 percent of us, keeps you from balancing your checkbook, or calculating your investment return, or from doing your tax planning in advance of the spring thaw. An adding machine, calculator, or home computer combined with the taste of success may be all you need to overcome your fear of defeat and difficulty.

Maybe you come from a family which revered fiscal conservatism to the point that you panic at the though of any risk at all. Investigating to find out what is *average* risk in mutual funds, *average* risk in stock investments, *average* risk in real estate investments, can allow you to take *less* risk than most others while *increasing* your own level of acceptable risk. On the other end of the scale, confining yourself to those same levels may be the perfect way to tame the overactive gambling urge that sabotages some financial lives. In other words, *knowing* the risk allows you to be realistic about the risks you take.

Setting things up to succeed is very different from merely acting in complete or partial ignorance and then hoping things will turn out all right. Let's say there are 20 million investors in mutual funds. Eighty percent of them pick their funds on the basis of advertisements, availability (their broker has it), or recommendations from friends. If you select your funds instead on the basis of past-performance statistics, outlooks for the industry each fund is heavily invested in, general economic forecasts, and a comparison of the managers who manage the funds, you are going to succeed more often than those 80 percent of your competitors. If you walk into a bank and announce that you need a loan, your odds are very much worse than if you have already introduced yourself to a loan officer, gathered the data he or she will need, have assembled support on your behalf, have a plan for repaying the loan, with contingency plans built in, and pick a time when the bank has lots of money to lend. The same strategy works on a fifty-year retirement plan.

If you are going to take time and effort to put your money in the bank, plunge into an investment, make a career move, you may as well put in enough extra "umph" to make sure you've done all you could, and that you've done it right. No one leaves exactly the same thing out of his or her financial efforts—for some it is research, for others it's the paperwork, yet others are shy about contacting those who might help expedite or explain details. Whatever your personal foible, you can master it once you identify it and create a plan for change.

Throughout this book are checklists of "typical" financial plans that you can apply to analyze and compare against your own circumstances. (Not all elements will apply to your unique needs; every financial plan has some holes in it somewhere.) By going through them, you can find what you need to seal up yours, or you may be able to organize your approach in a new way. At the very least they provide that most important of aids—something to compare yourself against.

The initial task described in each chapter is to question what you are doing. Even if it's working, look for a better way; look for an impending need for change. You may find that you are following the best possible route, and you can leave it intact. If not, you are helping yourself.

You may feel ignorant, or you may even be ignorant, as we all are to a degree, or even if you are very knowledgeable you may find yourself stumped in inaction. Perhaps you know how to study stocks, bonds, mutual funds, IRAs, and banking options, but do nothing. Just one month of action may be all you need to chart a new course and set new habits. Each chapter describes a plan that can be adapted and utilized for any individual's needs. Only you can bring it to reality for yourself.

Repeatedly, the methods I describe are familiar to those in the business world. They are the proven means of good business for individuals as much as they are for corporations. Take a businesslike approach, and if you mean business they will take you another rung higher on the financial ladder.

Some think of success in terms of luck, but the truth is that for the most part it will be your own determination, insight, and hard work that will get you ahead and headed upward. I hope you find the help you need in these pages.

1

Why Do You Need Financial Savvy?

THERE WERE TIMES in American history when financial savvy meant knowing how to handle bank accounts and perhaps how to invest in stocks. Paying the bills and counting the income were the essentials of personal finance. There were two kinds of bank accounts, and brokers spoke of "one-decision stocks" an investor could buy and forget about, confident in rising future value. Today there are a dozen or more types of accounts at every bank, more ways than that to buy and sell stocks, and investing may call for a computer program to figure the odds and variables. Experts tell us that it now costs upwards of a quarter million dollars to raise a child, and by the time we retire, our savings may be worth a pittance. In today's world of fluctuating currencies, legal notes, and moral codes, mastery over money is to one degree or another a measure of our success in society and life and an indication of our security. Possessing financial savvy has become a survival skill.

In America the average family moves every seven years, the average salaried worker changes jobs more often than every five years, and the average bank account can become obsolete within one year. Events move so fast today that we speak of "future shock" and "real time" because our old terms such as "time lag" and "out of date" aren't urgent enough. It's a time when the phrase "as sound as the dollar" has evolved from a worldwide truism to a joke. Until recently the peasantry of France was scorned for hoarding gold; now we find our countrymen emulating them. Perhaps financial knowledge can be therapeutic as well as enriching, but one thing is sure—keeping up with the Jones takes more energy than ever.

The question, once you decide to knuckle down and really learn about money matters is, How do I find what I need to know? You can read the financial sections of the newspapers and the magazines and all the wisdoms and bylaws, for although essential concepts and information will probably eventually bob to the surface, that process, though time-honored, is tedious at best. You can learn from friends, but you're lucky indeed if you meet someone who gives only good advice. You can take classes from experts, which I recommend if you've the inclination. Finally, if you already have some money to spend, you can hire experts to advise you. But even that's not an ideal solution unless you already have a head start, for you need some financial acumen in order to ride herd on your paid counselors. The difficulty is, what is ideal for one person doesn't work at all for the next, and what is appropriate for him is ridiculous for another. What you need is *the* plan that is best for you and your unique needs and preferences—and that's what this book will help you develop.

SET UP YOUR FINANCIAL BASE

Learning the basics of money management and investment need not be hard as many seem to fear. It's certainly not as hard as getting a school-of-hard-knocks education in gold speculation or trading unfamiliar stocks, or other involved investment strategies. You have to learn it the way the experts do—by first setting up your own financial base and then pursuing the opportunities that interest you and that you want to understand.

The idea of a financial base is not a new one, yet it is not often enough applied to personal finance. The Small Business Administration points out that the primary reason 90 percent of all small businesses fail within five years is that they start out with an inadequate financial base. I don't believe in Murphy's Law—"If something can go wrong, it will"—but the truth is that in your personal life, as in business, you must be prepared for a certain amount of bad luck and a number of false starts. Just like the entrepreneur starting out in business, you must have a financial base that will see you through a stumble or two.

Think of the other things that a business needs to succeed and you'll find many of the elements that will help you solidify your personal financial base. Cash reserves are essential, but often tempting to use up, or too well guarded to do any real good when they're needed. Your personal financial sheet needs a compromise somewhere between the two extremes of behavior to be sound and strong and yet meet your needs for growth and safety. If you are tempted to use up your cash reserves on living expenses, make them more difficult to access, say by putting them into an account that can be accessed only every three months. If you feel that you are too conservative and need more income from investments, find a financial counselor who can explain how to put your funds to better use.

Professional advice is another absolute need of both business and individuals. You don't need to retain a lawyer to have one on tap, but you do need one or more you can call upon. The trick is to find the right lawyer for your needs. These are items that the average person could investigate and uncover for himself or herself. But better yet, a smattering of legal advice *beforehand* would have obviated the need for back-tracking in the first place. In other words, even for people with modest means, competent legal service can pay off in cash dividends, just as surely as would a secure cash investment, and you may not even know when you need the assistance.

Accountants are members of one of the few professions in which the practitioners are forced to take part in continuing education (at least CPAs, Certified Public Accountants, are). When your taxes are prepared, your bookkeeper, or the accountant who hired him, had to go to school that year to find out how the tax laws changed over the last twelve months. That all fifty states require such measures is testimony to the complex and mercurial nature of the tax system. Its importance is evident every April 15.

The key point to remember about paying taxes and filling out your tax forms is that the system is dependent upon *your* decisions. Decide what to enter in your 1040 forms and what not to, and decide, subject to the IRS rules, how to report your finances. The accountant's value is determined by how well he or she can advise you to make the choices to best advantage without incurring a penalty from the IRS or an indictment from the justice department. Most tax services send your tax forms through a computer that is programmed to do the most work in the least amount of time. It can't decide to save you money or when to make a value judgment in reporting numbers on a form, but a good accountant can. For most of us, the expense of the proper accountant or tax preparer (even if he is seldom needed) is minor compared to the trouble, time, and, most importantly, dollars that can be saved.

Despite all the time, money, and aggravation they can save us, accountants and lawyers have a poor image in the eyes of many. Here, comparison with the medical professionals is apt. There are specialists in every field. There are miraculously endowed experts and there are incompetents; there are those who charge reasonable fees and there are gougers. Finding the one who is best suited to your needs need not be a problem, and once found, he or she is avaiable for your regular needs and emergencies alike—the times you are in most need and have the least time and objectivity with which to shop and choose. Best of all, today there are more lawyers in more specialties available and working than at any time in history.

Banks are too often viewed as merely service institutions, almost like utility companies. The most important thing to recognize about banks is that they are businesses and that bankers are competitive businessmen. Bankers do now and always have made money by using other people's money to take advantage of the spread in interest rates in different segments of the economy. They must compete with one another and other institutions for available funds, and they do this by offering competitive services and rates. They try to play the market to their advantage, and we, the customers, try to do the same for ourselves. That's us, if we learn how.

As anyone who is in business knows, banks are often very flexible when it comes to arranging deals, and can be either accommodating or intransigent. That is why it is important for anyone with money to know and understand a willing, knowledgeable banker. The idea of a "personal banker" isn't just marketing madness, it's highly desirable from the customer point of view. Having a close relationship with your banker can mean getting extra services, getting prompt service when you have a personal emergency, or even special assistance with major financial arrangements such as loans or legal services. Any way you slice it, knowing your bank and your banker can mean more than extra convenience and faster service—it can really add up to extra income and lower costs. Yet few customers take advantage of what banks offer these days. It does take extra effort, especially in this era of fast change. For nearly everyone, say the experts, the rewards are well worth that effort—and you can take that to the bank!

Each year countless best-selling books advising how to get rich in the stock market are published. Many of them contradict each other, and scant few have proven to be the gold mines their authors claim, but they continue to sell. Almost universally they promote the idea that the common investor can make a fortune by emulating experts who spend every waking hour analyzing the market or if the investor espouses the religious fervor of a particular strategy or approach. Neither works for long, as you know. An approach pushed by the financial advisers of the successful in our nation emphasizes something else—a balanced self-education process in which you master one investment vehicle at a time until you are successful at what you need to do. It's not a shortcut, but it is the most direct route to investment prowess and success. The proof is in the records of the New York and American stock exchanges and the surprisingly brilliant history of the associations of small investors and investment clubs—the smart small investor's success is history.

Instead of scanning all the hot-advice books and struggling to understand every nuance, what if you had someone you could call to ask about all the mechanisms and ploys you hear of? Wouldn't it be great if you could talk with someone who had access to dozens of financial experts and who follows the market closely every day? Most critically, wouldn't it be great to have a personal stockbroker whom you trust explicitly? You say that's what you'd like from your broker, but what you get is pitches to buy stocks that pay high commissions or are destined for the cellar, bad advice on trends, and a cold shoulder when you ask for service or advice that doesn't pay a fast fee? Some combination of these complaints is apparently the common experience, and for good reason.

Most account executives, as they refer to stockbrokers these days, have a career that lasts six months or less. The high turnover means that customers' accounts are too often handled by people with very little experience and little chance for success. Find the seasoned professional who will handle your account in a manner that makes you feel comfortable and confident and you have cut your risk factor considerably. You are also miles ahead of most other investors who are flying on their own or are suffering with revolving-door-type brokers.

As with finding other professionals such as lawyers, accountants, and bankers, the trick in finding a suitable account manager is knowing where to look and in being prepared with the right questions. Also, like other professionals, brokers and agents tend to specialize within their fields, meaning you can shop for people with characteristics that match your particular needs.

If your tastes run to overnight fortunes, you are going to be served best by a broker who studies the volatile end of the market. Or if you hunt around, you can find a good broker who specializes in long-term investments with steady growth. The point is, unless you specifically ask, neither type of broker is going to offer to recommend a more suitable alternative. Somewhere there is a broker who will serve you superbly, but it's up to you to find him or her. Finding the right professional for your needs can be done if you set out knowing what you're after.

Shopping for insurance is a constant, draining task for most of us, one that is made much easier when we can double-check the reputations and claims of companies with someone who is right on top of changes in the industry. For most of us that means a trusted agent with whom we have dealt before, and advice from other professionals on how and when to use insurance to best advantage. It is possible to shop for a certain kind of agent, and to find him. Doing so makes buying and updating insurance easier, more pleasant, and more effective. You can work around an undesirable agent, but it's a shame to do so when it's not necessary. It's possible to tell the good agents from the bad, as long as you know the questions to ask.

In summary, what the professionals can do is advise you on becoming financially secure, avoiding some of the attractive pitfalls, and handling emergencies when they arise. If you are motivated and wise, they can help you make yourself wealthy. It's a combination well worth the price (fees) involved, it's a strategy that pays, and it certainly beats the alternative. Used properly they satisfy the basic equation that defines all financial decisions—they pay back more than they cost, and they cost less than the alternatives.

When you have established a firm financial base from which to operate, the professionals can take on an additional role by providing referrals and contacts. They can advise you how best to attain your goal and can direct you not only to other professionals at the level you need, but also to other sources and services. Professionals may be people, but from a practical point of view they are terrific tools.

ATTAINING FINANCIAL INDEPENDENCE

Beginning with our childhood, most of us are ill prepared to handle personal finance in an adult, sophisticated way. Aside from the fact that we may grow up and graduate from high school and even college, there is no widespread education in finances. A high school may give spot courses in filling out 1040 forms or how to open bank accounts and balance a checkbook, but there is no basic instruction in real-life fianancial-planning skills. For most of us, it is difficult to learn it later on—difficult but possible for almost everyone.

Fear is too often a big obstacle to financial awareness and initiative. Most of the signals in our society tell us that young people should plan on spending all their money, and that learning enough to invest wisely in the stock market or in real estate is beyond most individuals. The truth is, you can be successful at working toward your goals. You may not achieve all your dreams, but odds are you can be very good at a much more sophisticated version of financial management than you are now practicing if you approach it carefully and give it your best try.

THE MOST COMMON FINANCIAL MISTAKES

1. **Working without a set of short- and long-term financial goals.** Lacking a financial plan for the immediate future and a destination for a specific date in the future is akin to a general without a battle plan: You are not going to conquer your own fate, it's going to conquer you. You *can* be the victor!

2. **Waiting until tomorrow—forever.** Procrastination, or waiting until you "feel" ready is different from a planned pause, and the effect is different, too. Wait to take care of your finances and tomorrow *can* turn into forever, financially. Today is the day to act.

3. **Lack of knowledge.** Ignorance is nothing to be ashamed of as long as you recognize it and remedy it when necessary. There is just too much

information and help available to excuse continued ignorance of basic financial skills. Now that picking a bank account can practically require a working understanding of the open money-market, the minimum acceptable level of sophistication is rising. Society is being segregated into those who are up to date and those who are left behind, so take your pick.

4. Negative thinking. If we prepare ourselves, we are all capable of making responsible financial decisions that work. Many studies have shown that the biggest reason people cite for staying out of financial markets and products that could bring them substantial return is—you guessed it—fear of the unknown.

RATE YOUR FINANCIAL HEALTH

Take a moment to honestly identify yourself and see if you can find some financial options to get closer to your goals.

0   advancing acceptably and under control
1   control and growth acceptable but seek more rapid growth
2   progressing but need tighter control
3   under control but need more growth to meet goals
4   need some improvement in all areas
5   could use more control but desperately need more growth
6   could use more growth but desperately need controls
7   urgently need growth and control

The more points, the more help you need. The options below are the first you should consider. The more points, the more options you should explore:

- Self-educate in financial affairs—courses, etc.
- Establish or tighten personal budget
- Establish net worth and actual financial status
- Hire (or request) financial counselor, manager, etc.
- Expand regular reading and monitoring of financial news and statistics, periodicals, books, etc.
- Document assets, income, and debt in a disclosure form
- Plan all financial moves in one-year financial calendar
- Establish, one-, two-, five-, and ten-year financial goals
- Explore, utilize, and expand in one new investment vehicle this year and at a set interval
- Pursue candid minimal advice from real estate agent, insurance agent, stockbroker, personal banker, credit manager, lawyer, ac-

countant, tax preparer, etc., and establish protection in all those
areas
- Turn over financial management to another in household or seek
regular assistance in planning and record keeping
- Seek our financially successful models to emulate in a reasonable
and careful manner. No matter what you are doing, you are following some model of financial behavior. If you want to lead a different
financial life, you'll have to be a different person, financially.

GROWING MONEY

There is a simple formula for making money grow: It is *seed money*
plus *opportunity* plus *time* plus *work*.

Seed money is your responsibility. You may take it out of your income
and enjoy the rewards. Or if you choose not to, that is also your choice.
Opportunity is what we manipulate together with our management of
time, through work, to build our wealth. Small opportunity and long time
can yield less or more than large opportunity and short time, but neither
can work for you unless you let them.

It pays to decide early on what kind of personality you have to cope
with. If you are nearing retirement age, you are forced by circumstances
to favor a more conservative investment philosophy even if that contra-
dicts your inner nature. If you are young, have expanding earning capacity and few financial burdens, you may do well to examine the rewards of
brave speculation and try to overcome the fear of being hard hit by
occasional poor judgment or worse luck, as long as you temper your
decision-making. Most of us want some degree of security, yet we want to
take part in the opportunity to make our money work for us. Too often,
say the experts, people spend their time vacillating from one position to
the other. Wall Street has a name for the individuals who wobble along
with this kind of approach—they're the odd-lot bunch. The ongoing joke
is that they buy after the market peaks and sell after it bottoms. In other
words, they fall victim to panic buying and selling and poorly thought-out
investing. You must know yourself and make plans accordingly.

WHAT IS FINANCIAL SOPHISTICATION?

Wall Street advisers are fond of pointing out that most investors have
access to nearly the same information most of the winners in the market
use. There is no reason that the small investors shouldn't use the same
principles to guard their investments—except that they don't. If they

aren't knowledgeable enough to make lightning raids, buying and selling with precision parries and thrusts, it is possible to improve odds in more conservative methods such as "dollar-cost averaging" and using second-tier markets. Too often people seem to want to take the shortcut of pure luck, which tilts the odds wildly against them. Sophistication is usually not a matter of insider secrets or membership in the old-boys' club, nor genetically endowed intuition, but rather investigations and homework, alone or in teams.

PROOF THAT THE SMALL GUY CAN BE A WINNER

You might be surprised to find out that investment clubs around the country average a better return on the stock market and money market than do the pension funds and all but a tiny minority of large institutional investors. These clubs are made up mostly of people who have little to invest, and elect to pool their time and knowledge with other folks who want to invest but need and want help in making their decisions. Finding them is as easy as contacting the organizations (see National Association of Investment Clubs and American Association of Individual Investors, page 250) and getting a list of groups in your area. There are even clubs that operate by mail and through home computers. At many clubs, factory workers, housewives, and newlyweds work together with corporate officers and preretirees to broaden everyone's knowledge and enjoyment of the investment world. Finally, clubs are an initiation into money-management success and terrific sources of information and literature! They are proof that the individual can come out on top.

Deciding to educate yourself to move into the financial position you aspire to and doing so are two different tasks entirely. A major argument I get from people who haven't ventured into new money-management techniques is that they think that financial management, especially investment planning, must be very boring. Of course it can be if you let it, but you'll find if you ask around that many of the most interesting people in the world find their personal finances, and the possibilities that exist for making their assets grow, fascinating. As with so many things in life, becoming involved allows you to discover how interesting it can be.

Think of what happened in the gold market. When Americans were not allowed to own gold and the dollar was still tied to a gold standard, there was little popular interest. You had to look hard in the weekly digest reports of *The Wall Street Journal* to find the price on the London bullion market. In hindsight it's easy to see that some smart investors were piling into indirect investments such as gold-mining stocks, and even when the gold standard was dropped and the public was invited to join the barter, the market was coldly distant and of little interest. Politics and war brought bullion buyers into the market in a big way, and soon gold skyrocketed. All at once the topic *became* interesting. And so it can be with many other investment possibilities, and all our financial opportunities, if only we take time to examine them more closely.

YOU HAVE PLENTY OF COMPANY

A couple of years ago, a major military and electronics contracting corporation had trouble competing with other high-technology and air-craft companies in hiring the best workers to fulfill its contracts, so its recruiters looked around for a special incentive to lure prospective employees. Along with health insurance, pension plans, and other side benefits, prospective personnel were treated to a new inducement—ongoing seminars in personal money management and investment strategy. The job quotas filled in record time.

The consultant who headed the seminars found that virtually everyone who was eligible for them attended throughout the series. Many brought their spouses, and a few who couldn't afford baby-sitters brought their children. "It surprised even me," he admitted, "to find out how eager these people are to learn how to improve their money-management skills." As he taught, typists and mechanics sat taking notes side by side with senior managers and vice presidents. The word is out: educate thyself or fall behind.

BE A DECISION-MAKER

All people have choices open to them in their lives, and that includes what to do about their money. Most of them, unfortunately, choose not to make choices. The result is that other people make decisions for them, decisions that are usually not in their best interest, but are in the interest of the small group of decision-makers. But we are all decision-makers if we decide to be.

At the very least, your money should work for you as hard as you worked to get it. That's only fair considering that you put out sweat and anguish for it, and money that is working for you is almost always also earning money for someone else as well, either through commissions or shared income. We often speak about a person's *estate* only when he or she is dead, or in terms of the object of a living trust and its concomitant "living estate." But the truth is that we all have estates, even if they are as small as $100. The idea that you have to die to have an estate is ludicrous—the only way that can happen is if you die penniless with a paid-up life insurance policy. The law recognizes all your assets as your "estate" while you are living and when you die, and you should recognize this fact while you are living.

THE FINANCIAL CONNECTION

Coordinating the many details that make up even a modest personal financial plan requires a system that is carefully documented. Happily, many of the forms of record keeping also create the framework for careful and effective planning. The structure of the net-worth statement, the personal budget, the investment calendar, and the portfolio summary all save time and annoyance at month's end and tax time, but more importantly, they enable you to handle your finances with the same foresight and cunning that other financially successful people do.

One of the few consistencies among the financially successful is that they know what their finances are and what they are doing with their finances. Spending time reading newspapers that discuss finances, magazines devoted to the subject, and discussing the topic with the people you know who are interested is no guarantee that you'll achieve anything, but it is a way to build a support network around your financial self. This can be very important, especially when you are tempted to let your commitments slide, when you feel overpowered by a run of bad luck in investments, or when you get a bit overconfident just because things are temporarily looking up. Make your finances a regular, important part of your daily life and you'll be rewarded with real accomplishment and not just the pride that goes with it, but also the financial rewards.

2
Your Financial Self-Analysis

THE TRADITIONAL FIRST TASK in a personal financial analysis is to figure out your *net worth*. Your net worth is the amount of cash that could be raised if you liquidated everything you own and paid off all your debts. The financial world generally defines it as "gross assets minus long- and short-term debt." Same thing. It can be either a positive or negative number. The important thing is to get the figures assembled and down on paper, for only when you have done that can you expect to analyze and effectively control your finances and make them work for you.

Along with your net worth, you should assemble records of all the financial instruments that could affect you now or in the future. Financial instruments are any documents or items that have monetary value or that form a contract for monetary value or liability. Stocks, bonds, loans, IOUs, mortgages, and checks are all financial instruments. Others include hidden assets, deeds on jointly owned properties and assets, those which are inherited; also upcoming balloon payments, loans or other debt for which you have co-signed, insurance or direct support for children, the elderly, or other dependents outside the home. In other words, all the deals, obligations, potential debts, and instruments that could bring you or cost you money. Once you begin itemizing them, the list from even the average household becomes impressive to behold. Don't be surprised if this takes some time to accomplish—if this is your first time around, you may be in for some detective work. Once you're sure you have identified and located everything, the next step is to organize and analyze. Then you are in a position to improve your position, put hidden assets to work, perhaps minimize debt, and generally accelerate your ride toward financial independence or wealth.

GATHER YOUR WITS AND YOUR WEALTH

We'll begin with the gathering process here. Later, in Chapter 4, on budgeting, we'll find out how to organize things so that we can put all our assets to work for us effectively while we save time and worry. Our mutual problem is that most people's financial lives are so unique that there is no way I could list all the possible things everyone should look for. So I'm going to present a list of questions that when answered will enable anyone to complete his or her financial-disclosure list. Once through this sample list, you can continue to organize with your own list.

When you're done compiling your list, you'll not only be far more cognizant of what your financial position is and what your goals are and should be, you'll have a prepared financial-disclosure statement ready to show your banker, a prospective business partner, or anyone else who insists upon seeing your financial records. Incidentally, if you go to the expense of hiring a good financial planner who has a record of good performance with others in your financial echelon and with your general financial goals, this is one of the things that he or she will insist on seeing first. Do it for yourself and you'll save a lot of time and trouble later on. Or, if you elect to go it alone indefinitely, you'll know that you are doing what the experts advise.

INVESTIGATING YOUR FINANCIAL SELF

1) *What are all your liquid assets with known cash value?* List them and note their location so that you can verify them later and locate them in an emergency.

Traditional items in this category include bank accounts (minus withdrawal penalties), cash, life insurance cash values, savings bonds, and money in other instantly accessible accounts, such as your brokerage house account or cash-management account. If it is accessible quickly, but not immediately, you can't list it here because it's not liquid enough by convention invented by bankers years ago, so we must have the next category:

2) *What are your investments and other assets, not including real estate or unmarketable securities?* List them and their estimated values along with an estimate of how liquid they are. (Are they accessible in two days, five, six months, two years?) The common eggs in this basket include

stocks, corporate and municipal bonds, commercial debt paper, and other marketable investments.

It is a legacy of the Crash of '29 that assets which cannot be cashed within a business-day hours of an emergency came to be considered illiquid. In more normal times we can consider most assets in this category to be liquid in the practical sense, but we'll differentiate them to conform to the conventions of the financial world at large.

3) *What are your assets, except for real estate and personal possessions, that can be liquidated if given time to take advantage of a fair market price?* The bread and butter entries here are business interests, investment real estate, group investment plans such as limited partnerships, pensions, trust accounts, tax-sheltered investments such as IRAs or Keogh accounts. The list here is really unlimited and may be as varied as any area in personal finance except number 4.

4) *What are all your other assets, excluding real estate?* Here you go with all the things you've accumulated one at a time and now add up to a considerable sum. All that furniture, those treasured collectibles, the cars, the boats (boats?), furs, jewelry, the stereo, cameras, computers, whatever you have of value. It's okay to estimate the value of "things," but record anything that's insured or is a financial instrument according to real value.

5) *What personal real estate do you own or have interest in, excluding limited partnerships listed as investment assets, or other entries?* This means property, land, buildings, etc.

6) *What are all your sources of income?* Salaries of everyone in the household are the obvious ones, as are investment income, taxable and nontaxable interest, profit-sharing plans, dividends, real-estate income, realized capital gains, winnings from any source, and other investment income. If you are inventive, you may have some unique entries here.

If you have been honest and successful you should have a complete list of your gross worth. Were you to show it to a financial analyst who planned to help you achieve your personal financial goals, this set of lists, together with your future ingenuity and earning power, would be the foundation upon which he or she would advise you to build your financial future. The potential you have, barring extraordinary income changes or a sudden inheritance, lies in what you have now and what you do with it.

The lists you compiled so far are the "plus side" of your finances, the raw materials, together with your increases in income and cleverness, which you have to attain your personal goals. Clearly, the other side of the books—your expenses—are just as important to your plans. To reconcile your income and outgo and to plan for the future, you must have a record of what's going on. Here's a sample of what your balance sheet might look like:

YOUR PERSONAL BALANCE SHEET

A personal balance sheet differs from a personal statement of net worth in that it deals only with the cash-flow segment of your finances. At this point, the two categories of information we are interested in are (1) your discretionary income, and (2), a comparison between your expenses and incomes over a span of several years.

	Last Year	This Year	Next Year	Etc.
Income				
Earned (work) (after tax)	____	____	____	____
Social Security (plus other entitlements)	____	____	____	____
Pensions (personal and group)	____	____	____	____
Profit sharing and other job benefits	____	____	____	____
Savings	____	____	____	____
Investment (interest, dividends, & capital gains)	____	____	____	____
Annuities, etc.	____	____	____	____
Other sources (including large gifts)	____	____	____	____
Totals	____	____	____	____
Expenses				
Household	____	____	____	____
Housing	____	____	____	____
Transportation	____	____	____	____
Recreation	____	____	____	____
Insurance	____	____	____	____
Debt maintenance	____	____	____	____
Taxes	____	____	____	____
Others	____	____	____	____
Totals	____	____	____	____
Total income minus Total expenses equals: Discretionary income	____	____	____	____

A Note About Discretionary Income

Your discretionary income entry is meaningless unless you have an idea of what it could be, what it should be, and whether you are satisfied with it. It's not so unusual for discretionary income to turn out to be a negative figure, too. Do you have plans for increasing your income in some area? If so, let's define those plans:

INCOME EXPECTATIONS

Source as above	Current Income/Yr	Changes Planned/Date	Expected New Income Next Yr	Expected Income/Date
———	———	———	———	———
———	———	———	———	———
———	———	———	———	———
———	———	———	———	———

Fill the form out for all your current and planned sources of income and you will have done more than project your taxes, you will have revealed your expectations for your job or career, your investments, indeed, the most important parts of your financial plans and expectations. Can you expect a raise at the job? Are your investments paying off? Will you have a major capital income coming up which might cause tax problems or open up some opportunities? All these bits of information impinge upon how you plan the next financial year, and the best way by far to define and organize them is to write them down.

If you are planning to upgrade your lifestyle, you must define from where the new income will derive. If your expectations of salary increases are inflated, sometimes the process of committing ink to paper will reveal a mental boast, a white lie, or a misunderstanding. Maintaining a higher lifestyle through debt maintenance can be a prudent plan for the upwardly mobile person with ambitious plans, but this kind of risk assumption requires more than a confident attitude. It demands careful record keeping and regular analysis of income and expenses to make sure that the cost of credit doesn't overpower the improved income potential. Comparing the bank account balances at tax time isn't an adequate method, but preparing your financial records as we're doing here is an excellent start.

TO MAKE DECISIONS, YOU MUST HAVE
THE FACTS AT HAND

Done carefully, and perhaps for more than the three years suggested here, these exercises permit you to analyze trends in your income. Sometimes an annual raise is spent before it arrives, canceled out by a foundering investment, the effects of inflation, or a miscalculation. If your income is on a steady rise in all areas, you may bolster your own confidence, or realize that your investments, as one example, may be a smaller part of the total picture than you had imagined. Regardless of your plans in life, an analysis of your income can only help you plan more efficiently.

THE AMERICAN GOAL

The more-or-less universal American goal is to live a better lifestyle and retire in comfort. Although the age at which we retire and the definitions of comfort are changing with the times, it is a goal that is pretty much forced upon us by history and our economic and governmental system. Anyone who doesn't have ample resources by retirement age must depend upon the goodwill of relatives or the government for a living. Despite the steady swing toward socialized economics, it is impossible to exist alone or as a couple with any combination of Social Security and welfare in any condition other than absolute poverty. All of us have to set our sights somewhere above that level—the question is, How much is enough for *me* to live comfortably and to retire on?

If you plan to use your net wealth to build an investment program, invest in a business, or otherwise expand your financial options, this is the very first worksheet you'll need. Once set up and compiled, it can serve as a consolidated record of what you own and are due.

Only you can answer the question of what is a realistic and satisfying goal for yourself. The limitations are the same as the tools of opportunity: the number of years until you plan to retire, the assets in your lists, and your ambitions. If you are satisfied with your present standard of living and hope to retire with that same comfort, here's the basic formula for figuring out what your financial needs will be:

Let's say you are fifty-five, you plan to retire at sixty-five, and you anticipate inflation will remain at 10 percent or more through the years. Retiring means not working, so we take your net income from all the sources except salary and job benefits, add potential income from all the rest of your assets minus your total debt, and this must provide you with

260 percent of your current total income if you want to have an equivalent income. (This is merely to compensate for the effects of inflation up until the start of your retirement ten years hence.) If you are average, however, your living expenses will be less at retirement and you will need just 60 percent of the equivalent of your current income (260 × .60 = 156 percent of your current income) to maintain the same standard of living you now have.

If it doesn't look like it will work out that way, something has to give, and you'll have to decide what, but at least you'll be able to figure this out with your new lists. Age fifty-five is a bit late to begin figuring all this out, but it sure beats doing it at sixty-five, when all your options are that much closer to running out.

If you have twenty years to go until you retire and inflation remains at 5 or 6 percent, you will need no more than the same 156 percent of your current income to maintain your present style of living, but on the other hand, you have twenty years to figure out how big a retirement nest egg you will need, supposing that your expectations about inflation are correct. The rule of thumb that planners use is to multiply your net worth times the rate of expected inflation and the number of years left until retirement and compare that with the prevailing interest rate (what your money can be expected to yield as income each year).

FIGURING RETIREMENT INCOME NEEDS

Investible funds × inflation × years to retirement + rest of net worth = *minimum nest egg at retirement.*

(actual formula is investible funds × (infl. rate + 1) and repeat for every year until retirement, then add the rest of NW)

Example: Given an investible fund of $100,000, an expected inflation rate of 5 percent, and ten years to retirement:

formula = 100,000 + (5% +1) and sum ten times
end of year one—100,000 × 1.05 = 105,000
end of year two—105,000 × 1.05 = 110,250
end of year three—110,250 = 115,760
.
.
.
end of year ten—155,140 × 1.05 = 162,900 = minimum nest egg

(Add rest of net worth, such as home value, etc., if you plan to sell it at retirement.)

Expected nest egg × expected interest rate + Social Security, pension and other income = *minimum retirement income*.

Example: $162,900 (expected nest egg) × .08 (expected available interest rate of 8 percent) + $2500 (Social Security estimated from published tables) + $1000 (we'll hypothesize no pension but $1000 income from a family trust)

$$\begin{array}{rl} \$162,900 \times .08 = & \$13,032 \\ + & 2,500 \\ + & 1,000 \\ \hline & \$16,532 \quad = \textit{minimum retirement income/mo.} \end{array}$$

To find your estimated *needed income* at retirement, take your *desired retirement income*, above, and multiply by the number in the table below that fits the number of years to your retirement and your expectation of inflation.

Example: Assume a desired income in today's dollars of $45,000. In order to maintain an equal retirement lifestyle, you need only 60 percent of the amount, so desired retirement income =
$45,000 × .60 = $27,000 in today's dollars
Assuming ten years to retirement, and expected 8 percent average inflation rate, the multiplier = 2.16
$27,000 × 2.16 = $58,320
$58,320 = *estimated needed income at start of retirement*
Estimate your likely lifespan and calculate what you'll need toward the *end* of your retirement years.

Needed retirement income (as in the 260 percent example on pages 32–33) − minimum retirement income = the amount of income you will lack, your *"income gap."* (If you obtain a negative number, then that means you already have enough wealth to support your desired lifestyle! You have a *retirement cushion*.)

Example: Assume a needed retirement income (as above) of $58,320 and a minimum expected income of $16,537.

$$\begin{array}{r} \$58,320 \\ -\ 16,537 \\ \hline \$41,783 = \text{expected retirement } \textit{income gap} \end{array}$$

EFFECTS OF INFLATION UPON RETIREMENT INCOME NEEDS

Expected rates of inflation

Years to retirement	5%	6%	8%	10%	12%	15%
5	1.28	1.34	1.47	1.61	1.76	2.0
10	1.63	1.79	2.16	2.59	3.11	4.04
15	2.08	2.4	3.17	4.17	5.47	8.14
20	2.65	3.21	4.66	6.73	9.65	16.37
25	3.39	4.29	6.85	10.83	17.0	32.91
30	4.32	5.74	10.06	17.45	29.96	66.22
35	5.52	7.69	14.78	28.1	52.8	133.18
40	7.04	10.29	21.72	45.26	93.05	267.86

Instructions: Select the rate of inflation you guess will prevail over the coming years. Then move down that column until you are even with approximately the number of years until your retirement. The number at the intersection represents approximately how many dollars will be needed to have one dollar of buying power in today's dollars.

Conclusion: Obviously this individual's expectations are out of line with attainable goals. In order to make up the income gap, he/she would have to use up all available capital, which is not acceptable, or obtain enough wealth within the next ten years to generate that amount (given an estimated 8 percent available interest rate, it would require $522,000 of additional nest egg, a figure probably unattainable for this individual). He/she has made a valuable discovery and has ten years to redefine retirement goals and to prepare his/her finances.

Unless you are very comfortable with numbers, you may find the whole process terribly involved, for we haven't even discussed any of the complications or intricacies other than inflation, and there are many more. The overall complexity is what the professional financial counselors and planners cite as the very reason people need to plan carefully, organize regularly, and assess their finances carefully and methodically. If you don't keep track of things, the finances can easily get away from you without your finding out until it's too late.

If your goals are more lofty than a comfy retirement, the analytical process is generally the same, but the final figures and the figure of what you'll need to accomplish in the intervening years will obviously be proportionally higher. The idea is to go through the exercise so that you have a realistic idea of what's going on. You may decide that your business plans haven't been ambitious enough, or you may decide that the added effort isn't going to be worth the final dividend and you will want to revise your plans and goals. The idea is to have realistic understanding years ahead, while there is still time to effect changes, rather than to fly by the seat of your pants, hoping for the best and awakening to a rude reality when your earning years are waning.

PLANNING FOR THE WORST CASE POSSIBLE

A major consideration in figuring your retirement needs is that you will obviously be able to spend your capital as well as your income as you near the end of your worldly career. For many that is an uncomfortable thought, for it presumes that we'll be able to predict approximately when we'll die. Clairvoyant I am not, and neither is anyone else, I'll wager, so unless you have an insider's tip, say from your cardiologist or oncologist, spending your capital must be planned very carefully.

Consider the case of two neighbors of mine who miscalculated rather badly. They amassed a personal fortune large enough to allow them to own three pieces of city property, a fine home in a prestigious part of town, and a comfortable monetary reserve as well. They anticipated living in comfort well into their seventies—considered a ripe old age in the 1950s. And they did. But about then, a heart condition for him and diabetes for her began consuming more dollars than the health insurance designed twenty years previously and Medicare combined could compensate for. A couple of costly operations and convalescent centers later, their properties were all gone and they had given up their fancy home for a tiny duplex that was more practical and allowed them some income, which they now needed. By the time they elected to move into a retirement home *in their mid-nineties*, it required the very last of their assets—the sale of their duplex—to pay the bills. When they both passed on, their rather tidy fortune was on the verge of running out.

YOUTH IS NO EXCUSE

If you are twenty-five to thirty and plan to retire at age sixty-five, historical evidence shows that you must begin setting aside about 15 percent of your gross income per year, every year (and obtain yields equal to the average interest rate) in order to retire at the same level of comfort and security that you will want to attain in your preretirement years (forty to fifty-five), when most people set their enduring habits. That's right, I said start preparing for retirement at age twenty-five! And why not? Financial independence is a long-term aspiration. In truth, it is what comes after a life of financial success and prudent planning. The problem is setting aside 15 percent when times are hard and money scarce. Sadly, the alternatives may be to trust in the government (Social Security), the future (hope that you'll get rich), or lower your standard of living (by this route the average Japanese family banks 20 percent of its gross income primarily for retirement).

WHEN THE FACTS ARE ASSEMBLED, ANALYZE

Once the client's records of income and assets are assembled, the financial planner moves on to the potentially embarrassing, more painful side of life—one's liabilities. It goes by many names, "expenses," "obligations," and many more, but the important thing is how liabilities apply against your assets.

HOWEVER DIFFICULT IT MAY BE, TELL THE TRUTH

1) *What are you and your dependents' ordinary living expenses?* The first step in figuring all that out is listing and analyzing the "minus side," no matter what your financial situation.

2) *What are all your interest expenses?* All mortgages, bank loans, consumer loans, insurance policy loans, private loans, the credit card payments and the finance company obligations—they all belong here. Painful though the list is to compile, this is the second thing a financial planner would insist upon seeing before counseling you on how to best pursue your financial goals.

3) *What are all your insurance premiums?* Health, life, property and casualty, specialty coverage—they are fixed expenses that change frequently as the priorities and risks in your life change. Later, in the chapter on insurance and agents, I'll discuss why the experts say it is vital that we keep our insurance up to date, and what disasters can befall those who don't. And I'll discuss those who don't need to bother with the expense of insurance.

4) *What are the gifts you bestow?* The average financial planner will probably ask you about tax-deductible charitable contributions, as a few of us do make major outlays in that direction as a tax-reduction measure in most cases. But, as the folks at Consumer Credit Counsellors point out, the biggest contributions many of us make are not charitable and they certainly are not tax-deductible. They are the cash to bail cousin Fred out of bankruptcy, to keep Grandma in groceries, to keep Junior in college because living expenses are suddenly 25 percent higher than the budget allowed for, and so on. Count yourself as lucky if this category isn't big enough to enter, for this is often a major expense.

5) *What are your total taxes?* Federal and state income, Social Security, property, and still other taxes are what make the government run. Isn't it curious that the federal budget lists several hundred sources of income, including competing segments of the federal government? It's the approximate equivalent of a father paying his child an allowance and then entering the amount as income on his tax forms. There is one ultimate source of US revenue, and we are it.

6) *What amount do you set aside as new discretionary investment/ savings additions?* Many planners list this as an asset, on the other side of the balance sheet, but this is a mistake. In order for your budget and planning to work, it must appear on both the assets and liabilities sides or else you risk fooling yourself into thinking that the money "just appears" when you are balancing your books. If you tried that with your taxes, the IRS would never stand for it, and neither should you. This is the category that usually separates the winners from the losers in financial games. In basic terms, the winners give this category high priority, and thereby achieve better rates of return than the losers, who usually don't even acknowledge this listing. If they do, they give it low priority when the funds are distributed at the end of the month. *If you don't do so already, start giving this category high priority, starting this month.* That is what a financial-planning consultant worth his fee would have you do, posthaste.

Although you can go into deeper detail, and you should, the basic summarized list of financial assets and liabilities in your personal financial disclosure statement should fit onto a page or two if you have answered all the questions so far. Just as an investment portfolio manager would ask to see a one-page summary of your financial condition and your investments, so any financial analyst could judge your financial well-being from the two lists we've just compiled. What's important is that you be able to find some meaning, and some solutions, in the information you have worked to assemble. Following the lead of the experts a bit further, we'll find how to improve your own financial-analysis process.

ANALYZING YOUR FINANCIAL POSITION

What we're doing here is going over all your answers to the above questions, evaluating whether or not you are satisfied with the situation, and if not, deciding in what direction you want to go to change things. (Something along the lines of, "I want to lower my monthly bills and increase my investment allowance" is more likely to get you on the road to economic fulfillment.) Later, when we assemble a budget, you can devise specific game plans to achieve your objectives, but for now we just want to identify problem areas and get a general picture of where you want to effect changes first.

The advice of most financial advisers at this point seems to be to *divide your sights into long- and short-term goals.* Long-term goals come first, for you can't devise appropriate short-term goals without them, but short-term goals often force themselves upon you and make their own priorities. *You have to decide what financial goals you want to strive for and weigh them against what you believe is possible and what you are willing to do.* Most of us realize that the psychological constraints that have produced our current financial modus operandi are going to affect the goals and expectations we set down now. If you want to effect a dramatic change, or even just a significant one, you'll have to begin here, in the planning process.

The reason for compiling your financial-disclosure lists before you define your financial goals and expectations is that they give you an solid idea of where you are starting from. Now that you have them in front of you (or soon will, right?), you need to begin defining your financial goals in very specific terms: *long-term, short-term, medium-range policies, priorities, and expectations.* Put these statements down on paper so you can refer back to them when you make future financial decisions.

Even if you are a person of modest means, there is going to be too much for you to remember, much less to keep careful track of mentally—and keeping track of things is what successful money management is all about—that plus being able to put it in the right place at the right time.

SET YOUR PRIORITIES—DOWN ON PAPER!

You have to set your own priorities, but I'll give you mine as an example:

1. My spouse and my children
2. My children's education
3. My business and investments
4. My home
5. My eventual retirement
6. Current standard of living
7. Entertainment and recreation

Your list will be different, but it will give you a guide to refer to, just as a businessman has his organizational chart which reminds him, or even tells him, what the day's priorities are. I have to review my list occasionally (and the list changes occasionally, too, but only slightly) to keep myself on track. In our home, we are willing to take time away from business, and thereby suffer reduced income in order to keep our children in special schools and involved in learning activities that we value. That is a financial decision as well as an esthetic one. A close friend has always kept entertainment and recreation at least in second place. His finances are completely different from mine. He enjoys a more affluent style of living, but he is approaching his forties with hardly a penny socked away toward retirement or, as I prefer to call it, "the emergency fund." What is important is that we are both comfortable with our decisions and our financial states. Perhaps when and if my friend assembles a family his values will undergo a basic change, but for now he is satisfied—and he knows it.

He refuses to buy life insurance, for instance, for he has no dependents and his family will not suffer if it has to go to the expense of his funeral. We've discussed this, and he thinks I'm wise to have insurance. Were the situation reversed, we both would be in sad straits—he from uselessly large premium payments, and me from undue risk that my family could be left in the lurch at the hands of one drunken driver or other deadly hand.

WHAT YOU HAVE —WHAT DOES IT MEAN?

While net worth is the single most vital figure in a personal financial statement, it means little unless it is viewed together with your age, your present and expected earning power, your financial history, and your financial goals. A small net worth means little to a young, aggressive professional with an advanced education and desirable experience in a fast-growing industry. However, for a middle-aged worker with no expectation of advancement at the job, or of an upward career change, and a history of abused credit, squandered savings, and poorly maintained assets, the same net worth could mean real trouble in the years just ahead. Seeing the whole picture is in many ways as important as assembling the parts of the whole, although you can't really do without either.

Every personal financial situation can be dramatically improved, and in almost every case you can make all the decisions that bring about desired changes. Perhaps you will need the assistance of a financial adviser to help you through the process or to help you understand the details, or perhaps you have the initiative and desire to go it alone, but almost certainly if you want to do it, you can.

Evaluating your current financial status in light of your age, goals, and other factors should give you the same thing it gives a financial planner, a bank loan officer, or other expert—a firm idea of whether you are acting in what the financial community considers a responsible way, and whether or not you are advancing toward the goals you have set for yourself. If you aren't sure how to make that evaluation, try looking at the same data the experts look at, and like nearly all of the financial-planner's clients, you will be able to make sense of it. (If you are stymied as to what the data are, work especially diligently with the sample formats at the end of the chapters.)

Speaking of bank loan officers, have you ever noticed all the embarrassing things they ask when you ask them for money? Like "Have you ever failed in business?" or "Are there any suits, judgments, or other legal proceedings active or pending against you?" How about "Have you ever failed to repay or compromised debt?" or "Are any of your assets unavailable for securing debts?" What are these people after, blood? No, they want to know if there are any ghosts in your closet, if you have hidden debt that makes you a poor risk—they want to know who you are financially, which is just what you want to ask yourself.

To realign their finances to fit with new goals or a new way of handling their assets and debts, most financial-planning clients are urged to write out statements specifying their financial goals and the areas in which they are dissatisfied with their past performance, and then specify what steps they think they can take to reorganize their financial-planning process. If you were in charge of evaluating and recommending changes in a business's finances, you would not think of failing to plot things out on paper and producing a written report. Don't settle for anything less for yourself.

SAMPLE FORM

Long-term financial goal _____

How well am I working to attain that? _____

Short-term financial goals _____

How well am I working to attain them? _____

Are short and long-term goals compatible and realistic? _____

Where am I likely to need major changes? _____

What is the next thing I can do to get closer to my goals? _____

FORMS ARE AVAILABLE IF YOU NEED THEM

If you don't want to create your own worksheets, even with the formats I provide in each chapter, a dandy shortcut is to use forms from your financial-service companies. Your bank, S&L, or finance company can provide you with their personal financial statements or financial-disclosure forms. Your banker, broker, or insurance agent can often come up with free financial-planning workbooks that let you list all your assets and liabilities in a prepared format which organizes things for you. Other possible sources included credit-reporting agencies and state consumer affairs offices.

You also have to deal with forms that are standardized to work for everyone but are not just right for anyone. If you have the hardware and the inclination, computerized programs can do the same thing for you, but they suffer from the same drawbacks. Personally I feel that at this stage you want to have records written out on paper so that you can look at them and handle them. There is something about having a physical object to hold and stare at that helps a struggling mind. A problem with computers, especially when you are dealing with a lot of information and new problems, is that you spend too much time moving data on and off the screen. You end up shuffling through superfluous data, and vital data ends up being hidden because you didn't think to punch it up. On the other hand, the feature of automatic calculation can make the monthly or weekly chore of record keeping much easier. Meanwhile, people in general are very good at screening and perusing large quantities of data in written form. If you enjoy it, it can be fun. What works, works for you.

When you begin to see the outline of your new financial plans and goals, you must compare the broad, comprehensive goals with the specific areas of action and control. Income, expenditures, investments, and risk must all be managed in new ways, ways you must somehow define. That means a new area of documentation, namely the nebulous area of intentions. If you commit your thoughts and intentions to paper, you know what they are tomorrow, a week later, a year later. It's not the only way to impose a structure to the decision-making process, but it is the most common and easiest to set up way I know of.

SOME GOOD SUGGESTIONS FOR BAD HABITS

Bad habits have a way of sounding worse when they are written out in plain language—there's no way to ignore the logical conundrums we all devise to uphold our unsupportable prejudices. If you have decreed that you must cut down on spending for dining out, it becomes difficult to rationalize a spur-of-the-moment trip to your favorite nightspot when you know you are going to have to eat crow just as soon as you read what you wrote at the last financial-planning session. Working with another person is another device you can use to enforce your decisions.

You may have noticed how much interest banks take in a business *after* they make a loan. Suddenly they are full of advice on how to maximize the chances for success, efficiency, and competing in the marketplace. They are there protecting their investment by helping the borrower to become stronger and more likely to be able to pay off the debt, and they are keeping the importance of the debt in the forefront of the borrower's consciousness. When a financial planner uses the standard procedures taught by the College for Certified Financial Planning, he or she also sets up follow-up sessions with each client to monitor the progress on a weekly or monthly basis. It follows that if this helps the planner's clients, it will help us to set up and follow our own formal review schedule and process, too.

BUDGETING DOES NOT HURT

When you have decided "who you are, financially" and what your new goals are, you are stuck with the problem of figuring out how to attain those goals in a workable fashion. You need a long-term strategy that you know will be modified as you and the world change, and a short-term strategy. The short-term strategy is your way of handling finances so that you move toward your goal and avoid obstacles and pitfalls. It begins with a simple goal, it requires some ideas of how that goal can be practically approached, and it involves the mechanics of planning before you act. Those mechanics are often called the budgeting process.

In business, budgeting is often considered the necessary evil or the unavoidable and odious task, but it is never shunned as unnecessary or undesirable. In personal finances, as in business, budgeting is a job that no one likes, but there is no substitute. As with balancing the checkbook and filing taxes, it's vital because it works so well. The following chapter details how to approach budgeting in a workable way and how to set up a budget that will work in your individual financial situation. Before we get down to the budgeting process, it may be helpful to you to evaluate one more element in your personal financial plan—the planner (or planners) in charge.

WHO'S IN CHARGE?

Widows and divorcees who spent their lives letting their husbands handle the household finances typically have very little trouble mastering their personal financial affairs after a very short initiation period. Surprised? You shouldn't be. These women were often either urged by their husbands not to bother with financial affairs or just abdicated the responsibility because society made it so easy to do so. This suggests a real truth: In many families the wrong person is in charge of the books, and if it isn't a matter of the wrong person in charge, it may be that more teamwork and broader input would help both in the present and later, when one spouse is left alone.

Moreover, as other members of a family or household are drawn into the planning and maintenance process, the importance and structure of the financial plan is better understood, and, I believe, more effectively applied. It is in many ways similar to large business deals in which corporations find themselves struggling to compete. Obstacles seem insurmountable and necessary change comes hard. Then, when the company joins forces with another firm via a merger or other form of cooperation, the financial solutions suddenly proliferate. Often analysts predict improved performance on that basis alone. And, as in a family, egos are often the major roadblock to constructive change of responsibilities. Just because you have been the person in charge doesn't mean you are necessarily best at it, and even if you are best at calculations or running the show, that doesn't mean you wouldn't profit by encouraging or even insisting upon help and cooperation.

BEING IN CONTROL IS OFTEN AS IMPORTANT AS HAVING THE MONEY

The very process of evaluating your finances can be used as a persuasive tool as well. One example which rushes to mind is that of individuals and families that are having severe credit crises. The credit-reporting industry monitors the process of identifying and dealing with credit abusers very carefully, and the companies and associations seem to agree on the following: Perhaps the most important thing someone with severely overdue credit should do to appease creditors who are breathing down his neck and threatening nasty legal action is to announce that he and his banker are reevaluating his financial situation with the specific aim of reorganizing and rebuilding his ability to repay the debt. To be believable, this must be done under the aegis of a recognized financial consultant, a banker, a credit agency, or some other responsible professional party. This is looked upon as the first believable signal of a new and better outlook for the individual's finances and for the company's outstanding-debt repayment. What a terrific alternative to hiring a lawyer—assuming that you are being sincere, of course.

Naturally this isn't an panacea or a permanent solution to severe financial problems, but when financial basket cases go to credit counselors or reporting agencies, that is the first recommendation they get. The usual response from creditors is to allow a renewed grace period following some verification that the person is trying to reorganize his finances and intends to meet all obligations. After all, the creditors are interested in getting their money back more than in legal revenge for late payment. Again, their response shows how much importance the experts place on this element of financial planning.

Financial records are not mere paperwork, they are also the tools with which we make our financial plans. Like any sound business, Yourself, Inc., needs its financial books readily accessible and in perfect order.

NET-WORTH STATEMENT FORM

Make a list of all the items listed below which you have. You may have to do some hunting or checking to come up with the exact numbers, but when you do, summarize them and put them in order. They'll tell a simple, one-page story about where you are financially right now.

ASSETS

1. Bank accounts
   checking
   savings
   certificates of deposit
   credit union
   money-market accounts
   T-bills
   others
2. Money-market funds
3. Government debt instruments (treasury bills, notes, etc.)
4. Bonds
   corporate
   municipal
5. Annuities and cash value life insurance
6. Mutual funds
   stocks
   bonds
7. Stocks
8. Commodities
9. Real estate
   residential
   vacation
   income
10. Limited partnerships
11. Personal business assets
12. Personal property (other than real estate)
13. Pensions, retirement & other tax-deferred accounts, assets
14. Profit-sharing plans & other noncash incomes

15. Other possibilities:
   Primary residence
   Other residential property
   Income property
   Others _____

   Secured property of other kinds
   Unsecured
   Auto, equipment
   Others _____

LIABILITIES

1. Mortgages and other fixed debt on property
   residences
   income property
   other

2. Commercial loans
   auto
   other secured
   other unsecured

3. Personal debts
   IOUs
   credit cards & other charge accounts
   medical & dental bills outstanding
   credit on personal property (as furniture, etc.)
   loan payments not listed above
   margin accounts
   education or other loans not listed

4. Future debt pending
   (balloon payments due at future dates)

5. All other obligations _____

$$\text{Assets} \quad - \quad \text{Liabilities} \quad = \quad \text{Net Worth}$$

_____ - _____ = _____

LIST OF ALL FINANCIAL INSTRUMENTS

(All legal papers recording financial responsibility pertaining to you)

Bank accounts
Equities (stocks or ownership in businesses)

Held-debt papers (bonds or any debts owed to you)
Debt outstanding papers (what you owe)
Insurance policies
Unrealized incomes (trusts, estates in probate, etc.)

List them, give face value, location and pertinent dates.

FINANCIAL-GOALS WORKSHEET

The financial goals we set need to be specific, and from the outset we need to get an idea of the extent of each goal. These are the broadest parameters that apply to all financial goals, business or personal. After you have filled out a worksheet like the one below for each of your goals, you may want to customize them to include other important data. For instance, if you are planning retirement assets, you may expand the worksheet to include all the ways you are saving and planning, perhaps including savings accounts, IRA or Keogh accounts, insurance, pensions, family assets, and so on.

When you have worksheets for all of your goals, assemble them for future reference and to refer to as you do more financial planning.

FINANCIAL-GOALS WORKSHEET

1. Financial goal   _____
2. Estimated amount needed (total) _____
      (all at once or in increments) _____
3. Date(s) goal is to be met _____
4. Amount currently available for goal _____
5. Additional amount needed (#2 − #4) _____
6. Amount to be available (per mo., yr., etc.) _____
7. Adjust #5 and #6 for est'd inflation _____
8. Goal appears attainable (date) _____
      (or reassess plans)

3

Laying Out the Basics

THE SIMPLEST FORM of personal financial planning is to establish a goal and then to follow the financial actions that will bring you closer to it. All too often those who are frustrated in trying to reach their goals are stumbling over the basics. This is probably inevitable, for the basics of personal finance today are much more involved and complex than was true just a few years ago. In our society, the types of everyday financial activity are so diverse that it becomes difficult to keep track of just what it is we need to achieve financial security and safety.

A financial planner described to me the case of a client who had invested almost half of his assets in a real estate partnership in the hope of making a big profit. Instead, it turned out that the deal was ill-devised and all but about 10 percent of his money was lost outright. As if that weren't bad enough, he was injured and lost his job. Suddenly, he was in big trouble. Not only did he have no income, he had inadequate health insurance, and very high medical bills which promised to wipe out his remaining assets in a short time. His family, he recognized, was unprotected by life insurance, but now that he would have loved to buy some, he could not, for his health was impaired. He needed to borrow money, but his investment adventure made the banks uneasy and unwilling. He would have liked to hire an attorney to pursue the possibility of getting some of his money back, but his was not a case that a lawyer would take on contingency, and his ready assets were already tied up in securing loans to live on and pay his medical bills and living expenses. Finally, desperate, he asked the financial adviser to help him begin again, for he saw that because of one mistake, all he had worked to build was destroyed, and not merely by the collapse of the real estate deal, but also because he had no safety net to fall back upon.

Notice that we did not need to know whether the man lost $5000 or $500,000, or how much he was left with, for because of his lack of planning early on, his predicament would have been the same. People's best hopes for the future are dashed every day simply because they do not count on bad luck, yet bad luck is what befalls us 50 percent of the time.

If you think about it, people who have good luck are those who prepare for likely contingencies as often as they can, so that when misfortune arrives, it can be handled. Instead of becoming an insurmountable problem, it is merely an inconvenience.

THE SETUP

This all goes to illustrate the most important principle in any kind of planning—*If you want things to turn out a certain way, you have to set them up*. You may fail more often than you succeed, but you will succeed more often than those who wait for divine providence to organize their lives.

I have a quote from Armand Hammer which applies to financial success posted on my office wall: "I was asked how I managed to be so lucky as to be so rich. I replied that I seemed to become exceedingly lucky when I put in fourteen hours a day seven days a week. I often hear, and it seems self-evident, that if you want to be twice as successful as you are now, you must to be ready to fail four times as often as you did before, or even more often than that. You know, you can argue with a man who stands still, but why bother? You can't argue with success—it's always new."

So you have to count on stumbling from time to time, or even all the time. To land on your feet each time, you must have a foundation that allows you to avoid economic disaster and to continue on your way toward your goal. The basics that form the foundation for every financial empire are:

1. Career and income planning
2. Cash-management system (bank accounts and a budget)
3. Health, life, and other forms of insurance
4. Legal planning, especially guardianship, wills and estate planning
5. Investment planning

Before you can make financial plans, you must have an idea of where you are going. Vague and generalized goals may reflect what you feel, but effective planning is based upon defined goals. Most people have varied goals at more than one level in their financial picture.

Typical Primary Goals for Newlywed Couple in Their Early Twenties

1. Paying new auto loan
2. Saving for home downpayment

3. Establishing credit history
4. Protecting assets with insurance

Secondary Goals

1. Establishing investment program
2. Saving for two vacations per year
3. Pay for night school

This couple has oriented their goals toward short-term, aggressive, and expanding activities. They need a credit history, one of them needs job training, and they feel they deserve vacations. When they sit down to lay out a budget for themselves and analyze their monthly and annual expenses, they are going to have a clear idea of which areas they want to move more money into and which they feel they can make more sacrifices in. Just as importantly, when they are planning their spring getaway, they are not going to make the mistake of abandoning all other goals to go first class when they can't afford it. All they need do is look back at their stated goals to remind themselves that they rank auto loan payments, regular savings, a good credit history, and regular maintenance of an investment program all *ahead* of vacations, say, in priority.

Typical Primary Goals for Middle-Aged Couple

1. Maintain mortgage and insurance payments
2. Upgrade investment program
3. Increase retirement savings
4. Contribute to children's college expenses

Secondary Goals

1. Increase standard of living
2. Save for world cruise
3. Finance part-time business

This couple's goals are entirely different at all levels, yet are just as conservative and logical as those of the couple in their twenties. What is important to notice is that their goals suggest rather different ways of handling finances. Their investments will likely be less risky, their insurance will be more important to maintain, and more costly, and their retirement will figure in every decision they make. By writing down their goals, agreeing upon them and defining them, these couples have a much better chance of reaching them.

The same process allows anyone, regardless of his or her circumstances and goals, to keep priorities in order and finances under control.

Just as important, it is necessary to make these kinds of decisions before you make a budget, an investment strategy, a savings plan, indeed any major financial decisions. It reinforces the positive effect to write down your goals and organize them.

YOUR *CAREER PLANS*

Career planning is not just a concern for the graduate entering the job market or someone contemplating a midlife job change. Nor is it merely a matter of applied determination, but rather detailed calculation. At the top end of the corporate ladder, company presidents and their peers must know their prospects for employment well, for they average less than five years at a job! For these people, talking to other companies involves not just today's business, but also establishing ties for tomorrow's job change. The principle is important for all of us, even if we expect to keep our present jobs indefinitely.

The people earning six- and seven-figure incomes have another trick that all of us can emulate and benefit from—they keep in touch with the many executive-search firms at their level (the corporate headhunters) who know the job marketplace and can give advice and referrals in upcoming opportunities. When opportunity calls or the ax falls, they are ready to jump ship if it suits their needs, for they know where to find a job, how to get a good deal, and how to survive mentally. For you, the equivalent may be a placement office, the local want ads, the union hall, or the local employment office. At all levels, however, the principle of testing the pulse of your job market *even when your job is not at risk* is a sound one.

Some positions are visible just watching the want ads. Business or trade journals may be other sources. The personnel offices and employment bureaus may have listings, or individual cases there may be accessible through your company's grapevine. However you do it, monitoring the demand on your type of job is a way of preparing for future employment and other financial considerations such as salary and benefits negotiations, allocation of responsibility, and other conditions that might directly affect your career and finances.

CAREER PLANNING IS A CHANGING CONCEPT

Career planning is becoming more important as the nature of our society alters and new jobs replace the old at a hastening clip. An increasing number of corporations are providing supplementary education to their employees in hopes that they will retain their workers in the future rather than having to let go obsolete people and hiring those with the new skills. If this is available, it is often the best education to be had for the dollar. Not only are just programs often a bargain, they are almost always tied into specific future job opportunities.

Even if your company or industry doesn't offer such courses, information about what skills will be in demand is available from a variety of sources. Often they include personnel directors, trade or industry journals, college extension programs, and quality employment bureaus. Continuing education is fast becoming a requisite for keeping many jobs, and is even more important in career advancement in most industries.

Job-search expenses, job-related education, and some other career-advancement costs are mostly tax-deductible. Check with your personnel office or your tax preparer to be sure. So are expenses related to learning how to invest, such as financial-magazine subscriptions, course fees, and the cost of finance books, if you can show that you used them to plan your investments for the year. If the government sees these as legitimate tax-deductible items, we at least ought to view them as prudent financial ploys! Preceding any strategy, however, a clear-cut picture of investment goals is necessary. Here's a brief outline of one way to clarify and state your goals:

INVESTMENT-GOALS WORKSHEET

Major Goal:

1. Select One From Each Group:

conservative long-term growth	maximum current income
long-term growth	moderate current income
medium-term growth (1-5 yrs)	some income
rapid capital growth	maximum tax shelter
short-term aggressive growth	maximum after-tax return
other	no current income needed

_____ and _____

2. Annual Yield Anticipated $ _____
   (income plus appreciation)

3. Current investments that fit your stated goals:

_____

_____

_____

4. Current holdings that do not fit your goals or are questionable:

_____

_____

_____

5. How can you increase yield and move closer to your stated objectives?

_____

_____

_____

6. Is the investment portfolio diversified enough to meet your goals for safety and growth?

_____

7. Is the portfolio properly divided into high-yield investments and liquid assets?

_____

8. If the answer to number 7 is no, which investments are inappropriate to your goals?

_____

INCOME PLANNING

Your plans and expectations for the future will affect every other financial decision you make, from the size and type of insurance policies you buy to job choices and estate planning you indulge in. To leave the future a big "if" isn't fair to yourself, for you will fail to optimize the way you spend and build your assets. As you look into insurance, estate planning, will writing and other financial-planning tools, you'll realize that it's easy to waste a good deal of money overbuying and planning haphazardly. Honestly anticipating your career changes and income growth will enable you to allocate your resources more efficiently and to have more funds available to work for you and protect you.

The most important resources for the average family are:

Work income. This may be salary or piecework, cash, or a combination of barter, benefits and credit. You may find that financial planners or career counselors can help you find a career or just a new job that increases your income and is acceptable to you in other ways. (Although career- and job-counseling expenses are usually tax-deductible, and by any standards can be a lucrative investment, watch out. It is also a business rife with fraud, especially in the mail order segment.) Also included here are the savings that are forced upon you—Social Security, pensions, profit sharing, company investment plans, etc. The problem is that most people overestimate the value of these assets, and they are penalized by finding out too late that their real value is ridiculously small. You can always save more yourself in the open marketplace.

Investments. The most common entry here is savings in bank accounts. Obviously related to work income, this is the most confusing yet most opportunity-laden arena for building personal wealth over the long haul. Credit counselors often ask their clients to draft and sign a pledge document in which they promise to give savings a higher priority than any other financial activity except paying household bills. For many this is a revelation. For financially successful people, this is as common and as natural as sunrise in the morning. Investments are chosen according to their safety, their sure return, their possible return, their term, liquidity, and marketability. Get a paper and make a chart—you can compare investments against one another easily and prudently.

INVESTMENT SCORECARD

Item	Safety	Expected Return	Sure Return	Min/Max Term
____	____	____	____	____
____	____	____	____	____

	Liquid?	Marketability If Conditions Change	Tax Preferred?	Overall Suitability
	____	____	____	____
	____	____	____	____

Equities. You may wonder why I list these separately from investments, and the reason is that ownership (which is what all equities, such as stocks, are) is different in the face of the law and taxes than are mere contractual arrangements (which is what all other investments, including bank accounts are). Real estate, types of insurance, stocks (as opposed to bonds, etc.) collectible valuables and other ownable things can be bought and sold, held and traded, so that large tax and appreciation advantages can be realized. If you want to give this type of investment a try, begin small, study the markets, and find or hire an adviser who will not tell you what to buy or sell, but rather how to trade sensibly.

Debt. Prudent debt returns greater wealth than is spent over the life of the debt. That is why financial advisers put a limit on the percentage of income they feel is wise to put into dept repayment. In the 1950s, families were advised to have no more than 15 percent of their monthly income in mortgage and time payments. Today banks are recommending 30 percent in many cases. Savings in the Happy Days era was over 12 percent per family; today it is under 7 percent. Then bankruptcy was as rare as a white tiger; today some 30,000 families, personal corporations, and individuals enter into it every year.

Miracles. I'm not talking about the religious kind, but the ones handed out by fate: inheritances, gifts, prizes, and other valuable windfalls. If you are not sure how to handle newly acquired wealth, make sure that the advisers you ask to help are responsible. Contact your accountant as soon as possible to determine what tax consequences will be forthcoming! Depending upon your state and previous returns, they may be significant, and, more importantly, you may be able to minimize them by planning ahead. Then you can begin calculating the best way to move the windfall into the investment category with the biggest possible portion intact.

"WHERE AM I?," HE ASKED

There are three periods in most people's lives as seen from the financial point of view—the early, planning years; the middle, earning and growing years; and the later, conserving years. Each period dictates appropriate economic behavior and proscribes other behavior. Sometimes it is difficult to recognize which period we are in. I prefer to think of the phases less in terms of age but more in terms of financial position and potential. If you are twenty-one, wealthy, and due for an inheritance, you will need to have the perspective of a person beyond your years. You will want to spend a larger portion of your time studying how to protect your assets and planning for possible disasters than would a twenty-one-year-old who has no personal assets, has nowhere to go but up the financial ladder, and who is destined to spend several years in the first financial stage.

PLANS AND CAREER SHOULD MATCH

Planning a career and other income means that you anticipate reaching a certain standard of living. Assuming that you anticipate an upward trend in true earning ability, you need to shop for financial products and services that will allow you to upgrade your service, and protection to meet your larger wealth and responsibility as they materialize. A whole-life insurance policy that meets the perceived needs of a $10,000-a-year worker is not going to protect the family of a $50,000-a-year manager, and further, it probably won't be worth keeping, even with a companion policy. The remaining alternative is to let the policies lapse, which makes them cost all the more for the period they were in effect. Therefore, if you anticipate a financial climb in life, you want insurance you can upgrade without penalty. In virtually all cases, that means guaranteed renewable term coverage with clauses allowing enlarging the policy. If you expect to be at the same company and in the same job for the next twenty years, getting the best plan for the money is all you are after. Other kinds of insurance should be shopped for with the same view toward tomorrow.

Other financial commitments should be approached with the same eye to the future and your plans for it. The products that carry a long-term frozen level of protection or return, or which have long-term obligation, must be examined very carefully. Although these may be very desirable for preretirees who want to lock in protection through the later years in life when it is difficult to obtain financial help, they may be real traps for the young who aspire to financial independence.

THE NECESSARY DOCUMENTS

A few legal documents are essential for everyone, regardless of age or financial status. The first is one we rarely hear about, for no one makes money selling it—it's a statement of intent, sometimes called a "living will," in case of the loss of legal competence. If you are incapacitated, as in a coma, or with paraplegia, you want to know who will take control of your assets, who will make the decisions concerning your health, where you will live, and other vital decisions. And accidents of fate or nature aren't the only possibilities—if you are judged temporarily insane or are recognized as a drug addict or alcoholic, you could quite possibly lose control over your assets and your life. Until you have dependents whom you care about more than yourself, this will be the most important legal document you create.

Later in life, the biggest single problem for couples is in having joint ownership of assets. When this is the case, as long as one of you is alive, you must have two signatures on every transfer of assets, or, if one is incapacitated, you must have a court-appointed guardianship, which is living hell for the healthy survivor. Courts can be capricious in their selection of a guardian, leaving you or your spouse paired with a hostile or unreasonable legal chaperone, and worse, you both have to report to the court periodically, often with disputes. Avoid it if you possibly can. The only sure way to sidestep the possibility is to prepare your affairs so that assets, accounts, and financial products can be handled with one signature, and by preparing your statement of intent and assignment of power of attorney. (On the other hand, if you want to keep track of each other, you may *want* to require two signatures on every legal or financial document!)

Among the things you want to include are a list of three individuals, in order of preference, to whom you ascribe power of attorney in case you are incapacitated. If you are married, your spouse has many legal rights according to state laws, but you would also find that there are many restrictions that can be financially crippling. It is possible to end up with all your assets frozen and your spouse unable to pay bills or use money for living expenses until a court appoints an "attorney-in-fact" (giving someone power of attorney over your affairs), or, heaven forbid, a guardianship. A carefully devised document hastens the process, may obviate the need for court proceedings altogether, and will certainly make sure that your wishes are followed. As with a will, it is best drafted by a lawyer, and a duplicate copy should be kept with him or her or with another responsible party who will be sure to know of any difficulties you have but who has no monetary interest in any of your assets if you are incapacitated or dead. This is not a write-it-yourself project unless you are careful, for in many states your wishes can be ignored if the document is improperly drafted.

Other directions you may want to include to reflect your wishes in case you are alive but unable to communicate, or are judged unable to reason, include:

- Whom you want to make your medical decisions.
- Whom you want to manage your finances, and perhaps how and where you wish to be taken care of.
- What events should precipitate a legal proceeding, such as the loss of the person with power of attorney or other responsibilities.

• What specific courses in medical care you wish to be taken if you are incapacitated. For instance, I have stipulated that if my brain is dead, I don't want to be kept alive by artificial means, and if death appears imminent, I want my bodily parts, as many as are usable, donated to research. You may have other conditions that are important to you.

IMPORTANT DETAILS

Estate planning is as necessary for the young person with few assets as it is for others if there are loved ones to protect, and that is what wills and estate planning do. Even if you are flat broke, just having a will that is properly put together can save your family from endless legal dates and arrangements. At the very least it's a worthwhile courtesy.

Often, people with few assets see no use for having insurance, for they see nothing to lose. In addition, as our government becomes more socialized, there is more and more protection for the underclasses. The problem is that in our society, you can also lose more than you have. Bankruptcy is one way out of this, and one that many more people are opting for, since it was made easy in the Carter years. But it is a poor choice for those who look forward to a stable financial future. You can still incur financial obligations that will outstrip your ability to pay and then haunt your future without mercy. Unpaid debts, whether medical or as the result of a lawsuit, just to name two, can ruin your credit for at least a decade, and longer if your history is sought out, as is becoming more and more common. If you abuse credit now, you may have canceled out all legitimate channels for obtaining it in the future when you may have even greater need for it.

Health insurance of the right kind can limit the unreasonable risk of this kind of exposure. For instance, insurance that you obtain through a group and that covers only major illness and has a very high deductible will not interfere with any of the Medicare or other forms of protection you count on for regular care, but will protect you in case of a catastrophic illness or accident. Further, it protects relatives whom you feel might step in if they knew you were in dire straits.

Health insurance must be analyzed not just in terms of its cost, but in terms of your future. If you have increased assets and more dependents, you may want more elaborate coverage just for peace of mind. On the other hand, you may be deciding that you can self-insure for a greater part of your risk and actually reduce your insurance cost. If your health is already a problem, large group plans may provide you protection that small plans would not accept. You probably review your insurance every couple of years, as all financially responsible persons do, but there are times when you should look at it with a new viewpoint, and this could be the year for you.

Along the same lines, life insurance might be immaterial to you if you have no dependents, but shouldn't be if you have loved ones whom you know will assume the responsibility and cost of a funeral if you die. Combined with a brief but correctly drafted will, a life policy can also keep your relatives out of probate court, which is a possibility in even tiny estates. A small, say $5000, policy will cost very little, yet provides protection for those you care about, as all life insurance should.

It should go without saying that if you are in the early stages of building a financial empire of your own, you have no business buying financial products designed for those with substantial assets and liabilities. I have had salesmen try to sell me deferred annuities and tax-free municipal bonds in the days when I had no taxes to save and my tax bracket wouldn't hold up my socks. Salesmen will sell what they have to sell as long as you will buy it, yet it's hard to know what makes sense and what doesn't. If you don't know, don't buy it—if you can use it, it'll be available later, but it you don't, they are not going to give your money back, ever.

THE MIDDLE YEARS

The young person who has built a financial base begins to adopt the concerns of the middle years, as I call them. Careers emerge and solidify, earning potential becomes more or less accepted (unfortunately), families form and grow, and habits weld us to the lives we have forged. The financial responsibilities that emanate from these aspects of our lives create needs different from those we had as young people and different from those we will have in later years. Often, this is the time in life when people need knowledge they don't know how to get, could use wisdom they haven't worked to gather, and want sophistication that comes from years of experience in financial planning, which they often did very little of. It's a time when people are glad they tried to keep up through the years, give up on themselves, or struggle like hell. For most, it is the time that defines their lives.

If all that is true, it is also a time of life to plan for, no matter how fuzzy your view of the future as a young person. If you told the average twenty-year-old to take his present living expenses, or worse, the level of spending he'd like to achieve someday, then multiply that figure by, say 10 percent for inflation, and extend that out for thirty-five years and tell him, "That's what you'll need the first year you retire," he'd probably panic. In some measure his fear would be justified, for many never do reach the goals and lifestyle they expect.

President Jimmy Carter's Commission on Pension Policy calculated back in 1980 that a working couple earning $30,000 needs at least $18,000 at retirement in spendable, inflation-compensated (and after-tax) dollars to maintain a satisfactory lifestyle. Take that $18,000 and multiply it by 10 percent inflation for just twenty years and that couple finds they need $110,000 *per year* in retirement income. (Now all you thirty-year-olds get a firm grip on yourselves.) After thirty-five years the figure jumps to over $450,000. What will we all do? Hope inflation stays low, and plan ahead.

Moral: If you wait until you're forty to start saving, it may be a real struggle to retire the way you really expect to. Add in the dream of a house and a business, and you may be too late if you are an average wage earner or anywhere in the middle category. People who begin saving in their fifties have to hustle all the way through their fifties, and perhaps their sixties and seventies as long as they are able, or so the statistics seem to say. The later you start, the more you will have to hustle later on and the longer the shuffle will persist.

The discussion of "statements of intent" or "living wills" on pages 57 and 58 addressed the broad needs of people in all categories of financial life, from the poor to the wealthy. Specifically for those with substantial assets, the best protection may be to establish a *living trust* with provisions for succeeding trustees. *You* are the trustee until something happens to you. Then the next trustee takes over until you recover or after you don't.

Among the listed trustees should be at least one institution, perhaps your bank trust department, which can take control if only minors are left to manage the trust at some point or other contingencies arise. Trusts are called "trusts" because you are *trusting* someone else to do right by you, so if you are innately trusting, be sure these documents cover all possible bases. Only a good attorney can ensure that. Happily, trusts, powers-of-attorney delegations, and statements of intent or living wills, need not be expensive.

With an established financial direction, your insurance needs change and probably need a major revision. Life insurance, which you originally wanted to be just cheap and reliable, now needs to be guaranteed renewable, if you can find it. Otherwise you may find that an upcoming illness will price you out of it altogether. Presumably you have increased earning power and have more to protect, so you may be buying protection, meaning you must go through the process of figuring whether to buy completely new policies or to buy add-on riders and policies. The problem with having more is that you are forced to spend more time and money on protection.

The will, trusts, and other documents you set up as a young family or a single career-climber may be far out of date in a short period if you assume new responsibilities, earn more than you used to, or set new goals in life. If you haven't been monitoring things, you can easily find yourself in a bind should something go wrong. A will that leaves out the latest baby, a trust that delegates fiduciary power to Uncle Fred and his newly acquired alcoholic wife, a statement of joint ownership that names your ex-husband as legal signatory for any and all assets—these little things can ruin your Golden Years.

Once you've "arrived," however, or see yourself on the way out of the middle years of financial life, you will want to assess all your plans, assets, and financial products to see if you are really headed where you had anticipated. Too often people wait until they are in their fifties or sixties before they start planning for their retirement. They're the first to tell you they should have planned sooner and more carefully, but they will also tell you that it is very easy to find the years slipping behind you one by one until your health suddenly fails, or to have a few emergencies erase your hard-won savings and leave you naked before the future, forced to work just for a living wage at a time in your life when you had hoped and dreamed to be partially, if not wholly, self-sufficient.

KEEPING UP ON KNOW-HOW

Membership in the AARP, its sister organization, AIM (Action for Independent Maturity), for those forty-five to sixty-five, or other associations or news services for older Americans is a good way to tune in on the concerns you will surely be facing when you reach that age group. If you are already in those categories, they are educational shortcuts to finding out how to prepare and guide yourself through the maze of problems during the later years in your financial life. You may also want to find yourself financial advisers in your age group who are likely to share your concerns and outlook. Your broker, lawyer, accountant, insurance agents, financial planner, among others may find it difficult to concentrate on your particular needs if they do not share some of your age-specific problems, and of course this applies to all groups. There are people who can rise above such biases, but I feel you should consider it at least.

Investing for your later years is as much a philosophical ideal as it is a practical one, as long as you accumulate assets regularly and continually. As long as you are trying to attain the highest interest rates or otherwise trying to maximize the return on your working money, you can say that you are preparing for the future, but you can do much better with a carefully and regularly considered plan than without one. The idea of opening an IRA or Keogh account may seem ludicrous to a twenty-five-year-old. It might be if he or she were to put as much into it as would a forty-year-old in the same salary range, but as a part of a diversified portfolio and a cushion in case of economic emergency it makes terrific sense. The only real arguments against it are: (1) you truly can't afford it, or, (2) you don't plan to live that long.

THE LATER YEARS

As you approach age fifty-nine-and-one-half, when you are eligible to begin taking out the IRA funds without penalty, you can consider some of the alternative uses for the accounts. A dandy one I have seen used is a way to phase out of retirement instead of stopping work cold turkey. Because the retirement plans provide the tax-deferral feature, the tax bracket in the year you begin withdrawals is very important. I have known people who arranged to cut their workload in half for several years before they retired, and instead of taking a full half salary, they accepted the maximum Social Security income allowed without penalty and the rest in employee benefits. These might take the form of a company car, travel expenses, office space, supplemental medical coverage, work-related education (many types of retirement seminars and related education qualifies under the law), work supplies and other eligible items. This way, the first years of semi-retirement qualify the person for the income, plus full or nearly full Social Security, plus income from the IRA taxed at a very low rate because the small total income results in a low tax bracket. The cost to the employer is the same.

Because this is unusual, you may have to propose such arrangements to your employers or business partners. Such a proposal requires that you have investigated the plan and found advantages for them as well as yourself. And if you can't sell the boss on the idea, at least it points out the fact that often creativity is the answer to the question, "How do I maximize my income and minimize my tax bill?" You must also keep in mind that this is just the sort of arrangement the IRS may argue with, not because it's illegal, for it's not, but because it is easy to make mistakes if you aren't careful.

Similarly, as you approach the retirement stage, whether or not you plan to retire (an increasing number of older Americans choose not to) you may want to "load up" your IRA and Keogh accounts with the maximum allowable contributions so that in the retirement years themselves, the tax deferral on invested monies works for you. Remember, the tax deferral continues to help you as long as there is money in the IRA or Keogh, and you are forced to withdraw it at a rate defined by the size of your contributions, so a setup in which you begin very early with small additions and end up with the maximum will also ease you into the withdrawals much better than if you wait until age, say fifty-five, to begin and then try to stuff in the maximum every year.

Other investment goals will change as you age, and you must plan to adapt your assets accordingly. Obviously you want to reduce your investment risk, and that will usually lower your aggregate return on investment, but it will also lower the likelihood that you will have a major loss in the years just before you lose your earning power. You will probably want to move out of growth investments and into income-producing ones, and you'll need to monitor your liquidity to ensure that you have ready cash to cover emergencies that you may not be able to obtain credit for any longer. If you are fortunate enough to have become almost entirely self-insured, you will want to monitor your liquidity to ensure that you can meet emergencies without disrupting all of your assets or incurring tax penalties.

PULLING HARD ON BOOTSTRAPS

If you are in financial difficulty and are in the lower- to middle-income ranges, there are numerous counseling agencies you can call on at little or no expense. Consumer Credit Counsellors is one nonprofit chain of such offices with outlets in most major cities. You can find others in the phone book (avoid the ones that charge you to consolidate loans) and through other agencies. Often your local chamber of commerce, state consumer protection agencies, ombudsmen offices, and bankers and finance companies can refer to you the good counselors.

Very often people who have been flying the financial skies by the seat of their pants and find themselves in a credit crunch or a cash-flow crisis discover that just by adopting sound management practices they can turn their finances around and not suffer any downgrading of their current lifestyle. Nine out of ten people who go to such agencies have already decided that they need a major new direction in the way they handle money. Of those, nine out of ten are successful in immediately restructuring their finances, the way they handle money, and more importantly, the way they *think* about money. Later some revert to their old habits, but it indicates that those who honestly want to find a way out of financial difficulty can do so. I think that's a significant statement, for most people who responded to a recent survey felt that there was no way for them to compensate for their financial difficulties. Although there were economic hardships on us all, the CCC found that most people could improve their position and had not simply because they didn't know the details of how to do so.

The principal actions the CCC and other similar agencies help their clients take are to:

- Eliminate or reorganize credit and debt
- Allocate funds through a budget
- Set financial and career goals to maximize income
- Select investments to optimize financial goals
- Establish a written record-keeping system

Turn those around and you have the mistakes people most often make:

- Abuse credit
- Spend and move money without planning
- Make spending and other financial decisions without long-term or even medium-term goals in mind
- Select investments on the basis of sales pitches rather than comparing the features of the products to their particular needs and management capabilities

FREE ADVICE BETWEEN THE TRACKS

But what about those who aren't fortunate enough to have wealth, which buys expert advice, no matter the price, or to be poor enough to qualify for the free advice that is so prolific in our society? You have to look for it and work for it, but thank goodness it is available everywhere. Finding the set of economic advice that perfectly matches your personal circumstances would be a miracle recalling Cinderella's fit into the glass slipper, only as you notice, there has been no princely ball. The fact is that you have to adapt the available information and the advice to your situation, and, yes, that is a difficult thing to do when you are trying to master all the principles at the same time. So the bottom line is: If you don't know what you are doing, either educate yourself, find a nonprofit qualified adviser, or hire an honest professional one. The only two alternatives are to hope that you get lucky and do things wisely from a base of ignorance, or to do nothing at all, which in this world of inflation, vacillating economies, and general uncertainties, is like okaying an arrangement to have your earnings and assets stolen from you at a larcenous rate, and I mean *in addition* to taxes.

ENTERING THE SYSTEM

To enter the social club of financial "can-do's," you must start with some of the same standard practices. Using a budget, keeping records, scheduling, and others are vital, but another is easy to adopt and can be a shortcut to the rest. It's the old consumer advocate's biblical law: *Comparison shop in the financial marketplace*.

It is a vital skill. Okay, here's an illustration: Suppose you want to buy a certain color TV and you have two stores you are willing to buy it from. Store A has a price of $500, cash and carry. Store B has the same price, but will negotiate down to $400 if you buy a $100 renewable labor-guarantee contract. Which is cheaper? If you never renew the contract, both prices are the same. Although the contract may give you some additional coverage, most products break down in the very early usage, when the warranty is in effect, or late in life, after long use, so the contract is unlikely to be needed the first year and actually constitutes duplicate protection—a silly thing under any circumstances. The store is gambling (with statistics very much on their side) that you will in fact renew your service contract. If you keep renewing it for the early years, the odds are very low that you will need it, and that money will be wasted. Later, say after five years when the product does begin to wear out, the average contract holder will have paid *400 percent more* into the contract than he receives in service. So, in reality, the odds are that the second store will cost you more unless you are very careful.

You must comparison shop carefully for most financial products, just like any others. That includes bank services, brokerage services, insurance products, investments, etc. And it means you must shop very carefully for financial-service businesses. Consult the *Consumer Reports* and *Consumer Guide* back issues and *Money* magazine for hair-raising articles about the differences between banks in the same neighborhoods and the differences in return on accounts and service charges and services available. The realty industry estimated that the difference between a superior broker and an average one worked out to over $5000 per residential sale. That is good money, certainly worth a couple of days, or even several, shopping for the right agent, wouldn't you say? The same holds true for other services. That is why successful, wealthy people hire the best, and why the rest of us should emulate them, at least in this one regard. To paraphrase a famous line, "It costs comparatively little more to hire the best, but it can cost you dearly not to."

FINDING FINANCIAL HELP

Self-education—are you successful at learning from books, magazines, and courses, and can you apply what you learn to real life?

Hiring an adviser—can you find one with the expertise you need, who has a proven track record, and whose services you can afford?

Using other professionals—can you trust your insurance agent, stock-broker, personal banker, real estate agent, etc., to give you honest, competent advice in other areas of financial planning? There is a natural conflict of interest here, meaning you must be very careful.

Using friends and family—is there another member of your immediate family who is more suited to financial planning and decision-making and is willing to accept the responsibility? And/or, is there a family member or friend with a proven track record who will help you with the basic tasks of financial housekeeping and planning? The problem here is in depending upon someone who may be well-meaning but full of inappropriate advice. You are not after hot tips in this case, but rather directions in sound economic basics.

WHO ARE YOU, FINANCIALLY SPEAKING?

Age _____

Financial stage_____

(beginning, growing with assets, maximizing growth, preserving assets with growth, preserving assets/retired)

Conscientious financial planner and record keeper?_____

Willing to spend time analyzing personal finances? _____

If so, how much per week? _____

How do you plan to update your knowledge of finances? _____
_____

Job and career oriented?_____

If so, income ambitions_____

If not, expected annual income from all sources _____

Approximate current assets_____

Approximate current income _____

Desired current income _____

Difference _____

Have a plan for making up the difference?_____

Are investments carefully planned? _____

How do you plan to upgrade current investments?_____

What is your investment personality? _____

(aggressive, cautious, middle-of-the-road, undefined, etc.)

Are you satisfied with your performance in planning investments? _____

If not, how do you plan to improve your performance? _____

What is your basic investment strategy? _____

Are the important things in your life adequately insured?_____

If not, how do plan to protect them and yourself?_____

Do you have an established banking system?_____

Does it meet your current and upcoming needs? _____

What do you plan to do to upgrade it?_____

OFFICIAL SOURCES OF INFORMATION

BANKS

Office of Consumer Affairs
Controller of the Currency (about discrimination in lending)

Division of Consumer Affairs
Federal Reserve System (problems with state-chartered banks that are members of the Fed)
Branches in Washington, D.C., New York, Boston, St. Louis, Minneapolis, Cleveland, Kansas City (Missouri), San Francisco, Chicago, Dallas, Philadelphia, Atlanta, Richmond

SAVINGS AND LOANS

Federal Home Loan Bank Board (for S&Ls that are insured by the FHLBB)
Office of the Secretary

Your state will have its own office.

CREDIT UNIONS

(Federally chartered—your state will have its own office)
National Credit Union Administration
Office of the Administrator, Washington, D.C.

SECURITIES SALES AND TRADES

Office of Consumer Affairs
Securities and Exchange Commission
Offices in Washington, D.C., Los Angeles, New York, Chicago

Office of Consumer Affairs
Federal Trade Commission
Offices in: Washington, D.C., Los Angeles

Surveillance Department
National Association of Securities Dealers
New York City

Offices of all nine stock exchanges have public affairs departments, though none have enforcement capacity.

To locate other government offices
check library
call state capital information office
call federal information office in Washington
(202) 655-4000

FINANCIAL DISCLOSURE

As with your net-worth statement, get a paper and pencil and copy the form below, listing the things that apply to you. Once you have the names of all the items, you can begin the process of finding the numbers and other specific information. When you have assembled the finished product in approximately the form I've outlined here, you'll have a financial-disclosure statement that will be adequate for your banker, should you apply for a loan, a finance company, should you decide to buy on the installment plan, a business partner, should you decide to enter into a serious business arrangement. In short you'll have a *complete* summary of your financial position, both long and short term, and active as well as enduring. It will illustrate your entire financial picture to anyone who needs to understand it—and that includes you! If you just want to fill in blanks, get a printed form from your banker or credit office.

FINANCIAL DISCLOSURE STATEMENT
(see your Net Worth Statement)

ASSETS	LIABILITIES
Cash—list banks, etc.	Notes payable—short-term and long-term
Stocks and bonds	to banks
Other securities	contractual agreements
Notes receivable	real estate loans
	loans against life insurance
Life insurance & annuities	IOUs to others
	(includes gross value of time payments
Real estate—improved	due)
unimproved	
trust deeds	Other liabilities
mortgages	
Personal property	
autos	
collectibles	
jewelry	
electronics	
other valuables	
Other marketable assets	

TOTALS: Assets _____   Liabilities _____

Assets
minus
Liabilities
equals
Net Worth

ANNUAL INCOME

Salaries and wages
Dividends and interest
Business income
Rental income
Other income
  (includes gifts,
  stipends, insurance,
  receipts, entitlements,
  and any other regular
  income)

ANNUAL EXPENSES

Mortgage payments
Payments on contracts and notes
Property and special taxes
Income taxes
Insurance costs
Estimated living expenses
Support of dependents
Legal encumbrances
Other expenses

TOTALS: Income _____   Expenses _____

Annual Income
minus
Annual Expenses
equals
Net Cash

INSURANCE
   Health insurance—company and gross coverage
   Auto—company and collision, liability & compensation coverages
   Life insurance—companies, face values (minus loans) and names of
      beneficiaries, plus special circumstances if any

SECURITIES
   listed and unlisted

   name and description, no. of shares or par value

   total cost, current market value

TOTAL VALUE ____

Total Value
minus
Total Securities Pledged as Debt Collateral
equals
Total Marketable Securities

REAL ESTATE

Address and description
Names and status of titleholders (who owns it, just you or partners)
   have you declared a homestead claim on any properties?
   how are properties owned?
      joint tenancy, tenancy in common, separate property,
      community property, partnerships, etc.

Date of purchase
Total cost
Current market value (ascertained by whom?)
Conditions of trust deed or mortgage
  held by whom
  loan rate
  monthly payment
  unpaid balance

     Total all above for each property

Leased property
  address and description
  names of lessors
  term and total price of lease
  annual and monthly payments
  special terms or circumstances

Is any of the property you own pledged as collateral for debt? If so, specify lienholder and terms.

Mortgages or trust deeds *owned*.
   This is just the opposite of ones you owe on. Name the address, payer, monthly or annual payments, terms and type of lien, balance owed to you and market value of the property, including a statement of who has decided the market value.

Long- and short-term goals both impinge upon each other, but short-term goals are most often what we can control. If your goals conflict radically with current reality, either they or your financial methods must bend. Well-defined goals and budgets are mutually dependent.

If you haven't already, run these goals through the Financial Goals Worksheet at the end of Chapter 2. With all the individual goals assembled, we can put together a composite worksheet that can be easily updated as years go by or your outlook changes.

COMPREHENSIVE FINANCIAL GOALS WORKSHEET

Goals	Amount Still Needed	Date Needed
Retirement goals	_____	_____
Long-term life financial goals	_____	_____
Twenty-year goal	_____	_____
Ten-year goal	_____	_____
Five-year goal	_____	_____
Next-year goal	_____	_____
This-year goal	_____	_____
Specific other goals	_____	_____

Amount Needed By	Dates Arranged in Order
_____	_____
_____	_____
_____	_____
_____	
	Total If Applicable
	_____

Personal Financial Calendar

Schedules for the Following:

   Mortgage payments
   Insurance premiums
   Other fixed payments

Budgeting deadlines
    Annual
    Monthly
    Other

Bank and other account balancing

Investment review/account statements

Tax-planning/preparation dates

Legal-planning reviews
    estate-planning documents
    investment status
    insurance and cash safety net
    tax minimization

Personal History

These are all the items that can be potentially embarrassing or on the contrary can be assets in the eyes of potential lenders, business associates, bankers, etc.

- Are you married?
- Do you have a legal statement of financial responsibility defining your spousal financial status? For example, have you declared all your possessions to be held in joint tenancy or tenancy in common, etc.?
- Are any of your assets held in defined joint tenancy, tenancy in common, or community property? If so, which?
- Are you a secondary signatory to other debts?
- Are any of your assets encumbered and unmarketable? (In other words, can you use them as collateral now?)
- Are there any legal judgments or terms binding against you? (lawsuits, liens, attachments, etc.)
- Are any of your assets pledged in any other way?
- Have you ever failed to repay a debt or had creditors initiate legal action against you?
- Have you ever failed in business?

Potential creditors can probably come up with other questions, but these outline the problems that typically hang up financial plans, especially loans. Your answers should give you a picture of how *safe* your financial situation is and what risk you can afford.

Personal Financial Goals

- Retirement goals
- Long-term life financial goals
- Twenty-year goal
- Ten-year goal
- Five-year goal
- Next-year goal
- This-year goal

Professional advisers appointments
    Annual necessary dates
    Quarterly dates
    Monthly dates
    Contingency dates
    Extraordinary dates ("What if . . ." statements)

Annual personal-financial review
    Goals and budget
    Investment strategy and progress
    Insurance needs and costs
    Legal needs and status
    Tax liabilities and opportunities
    Input from advisers

Transfer Schedules to Calendar or Date Book

4
Lively Budgeting

THE VERY WORD "budgeting" is enough to send chills of apprehension down the backs of the uninitiated. Even for those who deal with budgets in their businesses, the experience is often fraught with tedium or nervousness. It may help to alleviate the reluctance if you look at yourself as the president of your own company—Myself, Inc., or Our Family, Inc. As president you look upon the operations of the company as your primary interest and responsibility. And, as a prudent and wise president, you realize that the budget is the key to understanding what is happening in your organization, for measuring its very pulse. It is the pulse of your financial life.

So, you simply order one of your accountants to prepare the annual or monthly budget, and you bring your experts in to interpret it. The difference in this case is that you are also the budget preparer and the chief financial analyst, too, unless you abdicate to someone else in the family or enlist the aid of a financial consultant, in which case you'll still have to make all the decisions. The budgets that you construct, research, interpret, and deliver to yourself are going to allow you to make the most intelligent decisions possible about long- and short-term plans for your future. They're going to allow you to succeed in the marketplace, compete against adversaries, maneuver in the general economy, and weather the financial storms of the moment. They're going to give you control over your money by giving you the information and insight that can come no other way.

A budget is not one thing, but two. First, it is a *planning system* that lets you make decisions based on prudent logic and known facts rather than iffy intuition. Second, it is a *control system* that lets you steer the ship rather than being merely tossed about by the storm of monetary fate. What a budget is *not* is a "forecast." Forecasts are predictions about the future, and budgets try to minimize this guessing-game element. Economists and weathermen do forecasting, and you know what their records are! The aim of the budget is to plan expenditures based on what is *known* and what is *most probable*. Even astute businesspeople are often confused about this. Nor is it a prediction, per se, for no one can pretend to tell the future, at least not with money. They are guides for planning future actions, based on reasonable expectations. Like well-made battle plans, they should have plenty of room for contingencies and options built in. If you use them properly, they will help you achieve your goals.

Budgets are great tools, always have been, always will be, because they allow a careful person to plan for a specific result and maximize the chances of achieving that result. Budgets are "if, then" statements in monetary terms. Keep in mind that a budget's function is to simplify a complex picture, to sift out key patterns, to identify and call out important figures, and to present an outline that lets you see what needs to be done. Like a master painter who reproduces a scene, you use the budget to focus attention where it needs to be.

If you want an effective budget, you must design it with your personal aims in mind. If you are retired and want to keep track of every expenditure and source of income, your budget is going to be a detailed roadmap that guides you to money leaks and allows you to patch them up while planning for major expenditures. If you are a young professional on the way up in your career, job, and company, your budget is going to be less detailed in terms of small items, and instead will likely reflect the cash flow of a person who is trying to build a foundation for gain, growth, and a dynamic future. The two budgets assist in very different aims, and appropriately, they will look and work differently.

It's easy to see how differently these two budgets are being used to manage the same types of expenditures. For the Smiths, nearly every penny is accounted for, and the detailed analysis will enable them to quickly compare their year-end expenses against the budget to see where they had problems. Bob Jones, a young bachelor on his way up the corporate ladder, has different needs, and they are reflected in his budget. Household expenses don't play an appreciable role in his finances, and he probably doesn't want to bother with them anyway. Likewise, his car expenses are dealt with as unavoidable expenses, with callouts only for those outlays that have tax consequences. If we pursued the rest of these two budgets, we'd find a similar pattern. Your budget will match your needs in each area—listing in detail those outlays that are controllable and have a significant impact on your finances.

Honesty is a crucial aspect of budgeting. The personal budget is one area of your finances that should not reflect your hopes as much as it chronicles what you intend to do based on your best judgment of what is *possible* and *likely*. As any businessperson will tell you, only a realistic budget will work, for only a realistic budget can bring you closer to your goals by keeping you in control.

EXCERPT FROM BUDGET OF THE SMITHS, RETIRED TWO YEARS

1. Household Expenses
Gas company _____
Water & electric company _____
Grocery store _____
Health food store _____
Mortgage _____
Milkman _____
Bottled water _____
Household supplies _____
Unusual expenses, repairs, etc. _____
   Total Household Expenses $_____

2. Car Expenses
Gasoline _____
Maintenance _____
Parts & supplies _____
Parking, tolls, fees, etc. _____
Insurance _____
   Total Car Expenses $_____

EXCERPT FROM BUDGET OF BOB JONES, TWENTY-EIGHT, MARKETING MANAGER

1. Household Expenses
Mortgage _____
Others _____
   Total $_____

2. Car Expenses
Lease payment _____
Personal mileage, gas & maint. _____
Business mileage, gas, etc. _____
Insurance _____
   Total $_____

Think of a map of where you intend to go. A poor map would consist of a straight line between two points. The best map allows for all the turns and twists in the road, shows detail where it's needed, and summarizes information where clarification is of help. You don't expect to stick to the map if the road has changed, the landscape is altered, or the map is obviously misdrawn—you redraw the map correctly. Same with a budget, only the landscape is money and the options within the financial marketplace. If you are honest with yourself when you make up your budget, chances are you'll be able to profit handsomely from the process.

BUDGETING MECHANICS

When you begin laying out your budgets, you may want to follow someone else's format. I'll give you one, and you may want to look at others. The same rules apply to everybody, regardless, so let's begin with the basics: Every budget has two groups of figures—*fixed* and *variable* money flows. The point of separating the two, as is so often forgotten, is to keep clear what is *controllable and what is uncontrollable*. Often the entries are obvious—as in death and taxes, but frequently they are judgment calls. Here's where following the examples can come in handy.

If, like Bob Jones above, your household expenses do not have a major impact on your finances, lump them into one figure. As long as it makes sense for your purposes, it's okay to adapt the entries in your budget. Just make sure you don't delete the effectiveness of it.

If you glance at a budget, you notice that there is only one group of elements you can count on controlling—payouts. The structure helps you to coordinate, anticipate, evaluate and, if you are successful, control them. A budget is the tool that makes this feasible. Its effectiveness depends upon how well you can adapt it to your needs. A budget needs to be as simple as possible to make it easy to understand and extract meaning from, but at the same time comprehensive enough to include every important variable in your cash flow (expenses and incomes). The perfect balance is hard to achieve, but fortunately things usually work themselves out through the trial and error process.

Stockmarket analysts know that budgets are the most difficult thing to interpret when analyzing a company for investment purposes, but are uniformly the most revealing documents (and often are treated as state secrets). The reason is important: The financial statement of a company can be manipulated to show apparent health or aggressiveness within the limitations of creative accounting. The budget, on the other hand, shows how management really expects things to go. It shows whether expenditures are designed to go up or down; it reflects the amount of risk the company is willing to take. It describes in dollars and cents what the company thinks of its chances in the year ahead. When you compare that with the industry, the economy, and the business community at large, you can get a good idea of what is likely to happen.

If that company is Myself, Inc., you want to establish a picture through that budget which would inspire confidence and enthusiasm in the eye of the outside observer as well as the inside operator (you!). Some businesspeople nearly cry when they're forced to show their company budgets to outsiders, not because they are embarrassed by the contents or have done anything criminal or immoral; they simply feel that it is too personal a document to let strangers see. So it is with personal budgets: they're highly personal, but at the same time you want to feel sure that were you to show this personal budget to a knowledgeable financial planner, he or she would give it the stamp of approval for sound judgment and execution.

There are two sides of every budget, Income and Outlay, and the two are always equal. If you have one or more subordinate budgets, you begin with the income as "funds available," and you allocate them in the best way you can. If you have a master budget (you are the company president, after all), you can also go back and regulate the income, within limitations. It is easy to fool yourself into thinking that this last maneuver is budgeting, but it isn't. The old-fashioned name for it is "doctoring the books," and even in a personal budget, it won't work unless you really can control your income.

A common misconception about budgets is that they must be carefully engraved documents of enduring record. On the contrary, they are living, changing creatures right up until the time for which they are written passes. Then they become history for us to learn from. If the amount of income changes, then obviously the budget may be changed as well. If you look at your budget and see that you are falling behind schedule, then it must be revised in order to keep pace with your new circumstances. And if your budget doesn't at all reflect what you are doing, you had better reexamine what is going on, for someone is being fooled. That is the final proof of a good budget: is it really being used and are you deriving real insight and help from it?

A friend once told me that while the results of war are almost always overdone and overrated, sex is almost never overdone and cannot be overrated. I'm not sure just where he and I differ there, but I could have told him that budgets are more like sex than war because, while they can be overdone, a really good budget can't be overrated. (Sorry, that's the only tie-in between sex and budgets I could think of, but I thought there should be at least one.)

LAY OUT YOUR BATTLE PLANS

In any business the budgets are the central operating plans, the battle plans, the strategic guideposts for nearly everything that is done. Without sound budgets businesspeople remain unaware of their own companies' capabilities and make misguided decisions, hurting their chances of success. Privately we all are in the same situation, though some of us try to budget strictly on a daily basis, which amounts to short-sighted planning.

I once worked with the sales director of a major air carrier who figured out how to beat the competition to a multimillion-dollar market. He was ecstatic with dreams of bonuses and promotions, and was set to drop his other accounts in order to pursue his new bonanza. Then his boss, the vice president of marketing, sat him down to review the annual budget. Immediately it became clear to my friend that the sales department had neither the manpower nor the financial resources to service the new market that year. Had he pursued it, he would have lost six months' worth of commissions—his own income—would have alienated a number of major customer accounts, and would have alerted the competition to the presence of the new market.

On the other hand, by waiting until year's end and planning a budget for the project that could then be incorporated into the company's larger operating budget, he was able to scoop most of the new market for his company, bring in fantastic sales and commissions for himself, capture new clientele, and gain a useful reputation at his company, especially after the annual sales convention gave him star billing. All it took was a good budget and two people who were smart enough to use it. The same principles apply to personal finance and personal budgets.

One of the very first things a credit counselor or financial planner does with a client with financial problems is to work up a budget. Very often the response is happy surprise: The clients find that when they put all the figures down on paper in an organized, logical fashion, the reality pops out at them, and if they are thinking, so do the solutions. For the first time in their lives, many of these people have control over their finances instead of the other way around. That is exactly what budgets are supposed to do.

BUDGETING THEORY

Moving from nonbudgeting to budgeting is similar to what accountants call moving from a "cash basis" (knowing what is in your wallet and in the bank and what you usually spend) to an "accrual basis" in business (using a budget to stretch your awareness over larger spans of time and assisting your memory with detailed entries). Among other things, it means that you must have or develop a habit of servicing your budget. The annual budget has to be assembled every year—once is not enough— although it gets considerably easier after the first go-around. The monthly budget (which can be considered separately or as an element of the annual version) must be updated as regularly as you pay your bills, or else the system isn't up to date, and neither are you.

MAKING THE FIRST BUDGET

First, you need a record of expenditures from past years or past months, if you are doing a monthly budget. If you are lucky, you can read off last year's items and set up the outline of most of your budgets by rote. If you are like most of us, there will be significant discrepancies between the coming year and the past, and that gap between the two is where we want to concentrate our attention.

As you itemize your regular and irregular expenditures, problem areas will begin to stand out. Did you have cash-flow problems? Make a note of it. Were bank reserves exhausted before the Christmas buying spree? Circle it in red. Did commitments to investment nosedive? Make plans to give it higher priority so you can budget in some new foundations for success. That's what budgets are for.

Beginning with our basic budget items, namely outlays and your complete list of them from your records, you can use the judgment that this process relies so heavily upon. If inflation was 10 percent last year and you anticipate it will be repeated this year, you must add that to all the purchase expenses. Did you move into a higher tax bracket or move a larger proportion of your assets into taxable interest or dividend income? You'll have to adjust your income statement accordingly, and therefore the top line on your budget. You can expect an annual increase in utility rates (for the exact amount just look at the past and expect a bit worse). By the time you go through all your expenses and have adjusted each one for anticipated inflation and other increases, you will have created a basic budget-model for the month, or year, depending upon your purposes. Naturally you will also revise according to new plans you have for the period ahead.

This all sounds simple, and it can be. The common problem is that many of us decline to do it thoroughly and honestly enough to work as well as a good budget can. The budget can be only as good as what you put into it. Conscientiously done, it becomes a window into your financial future, a future you can manipulate better than before because you know the variables.

The first breakdown inside the budget is between fixed and variable outlays. The fixed ones, such as mortgage payments and others, are set aside into a separate list, for while we are going to deal with them, they are not our main focus of interest. The variable outlays are the ones we can control initially. By sorting things out on paper or on the computer screen it becomes easier to compare figures, especially when they become more numerous.

SAMPLE PRE-BUDGET WORKSHEET
(a list of current and future expenses plus planned discretionary payouts)

Item	Expenses last term (year, month, etc.)	Expected increase (inflation, growth, correction)	Amount to be budgeted
mortgage	$_____10% +	_____	= $_____
home ins.	$_____10% +	_____	= $_____
utilities	$_____10% +	_____	= $_____
auto exp's	$_____10% +	_____	= $_____
IRA/Keogh	$_____10% +	_____	= $_____
etc.			

(Transfer "Amount to be budgeted" items to your budget.)

SORTING OUT THE DETAILS

That you spend $1200 per month on rent may not be as significant as knowing that by choosing the $1200-per-month home instead of the $800-per-month apartment you now have cut your discretionary allowance by $400, and you must choose where it will come from. Without a budget you could intuit where the most prudent expense cuts might be made and slice away, hoping that you are right. With a budget it becomes easy to see that the $400 will probably have to come out of, say, entertainment money, money you intended to invest, or money you were setting aside for a special purchase. Instead of guessing, perhaps wrongly, at how your pocketbook would look at the end of the year with the extra $4800 rent, you can pencil it in on paper (or type it in on a computer) and decide with great acumen exactly where to compensate—ahead of time. This is the ideal way to avoid unexpected disappointments and really take control of your finances. Many of us begin with a definite plan in effect, one I call "the inertia plan." It means that we don't change our ways or ideas until some irresistible force, like overwhelming debt or the death of a spouse, comes along to spur us into action, preferring to expect the financial-planning process to take care of itself. Since it won't, the first exercise we need is to set up a budget, and kick that darned inertia into a rolling action plan.

MAKING YOUR BUDGET WORK

A savings and loan conducted a survey of its customers to find out why more of them weren't buying into the new types of accounts. One reason, as you might guess, is that many of them didn't understand the new services and products well enough to take advantage of them. But they also weren't sure how to tell whether the new accounts would be advantageous or not, so the attitude was, "Why bother?" The bankers' conclusion was that people don't know enough about their own finances (meaning they don't keep financial statements or budgets) to understand whether a change will cost them money or save them money. The savvy all starts with your personal budget.

You may remember the hilarious but at the same time tragic book that came out several years ago called *Getting By On One Hundred Thousand Dollars a Year*, by Andrew Tobias. The entire book was an object lesson in what happens when people don't work their finances through a budget or other control-and-planning processes that work. Here were successful doctors, lawyers, executives, self-made businesspeople, and others who were earning $100,000 per year and had nothing in the bank. A few knew the game they were playing, but the disturbing parts of the book were the passages in which these people would break down and cry, "I just don't understand where the money is going!" The author never seemed to ask (or at least he never mentioned having asked), "Why don't you know where the money is going?" Perhaps the answer was painfully obvious: They did not keep track of what they were going to spend, or, having spent it, where it went. Yes, you guessed it: no budget, and ergo, no control. These people must have been pretty smart. They were doctors and lawyers and mostly college graduates or else seasoned business people, yet most of them were stumbling over their own checkbooks. Their experience provide ample food for thought.

THE MECHANICS

The mechanics of budgeting are only as simple or as complicated as you make them, giving you the choice of how you want your budget to work. If you need a detailed, intricate version with entries for every expenditure, you will be doing a lot of entering and posting of figures, so

BUDGET SCHEDULE

Date to Be Checked or Posted	Item	Comments
_____	_____	_____
_____	_____	_____
_____	_____	_____
_____	_____	_____

you will need another device common to business budgets—a schedule. The simpler and smaller your budget, the more flexible and forgiving the process is. If you are new to the system it may be a good idea to begin with a highly detailed version that you can then pare down, condensing it as you see the categories of expenditures that naturally go together and those you wish to control most carefully.

If you are assembling your budget with the help of someone else, for instance a financial planner, you will need to write down a description of your goals for the budget as well as your general financial goals. Personally I think that is a great idea for all of us who are going the process alone, too, for it serves as a guidepost and reminder of what our original intentions were or are. Later, as our ideas change, we have a record to refer back to that reminds us why we budgeted or made other financial moves as we did.

Your financial goals impact upon the budgeting process in different ways, depending upon their nature. As you review each item in your budget or each budget revision with each goal in mind, you alter the plan that your budget represents. Is it a long-term or short-term goal? In either case you must ask yourself, is it high or low priority? Maybe you can rate it on a scale of one to ten, but however you rate your goals, try to do so before you begin writing a given budget, for they will affect every decision you make in it.

This is vital to understand because in addition to everything else, and as a part of what it does, a budget *accounts* for all movable monies in a given period of time. If you change one entry, it impinges on the plan somewhere else; there's no escaping it. It's *quid pro quo*. You spend more in one place, it has to come from somewhere else. If you don't have clear goals, at least while you are budgeting, you have the same problem that you had with no budget at all: no control.

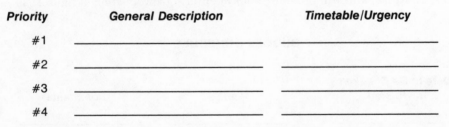

BUDGETING/FINANCIAL GOALS
(to be assembled and refined before budgeting)

Priority	General Description	Timetable/Urgency
#1	_____	_____
#2	_____	_____
#3	_____	_____
#4	_____	_____

The budget for each succeeding period is usually built upon the actual expenditures for the preceding one. You see where the money going out conflicts with your goals and try to devise a reasonable alternative for the upcoming period. Usually budgets do not work out exactly; they're living, breathing, heaving things that fight back when you try to bend them the wrong way and hum along when you coordinate everything conscientiously.

If you can't imagine where to begin, you can get a copy of the average budgets for a wide range of income levels for the average individual and the average family from the U.S. Department of Labor or the reference/business section at your library. It'll tell you what proportion of their income other people in your earning category spend for each major expenditure from transportation, to rent, to Christmas presents. The best place to begin, however, is with last year's and last month's records, for only they can tell you what you have been doing and how different that is from what you want to do.

Fixed expenses are the first entries in a budget because they are the parameters within which you maneuver your variable outlays, and if there are any changes here, you want to know it before you go making any discretionary payments. Allocating funds to entries progresses from the most important items to the least. This is why you want to control the form of your budget; otherwise the form can end up controlling you. You want to end up having allocated every cent into every category, but if you run out of money before you get to the end of the list, you don't want to have your priorities confused. At this point it becomes clear why you organize the budget before you actually use it.

Talk to people who help others prepare personal budgets and the same complaint reverberates: "Why aren't they more realistic?" The temptation is ever present to project what you *wish* would happen onto the budget you are preparing. When businesses do this they end up with the same product you will—"end-of-the-month discrepancy." You find that money you really needed for one expense was instead allocated to your pet project, priorities begin to conflict, the budgeting process begins to fall apart, and you are no better off than if you had no budget at all—except that you have everything written down and ready to try again next month.

Unlike your financial statement, in which sources of income are separated and called out individually, the budget sees just one income figure for the period. This is known as "the top of the sheet" or "top line" and is the beginning from a mathematical point of view. From there the budget is a series of subtractions in a pattern we hope coincides with your needs. Only you can make sure that it does.

SMALL DISCREPANCIES ARE JUST RIGHT

The times when you know that your budget is working for you, saving you money and redefining your financial situation, are when you reach the end of the month and say, "Hey, something is wrong here!" and you realize that you have violated your budget or you must revamp it. Then you are really profiting from the active process that is "budgeting." You adjust here, scrimp a bit there, perhaps splurge over there, and soon you have things back on track, humming along splendidly until the next danger whistle blows and you are back fine-tuning things. You may recall that "fine-tuning" is what Jimmy Carter and Ronald Reagan promised they could do to revitalize our economy. Fortunately, it is a realistic expectation in a personal budget.

USE ZERO-BASE BUDGETING AT HOME

Back when Jimmy Carter entered the presidency, the business world went agog with his announcement that the government would change from cost-plus accounting to zero-base budgeting. All this meant was that instead of taking last year's budget and adding new expenses to compensate for inflation and increased operating costs (using the cost-plus method), every agency, office, and section had to justify every expenditure every year (starting from a base of zero every period). A considerable amount of bookwork later, we were supposed to have saved billions of dollars. It was a nice idea, but it fell flat on its face for one very good reason—the managers in government had no incentive to make it work or to save money. But the principles of zero-base budgeting are perfect for the personal or family budget, for they assume that you'll rethink your budget every time you use it.

The idea that every item can be reevaluated in light of the goals and limitations of the current period makes obvious sense. The tendency is to assume that if an entry was worked out last period, there is no way to improve it this period. The urge to save time and paperwork can be self-destructive, for in actual practice what happens is that the budget begins to get "flabby" and "loose." Alternatives are hard to see if you don't take the time to reexamine the facts. Two stories, one from a credit counseling office and another from an accountant, illustrate how easy it is to lose perspective.

One gentleman was referred to the credit-counseling office by a collection agency which represented one of his creditors. He owed over $15,000 in unpaid bills, had no assets, and had already asked a lawyer to prepare a bankruptcy filing. The counselor went through the man's budget and found that he was diligently paying about half of his bills in full and leaving the other half totally unserviced. A heart-to-heart discussion revealed that the man didn't actually want to go the bankruptcy route, but he felt he had no alternative. The counselor helped him work out a plan where he paid only a portion of all of his bills, leaving none of them untouched, and only a couple were paid in full. When presented with the man's grim picture and the possibility that he might declare bankruptcy and skip out on future payments altogether and be able to stop paying the few bills he was now meeting, the lawyers and accountants representing the creditors agreed to the counselor's plan and also to accept less than 100 percent of the man's true legal debt.

The moral obviously is that by restructuring his payments through a budgeting process, the man was able to drastically improve even a disastrous situation. Of course the counselor's experience and insight helped, but the budgeting process is what turned pandemonium and panic into a controllable, analytical approach.

The other story revolves around a small film-production company that had tapped a new market in educational movies in the 1960s and '70s. A small family operation, the owners had always done their own books as part of their personal financial planning. After all, they lived and breathed the business and there was no separating it from their private lives. The business was growing by leaps and bounds, and yet they always seemed to be able to get just enough out of it to live on. So they finally found an accountant who understood their business and was willing to look at their books. It turned out that they had a huge cash flow they were not taking advantage of. As money came in, they had paid bills directly, without going through the budgeting process and controlling their payouts. By reorganizing their books and controlling their payouts through a budget, the accountant freed extra money at the end of each period, and the business suddenly carried a hefty paper profit. In fact it was so profitable that a nearby corporation bought them out a few months later for several million dollars in cash. Again, the insight of the accountant helped, but the budgeting process is what made it all possible.

BUDGET FORMATS

If you run a steady financial household, there should be very little difference between a list of your current, ongoing expenses and your personal budget. The first budget you make will be time consuming, but subsequent ones are greatly simplified by your planning experience and serve primarily as "red light mechanisms" to help you identify and deal with individual problems or problem times.

SAMPLE MAJOR BUDGET ENTRIES—ANNUAL

Housing & utilities
Taxes
Reducing debt (loan payments, etc.)
Transportation
Food, clothing, and other living expenses
Personal business (must produce income)
Insurance
Medical
Savings—subcategories may include retirement accounts, investment
    planning, planned purchases, college fund, etc.
Education
Religious or familial gifts
Vacation and entertainment
Gifts and holidays
New-investment capital
Fun money

FORMS

The easiest form for most households is an all-in-one budget that includes all entries on a monthly basis and in which the monthly totals are conveniently available for review, comparison, and for totaling at an annual figure for each entry category. No matter how complicated your budget, you can buy bookkeeping forms that will accommodate an entire personal worksheet. As do companies, you may also have subordinate budgets that allow you to manage smaller areas of your financial empire while giving you totals and parameters you can then plug into your central budget. Typical subordinate budgets that deserve meticulous planning on the micro level are travel in business, education (especially college), household expenses, vacations, and investment funds. You set your own priorities and set up and use whichever budgets will help you plan and monitor those areas of your finances you want to and need to control.

SIMPLIFIED ANNUAL BUDGET

Entries	Jan Feb Mar Apr May Jun Jul Aug Sep Oct Nov Dec	TOTALS (together equal total of your annual budget)
Fixed		
mortgage		
utilities		
(or list them separately)		
insurance		
(or list them separately)		
etc.		
Variable outlays		
household		
vacations		
dining out, etc.		
Totals		
(these make up your *annual* budget)		

BUDGETING HIERARCHIES

Annual Budget
Variable outlays
Fixed outlays

Monthly Budgets
Variable outlays
Fixed outlays
Subordinate budgets

Jan   Feb   Mar   Apr   May   Jun   Jul   Aug   Sep   Oct   Nov   Dec

SUBORDINATE BUDGETS

The totals of the subordinate budgets become entries on the monthly budget; the totals on the monthly budget become entries on the annual budget. Example:

> Household budget
> Vacation budget
> School expenses budget
> Auto expenses budget
> Education budget
> Other budgets
>   plus individual entries

Become Entries in
> Monthly budget

Which Is One Entry In
> Annual budget

USING BUDGETS

Generally budgets are used in two practical ways. One, you examine them at the beginning of the month *to plan* how much you will spend during the upcoming period. You allocate your funds to specific purposes. Second, they are used after the period *to review* how closely you have adhered to your budget. If you have deviated from it, you may have to adjust the entries for the upcoming periods to compensate for a sudden expense or to revise the later entries upward to compensate for higher needed outlays. The government recognizes the validity of this approach by allowing people with extraordinarily good or bad years to average their income taxes over three, five, or ten years. It works great in budgeting, too.

Budgets are always slightly off, but barring major surprises, should not be far off. Their success is dependent upon your ability to *anticipate* when you are building the budget, and to stick to your plans afterward. If you can do both, budgeting will be a powerful tool for you, regardless of your tax bracket.

You truly interact with the budget after you have set it up, let it run, and then revised it. It is during the revision process that you find out where your planning works and where you need more work; where you are honest with yourself and where wishes have overpowered honest reporting. Revising a budget before the period is elapsed is both bad and good news. It shows that your budget didn't work, but it's also good because you are taking your finances and the budgeting process seriously, and are working toward solutions to your financial difficulties or are improving upon your successes.

A final note on budgeting. Setting up a personal or household budget is but one way to formalize the financial record-keeping and planning process. Some people find it becomes a trusted habit while others feel they do not need it. Regardless of what you feel now, I urge you to try it for at least a couple of months and find out whether or not it can assist you the way it serves thousands of businesses and millions of individuals already.

PRE-BUDGET WORKSHEET

Income

Source	Column for each person in the household	Period (monthly yearly, etc.)
Earned Income		
Salary		
Wages		
Self-employment		
Bonuses, etc.		
Investment Income		
Interest		
savings		
bonds, etc.		
Dividends		
Capital gains		
Rental income		
Trust income		
Tax-Sheltered Income		
Social Security		
Pensions		
Retirement accounts		
Other income		
Gifts		
Windfalls		
Unemployment, disability, etc., insurance		
Alimony, child support		
Other		

Totals, monthly _____

Totals, annual _____

The totals then become the top of the respective budgets. All the entries in each budget are *deducted* from the top lines.

SAMPLE ALL-IN-ONE BUDGET

Entries	Jan	Feb	Mar	Apr	May	Jun	Jul	Aug	Sep	Oct	Nov	Dec	TOTALS (together equal total of your annual budget)
Fixed													
mortgage													
utilities													
(or list them separately)													
insurance													
(or list them separately) etc.													
Variable outlays													
household													
vacations													
dining out													
other													
Totals (these make up your *annual* budget)													

A SAMPLE MONTHLY BUDGET

Fixed Expenses	This Month	Same Month Last Year
(Uncontrollable)		
Mortgage/rent	_____	_____
Property tax	_____	_____
Income tax	_____	_____
Utilities	_____	_____
Insurance	_____	_____
life	_____	_____
disability	_____	_____
medical	_____	_____
auto	_____	_____
homeowners	_____	_____
liability	_____	_____
Loan payments		
autos	_____	_____
credit cards	_____	_____
gas card	_____	_____
etc.	_____	_____
Uninsured medical & dental expenses	_____	_____
Miscellaneous obligations		
alimony, child support, lump sum		
debt, etc.	_____	_____
TOTAL	_____	_____
Monthly average & difference between	_____	_____
same month last year	(average)	(difference)
Last year's average & difference	_____	_____
between same month last year	(average)	(difference)

Variable Expenses

(Controllable)

Groceries _____ _____
Housekeeping _____ _____
Laundry/cleaning _____ _____
Clothing _____ _____
Recreation _____ _____
Entertainment & dining out _____ _____
Vacation & travel _____ _____
Gifts _____ _____
Hobbies, periodicals, etc. _____ _____
Other _____ _____

   TOTAL _____ _____

Monthly average & difference
  between "this month" and
  "monthly average" _____ _____

                        (average)   (difference)

Last period's average & difference
  between average of all months
  last year _____ _____

                        (average)   (difference)

SAMPLE SUBORDINATE BUDGETS

Auto Expenses

gas/personal _____ _____
gas/business _____ _____
maintenance, average _____ _____
repairs, average _____ _____
improvements planned _____ _____

   TOTAL _____ _____
(becomes entry in main monthly budget)

differences compared in prior terms _____ _____

5
Finding Your Financial Place

THE FIRST PREREQUISITE to making financial plans that will work to reach your goals is to define who you are in financial terms. Your age, assets, income, career, and more all go to make up your financial profile. When you lay out your financial profile alongside your goals, financial planning is easier, and money management is much more effective. Alert, conscientious financial management makes your money grow, and makes it go further—it's like making extra money, and the only work you do to earn it is to be your own conscientious money manager!

Only you can know what your financial goals are, but no matter what they happen to include, you will find yourself sharing certain needs, problems, and solutions with others. If you are a young person just beginning a career and making long-range economic plans for the first time, you actually have many things in common with the middle-aged couple that is trying to attain a desired lifestyle while preparing for retirement, and also with the older person who is making sure that retirement is taken care of.

The elements in common are:

Income need
Savings need
Investment need
Protection (usually insurance) need

The ways in which we handle our financial needs and goals depend upon our emotional makeup, life goals, abilities, and opportunities, and all of these define the big variable—our idea of acceptable risk. If you are twenty-five years old, have a secure job with promise of expanded income, and few monetary responsibilities, your level of acceptable risk will obviously be higher than that of a sixty-five-year-old who faces forced retirement and the prospect of taking care of an infirm spouse. Different as the challenges facing you are, both of you have the challenge of evaluating your finances and positions to decide whether or not you can make new and better decisions to get closer to your goals.

The first task for everyone, then, is to identify and clarify his or her present goals. Put yours down on paper so that you can plot a course for reaching them. Here's a sample self-analysis:

Age: 29
Income: $28,000 as technician, expected advancement in two-three yrs
Net worth: $15,000 (car, furniture, savings, insurance, and investments)
Savings: $5000
Investments: $4000 (mutual fund)
Insurance: no cash value. Coverage on car, home, life

One-year goal: increase savings to $8000
              investments to $6000
              increase income to $30,000
              net worth at least $19,000

Five-year goal: increase savings to $15,000
              increase investments to $12,000
              increase income to $35,000
              net worth at least $30,000

Ten-year goal: own home
              maintain savings at $15,000
              increase investments to $50,000
              increase income to $40,000 +
              net worth at least $75,000

Investment goals: return of at least 10 percent, and preferable as close to 15 percent or better as possible

Retirement goal: Complete financial independence with above median income by age 60

These goals are probably a bit lofty for the average low-income American, but not out of line for an upwardly mobile person. Notice that by setting the goals up in terms of one, five, ten years, and retirement, our imaginary person has identified them and set parameters for himself. This is vital to most people's planning process. When he contemplates buying that new car, he'll compare that decision against the goals he has set and decide whether it is within his budget, whether it is a justified business expense, or whether he wants to forego the car in favor of increasing his savings this year. The plan gives a future to his annual budget. If some of the goals are unreasonable and unattainable, this gives him a solid piece of evidence that a reexamination of his finances and his goals is in order.

In each category he has broken down his goals into savings and earning components. If he suddenly gets a bigger raise than anticipated, he can revise the goals upward, compress the timespan (make the five-year goal a three-year objective, the ten-year original a five-year option, etc.), or use the money to upgrade his lifestyle. As in budgeting, the written plans work as a *control system* for regulating decisions.

ANOTHER ANALYSIS

Age: 59
Income: $58,000 expected 10 percent raise, retirement in six years
Net worth: $200,000 ($140,000 in home)
Savings: $20,000
Investments: $30,000
Insurance: $4000 cash value. Coverage on home, life, health, car, vacation
    home.
Investment goal: Safety primary. Willing to maximize return
    as long as risk remains low. All available money to be invested as
    soon as possible. Tax savings important.
One-year goal: income increased to $64,000
               savings increased to $23,000
               investments increased to $33,000
Five-year goal: income increased to $70,000
               savings increased to $25,000
               investments increased to $40,000
Retirement goal: retire with pension income of $15,000
               reduce savings to $5000
               increase investments to $65,000
               realize investment income of $7500
               travel

The figures in this plan suggest that there have been serious major expenses (perhaps a family and college expenses) or poor management in the past. The progressive stages show that there is an expectation of continued salary increases until retirement and establishes a miminum expected retirement income. His tax bracket affects which investments he considers, as does safety, which he considers paramount. If this person fails to get pay raises, loses a job, or realizes a loss in his investment portfolio, he will have this plan to return to, to revise, and to reorder his objectives. Much like a budget, which helps give structure and control over a short span of time, this plan lends an overview to most of a lifetime or career.

Much has been made of the idea that American companies are very good at making plans for next month and next year, while Japanese companies are good at planning ten years in the future. The individual needs to do both, for he can't go out of business if the going gets rough or a plan is misguided. Indeed, these "business forecasts" into various points in the future are a vital element in planning for both the individual and family, just as they are for business.

Assemble your own worksheets for one, five, ten years, and retirement goals based on your ambitions and your current net-worth statement. As with all companies, the plans give you an overview of what you are trying to do financially and serve as guideposts for decision-making. They bring you down to earth if your expectations are out of line, and they serve as an aid in self-discipline, if that's what you need. In any case, they are another major link in the documentation most people need to organize and monitor their financial growth.

Finding yourself in the overall financial landscape can be an imposing task if you have not assembled your goals, assets, and strategies together. Where you see yourself comes from the information on your financial statement and the game plan you have in your head and on paper. Formulating that strategy can be a real boon to your eventual success, for it affects all your earning, saving, and investment decisions henceforth. The trick is to define your strategy well enough to be able to write it down, and then, even if you don't, you can be confident of where you are headed.

Before you frame your strategy, you will need to collate at least four things:

1. Your present financial strength (from your net-worth statement)
2. Your tolerance for risk (an emotional and logical problem)
3. Your tax situation (mostly for planning later safety, income)
4. And your commitment to investment success

All these must of course be framed in light of your age, your legal responsibilities, and your moral constraints.

Your present financial strength is a limiting factor in how aggressively you can approach financial alternatives. With limited assets you can stake only a small investment venture, and more importantly, your ability to diversify is limited. You are like a gambler who begins to work the tables with just enough for the minimum bet. A very few turns of bad luck or poor judgment and you are out of the game. If you are thus limited, you may decide to join forces with others in investment opportunities that pool resources.

Your tolerance for risk is not just a matter of nerves or psychology, it is something you must define before you look into any investment. Should you lose your nerve and your ability to think rationally when your investment is fluctuating wildly, you will want to avoid commodities trading, for instance. If you are nearing retirement, you may be ready to reduce your risk to nearly nothing by playing only secure investments, even if the return is low, and by broadening your insurance protection. If you have a well-diversified investment plan and a growing asset-base, you may be in position to increase your risk with the expectation of increasing the return on your investments. However, you must keep in mind the principle that has kept the insurance industry afloat for centuries—you must average out the total risk of all your investments so that you come out ahead in the long run, even if that means limiting some of your investment capability in the early years. If you are young and have time to replace lost assets, risk may well be justified, as long as you have planned what to do if your plans don't work out. So how much of a risk is right for you?

Your tax situation has an inordinate effect on your investment decisions in this country. Tax laws define savings accounts, pension plans, investment opportunity, and more. It's the largest single moving force in the economy, aside from ambition itself. While taxes are inevitable, and many taxes seem immutable, the fact is that your tax burden can be manipulated through planning. Common examples include the use of deferrals, retirement funds, redirecting of income to other family members, and selection of tax-preferred investments. The caveat accountants mention most often is, "An investment is an investment first and a taxable item second." It must be a good investment before it can be the other. Your marginal tax bracket (the tax rate on the next $1000 you earn) can eliminate investment opportunities. For instance, you probably need to be somewhere between the 32 and 40 percent brackets before tax-free investments provide a decided edge for you. Real estate, municipal bonds, and other tax-favored investments may allow you to lower your investment risk while increasing returns if you are in a high enough bracket; they can destroy you if you don't have the assets to support a cutback or a demand for unexpected losses or expenses. You and your accountant can spend hours defining where you are, taxwise. His or her fee is tax-deductible.

All the other elements in your financial statement come to nothing if you have a weak commitment to either success in investments or to earning a certain, larger income. In broker's parlance you are "a sitter," going nowhere. You are the only one who can effect a change here or decide what the facts are. If your investment actions do not coincide with your goals, it may well be that your acceptable risk and your commitment to investment success are out of sync. If you feel sure that you could get 15 percent return on your assets but you always opt for conservative investments that yield under 10 percent, something has got to give. Either you bolster your commitment, you accept greater risk, or you accept your present plan of action. Part of the responsibility of commitment is accepting the responsibility for educating yourself, for devoting the necessary time and effort, for reorganizing your priorities so you can devote the necessary energy to investing to make it meet your goals. Accept your own characteristics and you'll feel better about how you invest.

Career plans can be a very important part of your financial planning, for they give you an idea of what you may expect. If you look forward to working as a city attorney for the next twenty years, you obviously have different financial expectations than does a would-be corporate partner. It is easy to fool oneself into believing that the future will take care of itself.

Not only might you make different career changes if you see your income planned over a long span, you may come to realize other things about your financial plans. Are home ownership plans realistic? Can you afford the credit load you had planned upon to maintain your lifestyle? Are you exposing yourself to unreasonable risk by underinsuring or allowing excessive risk in your investments, given your plans and prospects? These are all difficult questions under any circumstances. All are made easier to understand by putting your dreams and your limitations down in black and white.

FITTING INTO INFLATION AND THE ECONOMY AT LARGE

Over the span of decades, and with double-digit inflation, the figures that come from financial projections soon begin to appear astronomical, and the tendency is to wonder how it can be possible to accumulate enough savings or assets. The answer is that the other elements of the economy must be taken into account as well. For instance, the same inflation that makes your needs so great numerically will also work multiplication magic upon your savings. Also, each year as you get older, you will be earning more for the same quantity of work, enabling you to save more annually as time passes. If you are typical, you'll increase your earning power into your fifties, when most people reach their peak, and, presumably, your skill at handling money will have made saving less painful.

It's impossible to make specific plans for retirement until you establish at least some tentative goals. The standard of living you expect to be able to maintain obviously makes a difference in your projected needs. So does the area you plan to live in and the type of home you hope to maintain. The activities you anticipate engaging in may be a large expense, as will your feelings about whether or not you might want or be able to work. The more extravagant your goals, the more demands you place on your annual savings needs. If you set your goals too low, however, the effect is similar to neglecting your savings. You risk being left in the lurch, living on too little for too long, in a period of disappointment and discomfort in your declining years.

As you form your goals, your idea of what is realistic will change with your perception of how your savings program is proceeding and the future you see for other sources of income. If you have faith in the future of Social Security and the growth potential of your pension plan, you can feel confident in a modest savings plan (you will be among a microscopic minority, too). Otherwise you may expect to spend your life annually updating and improving your retirement fund to pursue your expected needs.

Part of this planning process is defining priorities in your budgeting system. If you have faith in your ability to build net worth through your investing skills or your success in your own business, you may be willing to place savings below these goals temporarily, or even for a long period of time. This reshuffling of priorities can be a real gamble, while playing the conservative role is no guarantee of success. If you win the gamble, your retirement may be more comfortable than you dreamed possible, while if you lose, or you are beset by bad fortune, you will be forced to deal with insufficient funds at a time when earning is difficult and change harder.

CONTINGENCY PLANS ARE NECESSARY, TOO

The recommended precaution against both these eventualities is some careful contingency planning. Emergency funds are one part of this. An emergency fund might consist of money you plan to give your children, but which you hang on to for a few extra years. It might consist of equity in your house, which you are willing to live without. There are many possibilities. The other major contingency guard is insurance—in a number of forms. A solid insurance program encompassing health, life (possibly), and protection of your assets can provide a guarantee against ordinary financial disaster.

THE NEW RETIREMENT

Disasters are especially devastating in the retirement years. Major illness may rob you of the final and most crucial income-earning years, and tends to last longer and cost more than at any other time in life. Catastrophic health insurance is clearly a vital need. It is sold in every conceivable form, often fraudulently and as duplicate insurance to existing plans or Medicare, but it is no more important than maintenance-type insurance for the elderly. The urgent need for health insurance *and* a life will are summed up in this terrifying fact: The average middle-income American male spends as much on health care in the last three months of life as he earned in his adult life. The years after age sixty-five are typically ones of declining health, and almost two-thirds of Americans in that group have persistent ailments that require regular prescribed medication, and/or other regular medical attention. Odds are very high that you'll need major and regular medical attention for a number of years, and without protection, even a substantial nest egg will be wiped out in short order.

OPTIONS HAVE PLUS AND MINUS SIDES

Extremists have moved to Sri Lanka when they retire in order to escape income taxes and to enjoy the low cost of living. However, you must weigh the consequences. Many Americans have discovered that a move to the U.S. sunbelt is not only economical because of the tax advantages in some states, notably Arizona, but the living expenses in moderate climates are also lower.

A major drawback from my viewpoint is that this often separates families. Only 5 percent of the elderly spend their final days in nursing homes, but 50 percent end up living with next of kin in their final years. What is the impact of separating yourself from your family in the years just before you may need them most? I don't know the answer, but it certainly can be a major one. This is a good example of how seemingly unrelated actions—such as maintaining close family ties, especially with children—can have major financial ramifications, and callous though it might seem, should be considered in terms of your financial goals and future.

Choosing the location of your retirement home is one consideration, but selecting the actual living place is another complicated task that can have heavy financial implications. If you own your own, you may have increased your net worth by taking the once-in-a-lifetime tax allowance, which is currently a break on the first $175,000 in capital gains when you sell and repurchase your dwelling. This may make it worthwhile for families who had previously thought renting the only alternative to trying to enter the home market. Also, the ownership of a home is the final and largest single reserve asset for most retirees. When and if other funds run out, it is possible to use the equity in the home for living or emergency expenses. A recently popular twist on this is the reverse-amortization mortgage which is available in nearly every community. Instead of selling the house and moving out and then using the cash to live on, the reverse mortgage involves selling the house to an investor or institution and then continuing to live in it for the life of the mortgage *while* receiving monthly payments.

The built-in problem here, as it is in all retirement planning for everyone except the comfortably wealthy, is that you can't plan when you will meet your maker. I've described the plight faced by my ex-neighbors who carefully planned their comfortable retirement to last well into their late seventies and perhaps beyond. They both lived into their late nineties, with plenty of unexpected medical bills, and toward the end, money was running out. It points up the truth that when planning retirement, the strategy is to allow for plenty of leeway.

If you plan successfully, you'll retire with a mixed bag of income sources and assets which you can liquidate. Balancing the act requires that you examine and understand each element of your estate so that you are sure the aggregate will be adequate to last as long as you do, providing you with the comfort you desire. Organizations that regularly research the retirement situation in America report that most people in the middle class overestimate the value and lasting power of their assets and end up retiring at a substantially lower economic level than they had expected. Most of the problem, they say, arises from misconceptions and misunderstandings about what various savings plan provide and how they fare in the face of inflation.

DON'T LET STATISTICS TRIP UP YOUR PLANS OR EXPECTATIONS

Figures popularly used to calculate insurance actuarial tables, retirement needs, and other financial markers can be misleading, as we all know. For example, in 1980 the average life expectancy was seventy-three—a commonly quoted figure. However, that mathematically compensates for all the people who die between birth and old age. If you make it to age sixty-five, then your life expectancy is eighty-one. And every year the figures climb. At the present rate, the average person who reaches age sixty-five at the turn of the century will expect to live into his/her late nineties! Suddenly the pension/Social Security/savings plan that was designed to be effective with the 1958 census figures is revealed as woefully inadequate. And many of the other conventions we accept today are, too.

For instance, imagine a person born in 1935. He'll be sixty-five in the year 2000, with a continued lifespan of almost thirty years. Let's say he began saving in earnest at age twenty-five. That means he would have forty years, less than half a lifetime, to save for a thirty-year retirement. Every four years of savings will have to last for three years of retirement! Inflation will help him or her save during the earning years, but perhaps it will be worse during the later period. Clearly, for the average American this is an unworkable plan. Either he has to accept a drastically lowered standard of living through the retirement years (even assuming he is able to build a substantial asset base to live on) or he will be forced to work past age sixty-five. These are the realities tomorrow's retirees must work with.

Social Security is a major source of income for most retired Americans, and it should not be. It was never meant to be, but was implemented with the idea of providing a cushion of relief for those who failed to adequately provide for their retirement. It was meant to provide a *subsistence* living in a state of destitution, and it does. Little did Roosevelt or the Congress anticipate that people would expect Social Security to be a security blanket to provide the bulk of their continued income. In the intervening years Congress has tied the benefit schedules to inflation and increased them in order to help the recipients, but this has inflated the system beyond the capacity of the economy to support it, and as tax rates decline in off years, the system has threatened to collapse.

The fact is that Social Security, like all pension systems except those for federal employees, is a weak link in the average person's retirement future. If you can bring yourself not to depend upon it (after all, we've heard threats to cut benefits for years), then you can concentrate on planning to maximize it and your savings. If benefits are not cut, other changes will have to come about, so we can anticipate those. Among the ones most often mentioned: The age for receiving full benefits may be raised to sixty-eight or possibly even seventy-two; partial benefits may be reduced and the age raised from sixty-two to sixty-five or even sixty-eight; FICA taxes may be imposed on all income, not just salary and self-employment work income; cost-of-living increases may be cut or eliminated; eligibility requirements may be redesigned, effectively closing out all but the truly needy and destitute. Either way, long-term financial plans must suffer, for those who retire will either have to enjoy severely limited Social Security payments later, or suffer much larger taxes now, which will restrict their ability to save for retirement.

To qualify for Social Security as it is now set up, you must accumulate work credits, and the number required is increasing every year. In 1979, twenty-eight WCs were needed to qualify; now it's forty, which require at least ten years of full FICA payment. This is another area where changes may be made, but for now, if you are over forty, it is important to keep track both of your earned credits and the requirements. Checking your credits is a hassle that should be repeated every three years. The reason is that if the government makes an error in your record and reduces your credits, the mistake is uncorrectable after three years. Yes, that is terribly unfair, but then the government is always protecting itself. The procedure is to obtain Form 7004 from any Social Security office, fill it out and mail it (it is a postcard, actually) to the Social Security headquarters in Baltimore. Ask for three years of records and check them against your work records or tax forms.

Another check worth making at tax time is to have your accountant verify that you haven't overpaid or been overcharged on your FICA/RRTA tax. This can easily happen when you change jobs, get a pay increase or have other changes in your pay. Along with other records, you want to leave a record of your FICA/RRTA taxes in an accessible place in case you die or are incapacitated so that your dependents can easily find them. They may have more need of them than you do now.

The best thing about Social Security is that while you may be restricted in the amount of income you can earn on a job and still remain eligible for all benefits, there is no limit on the income you can gain from investments. You can receive $500,000 in income from interest, dividends, and other investment income and still retain eligibility. For middle-class and lower-income Americans, this points up another reason to save as much as possible during the early earning years—you are actually saving up your work through savings, which will allow you to work very little at age sixty-two or sixty-five and later, yet still obtain your full Social Security benefit, whereas if you work for a living at that point, you will be penalized.

The schedules change each and every year, so get your free copy of them from the Social Security office, your post office, or wherever is convenient. If you are near the minimum qualifying age, it may be worth it to plan a couple of years of extra work to pile on the credits, as this can affect the size of your benefits from now on. To find out how to apply for the most benefits, you'll either have to work your way through the current year's tables or get the help of a financial counselor, perhaps an accountant who specializes in the affairs of older clients and is well versed in the tables, but someone who can sort things out. There are many ways to file, and they all yield different size benefits, so please be careful. There are a number of tricks you can legally pull to stop working a few months early or collect a few extra paychecks after you file without affecting your status, so check in with someone who knows the ropes. Whatever you do, don't settle for knowing just what the government sends you on those little forms—that's not enough knowledge to protect you.

There are three good reasons for not having any Social Security credits—you have a railroad pension, a government pension, or you haven't been paying federal income taxes. The bad reason is that the government miscalculated your credits and you did not ask for a correction within three years. Railroad Retirement is the biggest can of worms in the pension world. You may have been exempt from Social Security or you may have both coming to you. Dependent benefits are entirely different than under Social Security, but benefits are tied to the consumer price index, just as Social Security is. To further complicate things, the two can be merged in a variety of ways to maximize the total benefits you receive. The only way to sort things out is to master the rules and table yourself or find someone who has done it, perhaps at the Railroad Retirement Board office, a railroad employee association, or an accountant who specializes.

Government pensions are the featherbed of a lifetime for the average American. They have all the vital protections that private pensions lack, and they accrue full protection in fewer years. Each branch of the government has its own set of rules, so you will have to do some research to find out how to maximize your benefits, but predictably there is a panoply of literature, information offices, and counselors ready to help any fellow government employee get the maximum possible from the general fund. Government pensions are tied to the CPI and are adjusted every six months, meaning they pay out at a better rate than any other pension system in the country. Vesting schedules, which determine how long you must work at the job before you are eligible for full or partial pension benefits, are shorter and more generous than any other system, too.

The future for all the government pension and protections systems is cloudy. They are all in arrears and getting weaker. So many people depend upon them, however, there is no real chance that they will be allowed to fail, although benefits may be affected in future years. This can also have an effect on career planning, for many people who have sought government jobs specifically for the pension benefits may now have second thoughts.

CORPORATE PENSIONS

Corporate pensions have been compared to a cruel joke. The view is gruesome from the inside, and even from without the humor is difficult to see. With very few exceptions, they have been instituted as means of attracting employees and pacifying them once they are aboard. They often have ridiculously unfair vesting (acquired eligibility) schedules, and because 99 percent of them are not tied to inflation in any way, they prove to be paltry shadows of the security they are advertised to be. A good source of information about pensions of all kinds is the Employee Benefits Research Institute in Washington.

As an example of what I'm talking about, a frequently seen vesting schedule in older pensions is the "ten-year, 100 percent rule." This means that an employee must work for the company for ten years in order to receive any pension eligibility (vesting) and at ten years he or she would be fully vested. (Most vesting schedules are graduated.) Since the average salaried worker changes jobs every five years, comparatively few qualify at all at companies with these plans. New laws have set minimum vesting schedules, but they may not be much better. It is possible for a pension to require up to thirty-three years of continuous employment before full vesting occurs.

There is talk of forcing pensions to allow full "portability" of vesting between plans via a federal balancing agency, similar to the Federal Reserve in the banking system. But until that happens, nearly all pensions are stuck where you earned them, and it may behoove you to analyze the vesting schedule before you change careers or quit a job. It may be that another year or two could spell the difference between having a pension, weak though it may be, and having none. The EBRI also reports that about 20 percent of pension benefits go unclaimed, so keep track of the benefits as you move from job to job—gathering a handful of small checks could be vital when you retire, and besides, you're entitled.

The 1974 ERISA (Employee Retirement Income Security Act) set standards for company pension plans and established the Pension Benefit Guaranty Corporation to protect those whose pensions fail. These were giant steps against the abuses that used to take place, as the firing of employees in the years just before they became eligible for full benefits (remember the rain of fired employees from sixty to sixty-three years old back in the early 1970s?), but most company pensions are still paltry by the time they take effect.

The biggest protection you have with pensions is to stay informed. The reason is that pension rules change continuously. Some plans are absorbed by larger ones, benefits change, some plans require formal requests in years before benefits are due. Insured plans may have different eligibility if they fail and the insurance is invoked, and uninsured plans may make it important to take any and all possible benefits in a lump sum, depending upon the strength of the fund and direction of the economy. Often you are required to provide evidence of your eligibility, and if you are disabled or have moved, your company records are inaccessible. Or if you have died and your dependents are trying to claim your benefits, the process can be nigh unto impossible. Better to find out in advance and have the documentation waiting in a safety deposit box or some other secure but obvious place.

There are also so many options in pensions, it is easy to make big mistakes easily. Some plans allow "participation," enabling you to add to your pot. Some can be discontinued without notice, others may be affected by union activities, illness, or other factors. Payout may be restricted, some variables may require that you ask for them years in advance, and options for survivor benefits are as complicated and varied as the federal tax code.

Finally, you might want to investigate to see how the funds in your pension are being invested, for this has been the downfall of many pensions over the years. Half of all Americans are covered by a company pension, but only a small fraction will receive the full benefits that they might have because they don't keep track of their pensions and will not do what is necessary to maximize the benefits. This will leave more funds available for those of us who do.

THE BEST PENSIONS ARE SELF-MADE

Personal pension plans on the other hand are a step in the direction of fiscal and financial responsibility on behalf of all parties. The Keogh (HR-10) and IRA (Individual Retirement Act) accounts are the first major steps since the establishment of Social Security that this country has taken toward helping the working American take care of his or her own retirement. They have the superb advantage, which company pensions lack, of being excellent tax shelters. The three big advantages are: (1) you don't pay tax on your contribution, so you reduce your taxable income every year you put money into your accounts, (2) you don't pay any tax on the interest or income from your investments in the account, so that over time, the tax exemption builds equity two, three, or four times faster than would be possible in a taxable account, and (3) you pay taxes only when you retire (beginning between the ages of fifty-nine and one-half and seventy-one and one-half), so you can arrange to have a low tax rate, and most people do anyway. Even if you do so well that you have a high tax rate, the tax deferral will have made you extra money.

The disadvantage of the IRA is the comparatively low maximum allowable contribution. Just $2000 at the beginning, it is being raised periodically as inflation makes it less valuable, but it will always lag behind the rather generous allowance given in the Keogh law—which began at $15,000 per year, or 15 percent of income, whichever is less. The so called Super Keogh allows those with large incomes to save more. There is almost no working person who couldn't profit from using an IRA or Keogh. Given the condition of modern pensions, it is reasonable to say that in many, if not most cases, opting out of a company pension in order to put your money in a personal pension is probably a reasonable and smart move.

Fortunately now everyone is allowed to have his own IRA even if he has a company pension, and if you have vested pension benefits you may roll them over into an IRA when you quit your job. Be sure to look into this now, for when you lose a job and are preoccupied, you may forget, and there is a time limit within which you must act. Also, if your job allows you to opt out of the company pension, you can use the money that would have gone into it and fund your personal pension instead. Then you never have to worry about vesting schedules or eligibility requirements ever again. And as for growth of assets, pension managers, when they are honest, have traditionally been the most conservative investors, so you are fairly sure to match their investment success if you follow a prudent investment program.

There are a couple of dandy ways to set up multiple plans, and make extra use of the system. If you are salaried and want more opportunity to invest through the system, you can ask your employer to set up an SEP-IRA. The SEP-IRA works similarly to Social Security in that your employer sets it up, and both he and you contribute to it monthly according to a federally defined formula. But the kicker is that the maximum contribution is $7500 or 15 percent of your salary, whichever is less, and if the employer doesn't pay the full available amount, you *may* make up the difference at year's end. If you are trying to build up your pension, the SEP-IRA is a real asset. Members of Congress are heavy users of all personal pensions, meaning we can be confident that they will continue, and the allowable minimum contributions will steadily rise with inflation.

For lower-income families, the Mini-Keogh lets you contribute up to $750 per year of freelance income to your retirement account. Taxable income must be under $15,000 and freelance income must be under $5000. Perfect for moonlighters, and there is no percentage minimum, so you can moonlight just enough to fill your Mini-Keogh if you want.

If you have very high income, e.g., over $100,000 taxable, a Defined-Benefit Keogh can allow you to bring over $15,000 into your account. You must set up a retirement-income goal and contribute enough to meet that goal, based on some enormously complicated actuarial, interest, and economic-growth tables. Not many accountants know how to set it up properly, but it can be done to advantage. The thing is, those who are eligible often may have found other equally attractive and less complicated tax relief.

If you have enough money in your funds to make the maintenance fees negligible, it may be to your advantage to have more than one account in order to diversify your investments. You might have a plan at your bank, another through a money market or mutual fund, and another through your broker's office. It is even legal to have both a Keogh plan and an IRA at the same time, but you can contribute to one only in any given year, depending upon your employment status. Another alternative: if you are self-employed you can use an SEP-IRA instead of a Keogh to simplify the bookwork in many cases, but that is a decision to be made in concert with a lawyer and accountant. Whatever you decide to do or not to do, please investigate first. It would be a pity to let the best legal tax shelter ever devised go to waste!

THE SAVING GAME

A real problem faced by everyone who wants to expand his or her earning power and financial return is how to find, select, and monitor investments. In other chapters I talk about how to deal with securities and investment opportunities available through your bank or thrift, and insurance companies, but there are many other investments that will present themselves to investors. Handling them with the level of safety and profit that you desire can be a real problem, but one made manageable by finding and utilizing professional advisers and educational opportunities.

For example, choosing and managing a real estate or venture limited partnership is a process many very able and astute businesspeople pursue as a full-time career. The legal problems that can crop up demand the help of a lawyer who is familiar with the area of law involved, and the risk evaluation is probably more complicated than in any other investment the average person is likely to make. If we stick with the example of a real estate limited partnership, it's obvious that you can use a real estate broker, who can be another source of information and advice—or another person who tries to rush you into a compromising position for the sake of a few dollars in commission or other profit from your actions. If you are going to trust an individual to influence your decision-making, take the trouble to investigate that person first.

How does the beginner or the investor who wants to branch out into these kinds of investments guard against the pitfalls, the incompetents, and the crooks? The answer is that unless you have someone who is willing to do it for you, you will have to investigate every potential investment, learn the potential problems, weigh the evidence, and make an informed decision yourself. It can be a lot of trouble, which is why so many people make decisions without doing the work, and end up losers.

Recommendations from some of the large professional organizations may provide some clues as to how to approach the idea. The National Association of Realtors advises that unless a piece of property is clearly a good investment in itself with a good likelihood, based on sound, recognized evaluation methods, of making a strong after-tax profit for a single owner, it is not likely to be a worthwhile investment for a partnership. Thus, one of the signs of a worthwhile investment situation is a competitive marketplace populated with individuals and a mix of buyers as well as partnerships. There are a good number of undeveloped "planned" communities in the deserts of Arizona, California, and Colorado (that are to this day just patches of desert land) which attest to the truth of that and the folly of putting money into unresearched investments. Thousands of investors are bilked through real estate and venture capital schemes that are evidently contrived to generate investments but have no chance of ever being completed, much less sold for a profit.

The IRS and New York and American Stock exchanges all make the same recommendation about tax-shelter investments: *if it isn't an inherently good investment that has a possibility of making a profit, it's not going to be a good tax shelter, or certainly not a safe one.* On that basis alone the IRS disallows thousands of tax-shelter schemes every year, and some of the principals go to jail over it. The other recommendation made by all these organizations is simple, but often ignored at all levels: before you invest, *check into the people who are in charge of the deal.* The Brooklyn Bridge has been sold for scrap at least three times. A poor investment in partnerships or other person-to-person investments is separated from outright fraud by a cat's whisker. In fraud there is intent to cheat or rob, but in a poor investment there is the identical lack of care and investigation that makes fraud possible in the first place. In either case, the penalty is losing all your money. In either case, there is no cure, but the preventive medicine is the same. Honest people don't mind when you check up on them.

At the top of the financial world, investors trust in the people who do it best—professional investment analysts. Without such luxury you must be your own investment analyst. Like all other areas of financial management it requires time, effort, and a driving interest to make sure that you are really on top of the criteria that tell you whether or not to go with an investment. If your inclination is toward higher returns than you can get in safer deals, and your spirit soars at the thought of a gamble, you can at least protect yourself in the ways professional traders use:

One. Diversify. Limit your risk by spreading it around. This puts a load on you to investigate and understand more separate investments, but is perhaps the universal tactic.

Two. Specialize in the area of your highest interest and risk. In other words, diversify in conservative investments that require little special knowledge and then spend your research time looking into a narrow area where you can gain some bankable expertise. You can't be the Universal Man even in the area of investment finance—there's just too much for one person to know.

Three. Devise a complete plan for every investment that details when, how, and why you buy or divest yourself of an item or product, and stick to it—or modify it as the facts change—but don't forget it.

BEFORE INVESTING

What are the basic elements of a sound financial base that you can plan from? These are a good starting place:

1. Adequate savings for emergencies and opportunities
2. Adequate liquid assets (cash) to handle investments
3. A minimum amount of debt (you need a credit history)
4. Major secure assets, such as home equity
5. Prudent levels of insurance
6. A dependable source of income exceeding living costs

COMMON INVESTMENTS AND USES

Investment	Common Use	Risk Level
Bank accounts	safe income	L
Bank certificate of deposit	safe income	L
T-bills	safe income	L
Treasury and other federal pass-throughs	safe income	L
Money-market funds	income, growth	L
Commercial paper	safe income	varies
Treasury or state bonds	safe income	L
Federal agency bonds	safe income	L
Corporate bonds	safe income	varies
Convertible bonds	income, growth	varies
Bond mutual funds	income, growth	M
Bond funds	income, growth	M
Tax-exempt bonds, Treasury Bills, etc.	safe income	L
Municipal bonds	safe income	L
Corporate common stock	growth, income	varies
Stock mutual funds	growth, income	varies
Preferred stock	income, growth	varies
Convertible preferred stock	income, growth	L-M
Warrants	growth	L-M
Real estate	growth	varies
Commodities (including gold)	growth	H
Collectibles	growth	H
Business partnerships	growth	H

Before you make any investment, you must know the answers to these questions:

1. Why am I considering this investment, and does it meet my needs?
2. Is the risk involved acceptable?
3. Do I know enough about the investment to make a truly intelligent decision?
4. Do I know enough about the promoters or managers of the investment to trust them?
5. Am I willing to spend the time and effort necessary to investigate the investment before I decide to go with it, and assuming I do invest money, to monitor it properly?

SELECTING INVESTMENTS

Deciding which investment is acceptable for you involves two major decisions: One, Is the risk level acceptable? and, two, Which kind of investment opportunity are you willing to spend the time and effort learning about so that you have knowledge to intelligently weigh the investment alternatives?

Clearly the risks inherent in commodities trading make it unacceptable for anyone not already capable in other sophisticated investment methods, and even then ready to devote a good deal of time studying and working the markets. A beginner can very well enter the stock market by first investigating the mutual funds, then moving on to blue chip stocks, and eventually into short-term growth-stock trading. Collectibles may provide a way for you to accept greater risk, especially if you have an area of interest or expertise. A person shy of any paper investments or willing to accept almost no risk can settle on the government bonds, pass-throughs, and CDs in order to guarantee a fixed rate of return, yet still have a field of options from which to choose.

SAMPLE YOUNG PERSON'S EARLY INVESTMENTS

30% bank CDs and T-bills
30% mutual funds, half money market and half stock
30% blue chip stocks or bonds
10% growth stocks or collectibles

ANALYSIS

All but 10 percent is in conservative investments. All investments are fairly short term so they can be liquidated when the person finds a better alternative. This is a very easy portfolio to move into growth funds, then a more aggressive stock plan, money-market certificates and commercial paper as well as more in speculative collectibles, real estate partnerships, or gold as the investor's sophistication broadens.

SAMPLE MIDLIFE INVESTMENTS

20%   tax-preferred commercial paper and money-market funds
30%   mutual funds, bonds, and blue chip stocks
20%   growth funds and growth stocks
10%   gold or similar alternative to cash
20%   real estate, business partnerships, private loans,
      other nonstandard investments

ANALYSIS

The breakdown is typical in an even economy. This person has confidence in his or her skill in the stock market, and is confident that interest rates will not rise, although he is hedged against that alternative with the 10 percent gold holding. The 20 percent in tax-preferred holdings indicates higher income typical of the middle years and the need to manage annual income through tax planning. The 20 percent real estate or business partnerships must be well researched. From an objective point of view, a rather conservative, yet reasonably forward-looking portfolio.

SAMPLE PRERETIREMENT INVESTMENTS

30%   bank CDs, T-bills, government bonds
30%   conservative mutual funds, type depending upon markets
20%   gold or similar alternatives to cash
20%   real estate, collectibles, preferred stock or corporate bonds—
      investments capable of growth, very safe, easy to liquidate but
      may require time to do so

ANALYSIS

All investments here are conservative, indicating that the person does not feel he can afford any real risk. The breakdown is well balanced in an economy that is neither in rampaging inflation or severe recession, but will survive nicely in either case. There is some allowance for appreciation in gold and real estate, collectibles, etc., but the exposure is spread out and limited. Typical of a middle-class preretirement plan that has been twenty years or more in the making and will be easy to manage far into the future.

SAMPLE SINGLE MIDLIFE INVESTMENTS

- 10% commercial paper, thirty to ninety days
- 20% gold and gold-mining stocks
- 20% real estate limited partnerships
- 20% stocks, stock options
- 20% collectibles, art, antiques
- 10% bank CDs

ANALYSIS

These investments show acceptance of greater risk and more self-confidence than the previous examples. This person is after a higher rate of return and is willing to pay the price in terms of maintaining short-term, volatile investments in addition to higher risk. There is a substantial cushion, however, and if this person is a careful investor, there is nothing reckless about the portfolio. It is aggressive yet appropriately balanced.

SAMPLE YOUNG MANAGER'S INVESTMENTS

- 20% NOW and readily accessible mutual-fund accounts
- 20% growth stocks
- 25% stock options, half covered and half naked
- 20% a real estate partnership
- 15% investment-grade photographs and lithographs

ANALYSIS

This portfolio shows either aggressiveness or foolish adventurism. This person is after maximum return in every investment vehicle, and is willing to bet on which will bring the best return. For such an attitude, there should probably be a broader mix of investments in order to spread the risk around. However, he or she may feel confident in the investments shown because of personal research or other insight into them. The large portion of funds in quickly refundable NOW and selected mutual funds show that the investor is ready to make new investments soon and will make a quick decision if necessary.

Each of these sample cases shows how your position in life and your attitude toward risk affect investment decisions. They purposely lean toward the conservative side because this is where the less experienced or less confident financial plan must begin. With experience and success come the prudence and wisdom to win in more speculative investments often enough to win overall. Break down your own investment nest egg into the investments that match your present abilities and emotions. Then investigate the areas you've chosen. More speculative investments with potential for greater returns can then be a part of your one-year, five-year, and longer-range plans as discussed earlier in the chapter. Whatever you want to do with your investments, begin right now.

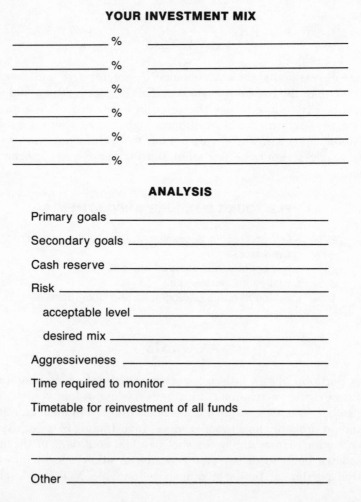

YOUR INVESTMENT MIX

_____ %   _____

_____ %   _____

_____ %   _____

_____ %   _____

_____ %   _____

_____ %   _____

ANALYSIS

Primary goals _____

Secondary goals _____

Cash reserve _____

Risk _____

   acceptable level _____

   desired mix _____

Aggressiveness _____

Time required to monitor _____

Timetable for reinvestment of all funds _____

_____

_____

Other _____

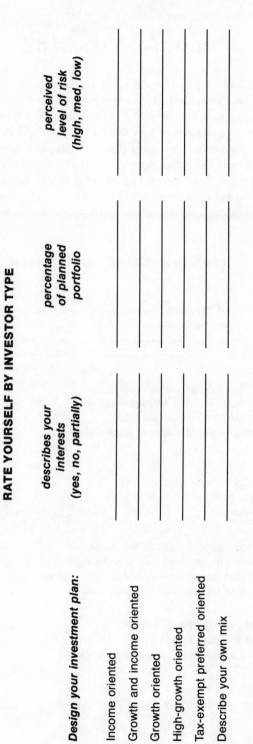

RATE YOURSELF BY INVESTOR TYPE

Design your investment plan:	describes your interests (yes, no, partially)	percentage of planned portfolio	perceived level of risk (high, med, low)
Income oriented			
Growth and income oriented			
Growth oriented			
High-growth oriented			
Tax-exempt preferred oriented			
Describe your own mix			

PLANNING A STRATEGY

When you have made the decision to go with an investment, your responsibility isn't over. In fact, it's just begun. Now you need to monitor the investment, you must decide why you have it, when you plan to sell it, under what circumstances you would want to sell it, what profit you intend to make, what loss you are willing to take, and the list goes on. The following form will help you decide whether to make an investment or not. And, once you have taken the plunge, it will help you to keep the important decisions regarding it in the forefront of your financial mind.

INVESTMENT-STRATEGY PLANNER

Date bought/invested _____
Price _____
Commissions _____
Total price _____

Periodic return (monthly, annually, etc.)   _____
Minimum acceptable return at any future time   _____
Salable value at which I will sell for profit   _____
Loss price at which I will liquidate in hopes of
   cutting losses   _____

Current cost (original price plus losses)   _____
Current gain (any gain minus original price)   _____
Current annual return   _____

Date before which I expect profit to materialize   _____
Date before which I expect loss risk to grow excessive   _____
Date at which I plan to sell even if profits don't appear   _____
Date at which I plan to sell even if a loss shows   _____

How often must I review this investment?   _____
Where will I find the data I need?   _____
Where can I find advice and further analysis on
   this investment?   _____

Current plans for this investment   _____

Successful investors study investments before they take the plunge, and then monitor them closely. It's a habit as much as anything else. They also make contingency plans so that when time passes, or circumstances change, they know *when, where,* and *why* to change their investments. Every time you fail to do these things, you raise the risk level of the investment, so maintaining your investments is actually a way of reducing investment risk and increasing return.

6

Insurance, Agents, and Risk

IINSURANCE IS AN AGREEMENT wherein a cash premium is paid against an eventuality of some sort, which, if it comes to pass, causes the agreed-upon value of the insurance to be paid. *Assurance* is just someone trying to make you feel good. *Ensurance* is a point of logic, similar to a guarantee, meaning that something has been done to make sure the event will come to pass, but if it does not, no repercussions are forthcoming. Only insurance pays cash.

What do you need to insure? That's easy—you insure what you can't afford to lose. If other people depend upon you or your income, you insure your life, making them beneficiaries. If you can't afford to be sued for a quarter of a million dollars, you insure your driving with auto liability insurance. If you can't afford to replace your house or the things in it, you buy homeowner's insurance, and so on.

Sounds easy so far, but answer this question: Why should Joe Smith insure his car and why is Bob Doe prudent when he doesn't bother to? Joe has a new car, low income, and he drives in the city daily. Odds are high that someday he'll have an accident, and even a relatively small repair bill would strain his financial position. A major repair or substantial lawsuit would wipe him out.

Bob Doe has a not-so-new Rolls-Royce, but even if it were new, he wouldn't bother buying collision insurance because he can afford to replace the car with pocket change. If you pressed him, he'd explain that over the span of one's lifetime, the sum total of insurance payments would exceed the total cost of the accidents for the average person. Otherwise, insurance companies wouldn't make any money.

For Bob, whose wealth makes him effectively *self-insured*, most insurance is a bad bet against the odds. For Joe, as with the vast majority of us, insurance creates peace of mind we can't live without because we can't live with the alternative. Millions of Joe Smiths don't buy as much insurance as they need, and millions of Bob Does waste their money out of habit, or because they simply enjoy the secure feeling insurance can provide. You can avoid throwing your money away in either of these ways as long as you *select your insurance based on your current personal needs.*

The reason insurance is on the whole a terrific deal is that it is a cost-effective way to save any person from accidental financial ruin. The competitive marketplace has kept the average insurance coverage at a relatively fair price, and the sheer numbers of insureds have enabled insurance companies to create policies for almost every conceivable need. There are exceptions, naturally. Some individuals risk their financial lives in ways that cannot be insured, and some insurance is not cost-effective, but for most of us, in most situations, using good insurance is a way to protect ourselves against the long odds—accidents, illness, death, and other acts of God that could wipe out a life's achievements in one fell swoop.

Another exception has to do with the widespread effectiveness and acceptance of automobile insurance. Liability coverage is required by law in some states, which seems to have the curious effect of inoculating the *uninsured* population against the financial effects of auto accidents in many cases. Of course what has happened is that all insured drivers end up sharing the cost, or at least that's the way it is supposed to work, and that is why no-fault insurance is supposed to be so great. Ironically, it has also created a situation wherein those who fail to insure themselves and have no assets reap no punishment for their irresponsibility. The responsibility has become solely monetary, so that those without assets have no fear of being sued. The courts will slap their wrists, effectively wiping their slate clean.

Meanwhile, the rest of us with savings, possessions, and general assets must protect ourselves and our fellow citizens by paying for insurance. So there you have it: The very rich don't need insurance because they are self-insured, and the insolvent don't need it because they suffer no penalty for not having it. That leaves the rest of society to carry the load.

A common misconception about insurance is that it constitutes real protection against all loss. The truth is that insurance is only a contract that guarantees payment of a carefully specified amount if and when a specified event comes to pass, and nothing more. The only real protection is spelled out in the contract, namely the policy.

Notice that this is very different from "indemnification." It is a word that is bandied about, but very few types of insurance indemnify against anything, for true indemnification is to guarantee that *all* the value of the damage or loss will be replaced, not merely a predetermined amount. Don't mistake insurance for indemnification—they can be the same, but even when the term is used, they almost never are.

If insurance is rarely indemnification, it is always betting. The law pretends to make a differentiation, but as a practical matter, they are variations of the same game. You get to bet against fate at specified odds. The bet at the track may be 12 to 1. You know your odds and you place your money. If you put down $10 and the event comes to pass, you get your $120, no more, no less. If the event doesn't come to pass, you get nothing but a thrill. Insurance operates in the same way, only the company can pay less than the odds seem to state. And, like the casino, the insurance company sets the odds and stacks them to guarantee that the company wins overall.

In business, insurance is part of the management area known as risk management. The steps in risk-management theory involve (1) identifying risk, (2) evaluating risk, and (3) dealing with it in one of three ways:

1. Accepting risk
2. Avoiding risk entirely or in part
3. Transferring risk to another

Anyone would choose option three if there weren't any catches, but of course, there are. The people who accept transferred risk are mostly the insurance companies, and naturally they charge a fee for their service of spreading risk more or less evenly among a large population.

To get a better idea of how this all works, apply risk-management theory to automobile driving. First we identify the risks:

• Accident-caused repair expenses
• Medical bills in the event of injury
• Legal and court-imposed fees in the case of suit (liability)

These happen to correspond to the three major elements in comprehensive auto insurance.

Next we evaluate the three. Repair (collision) costs are prohibitive for some of us, inconsequential for the wealthy or those driving junk cars. Medical costs are prohibitive for everyone except the very wealthy. In the final area of risk, liability, the potential cost can run into the millions of dollars the way courts are running these days. Even a multimillionnaire is vulnerable to financial ruin, but someone who is broke and has no possessions has little to lose.

Now we must deal with the risk according to our circumstances. A poor person may *accept* all risk on his own shoulders, for he has no assets to lose, he can transfer all medical costs to the government, and he probably cannot afford adequate insurance, or thinks he cannot. He counts upon the system of socialized medicine and nearly universal insurance to protect him.

The wealthy person decides on a matter of discretion at what point he wants to be self-insuring, and buys coverage only to protect against financial disaster beyond that level. That may mean buying only major medical and liability insurance, or only liability.

The middle-of-the-road person enjoys none of the options of the poor or the wealthy, with the exception of limited self-insurance. None of the three areas of risk are supportable, so the alternatives are to avoid risk (by not driving) or to transfer risk by buying insurance.

The idea and winning tactic in the insurance game is to go through this process not just for every area of risk, but once an insurance policy is being considered, to go through the risk-management alternatives with every area of coverage and every feature in the policy. The goal of risk management is not just to buy insurance when it is needed, but also to make sure that the prudent amount of coverage is being bought at a competitive price. This applies to the deductible as well as to the face value of the policy.

AUTO INSURANCE

Price and feature shopping are matters of detail. Analyzing your situation in terms of risk management before you begin comparing policies will help in deciding which policy features are more important and which are less so. The process of comparing policies can become an involved and tedious process. And remember, you must compare policies not only when you first shop for insurance, but also each time you or the company sees a need to modify the coverage you have, or when more cost-effective coverage becomes available.

To simplify the task you must impose a system on it. The following chart is a sample comparison chart of the major features of competing automobile policies:

	Coverage amount	Premium amount
Liability	_____	_____
Personal injury	_____	_____
Uninsured motorist	_____	_____
Collision	_____	_____
Deductible	_____	_____
Comprehensive features		
_____	_____	_____
_____	_____	_____

Unusual or excluded features

_____ _____ _____
_____ _____ _____

You can easily make similar comparison lists with other types of coverage. Often if you ask for the promotional material from several companies, they will supply the lists of features you'll want to compare.

INSURANCE PRE-EVALUATION WORKSHEET

Type/Company	Annual Premium	Deductible Options	Difference
_____	_____	_____	_____
	_____	_____	_____
	_____	_____	_____
_____	_____	_____	_____
	_____	_____	_____
	_____	_____	_____

Is deductible affordable in average monthly cash flow?
If not, is increased price of lower deductible affordable?
If so, does lower price of lower deductible justify that option?
What are significant policy differences other than price?

LIFE INSURANCE

There is no good reason at this point to have life insurance with a savings provision unless you already bought it and it is not worth your while to drop the policy to move into term insurance. Or you are a life insurance salesman and you need to support your product. There are many purported reasons for buying all sorts of life policies with savings elements, but without exception they are demolished by this analysis, which has been publicized by many consumer advocacy groups.

1. All life insurance consists of straight term insurance combined with a low-interest savings component.
2. If you divided those policies into their two components, the straight term can be bought for less. Basic economics ensure that this is always the case.

3. If you take the amount of the total premium for the entire combined policy, subtract the portion going to the term portion, and take the savings portion out into the general marketplace, you will always be able to safely invest that money in instruments that give you much better return than the insurance company is willing or able to give. This, too, is always the case, although the gap is narrowing as insurance companies struggle to compete.

There is a problem with term life insurance, however, and that is the lower profits going to insurance companies. The extremely low per-$1000-coverage price of the most cost-efficient term products naturally forces down the commission to the writing agent to the point where he or she simply cannot provide extensive service and counseling. The ramifications of this are twofold: One, if you buy term insurance, you cannot expect Cadillac treatment from the agent and his office. The alternative is to be personally better educated, to read and understand your insurance policy and the literature available from the company, and to discuss things with other financial advisers. Two, we're probably about to witness the demise of most of the old-fashioned insurance agencies. Ralph Nader labeled the insurance industry the most inefficient in the country, and he may have been correct. While part of the flab was sent to company profits and excessive numbers of employees, a portion of that excess went to provide extra service and neighborhood representation, at least in the better companies. Today, cost efficiency will revamp the entire business, and we'll have traded cheaper insurance for direct communication with the district office, and maybe direct interface with the central computer instead of your neighborhood agent.

The amount of life insurance (the face value of the policy) should be a function of whom you want to protect and how. If you overbuy, you end up pouring large premium payments down the tubes, and odds are you'll never get any back. If you underinsure, your dependents may have a difficult time coping with the loss of your financial strength. The average agent will recommend much more than you likely need, and that's a good place to begin.

The names of the first and secondary beneficiaries are important, for this can affect how and when the policy is paid off, in addition to determining to whom it is paid. The usual example case is that of a man who names his wife as sole beneficiary. Later they are both killed in a car crash and the orphaned children are left unprotected, the policy haven fallen into the taxable estate. Proceeds from insurance, like assets in a testamentary estate, can be redirected by the courts if the named beneficiaries are dead or incapacitated.

The strategy is make sure that all the beneficiaries are those who need protection, that the disbursement is defined, and that those who do not need protection are excluded except for matters of courtesy. After naming first and secondary beneficiaries, you may want to specify that proceeds go to your estate according to the instructions in your will. For example, a husband and wife might buy policies on each other, based on their individual earning power and probable needs as single survivors. Children or other dependents, or relatives and friends, can be included as contingent beneficiaries. The legal details are different in every state, so ask your agent or lawyer, or find someone else who knows the facts.

Other common problems arise from naming children by name, leaving subsequent offspring excluded, or by failing to modify policies when divorces occur, meaning persons outside the family may make undesired claims. Very often these problem clauses are written into the policies and people assume that they must sign the dotted line. Hogwash. Insurance policies are contracts, and the companies are used to dealing with added and deleted clauses. It may be a trial and error process to find out what the company will accept and what it insists upon, but this can result in superior coverage for you and your loved ones.

Properly written life insurance allows a surviving spouse to have money to operate with while probate clears the courts, while Junior gets through college, while the spouse figures out a way to make a living and keep the homelife going. If you love someone enough to protect him or her with life insurance, or you depend upon someone so much that you need to insure him or her, take the time to shop carefully for the best policy and then implement it prudently. This has to be figured on the basis of the cost of the style of living, the earning potential of the person or persons involved, and the income-producing potential of any assets involved. This is tough because it calls for judgment calls about the people you love. Can they get by with comparatively little or will you need to protect them against the smallest adverse breeze? The agent will be elated to hear of the latter. The process is one of compiling projected budgets for your dependents and figuring the income expected from their ability to work, Social Security, pensions, and other independent forms of income, and then calculating how much money will be needed to fill the gap and for how long.

CALCULATING LIFE INSURANCE NEEDS

Dependents	Current Income	Required Income	Sure Income	Earning Potential	Difference (Ri − Si)
_____	_____	_____	_____	_____	_____
_____	_____	_____	_____	_____	_____
_____	_____	_____	_____	_____	_____

(Difference = Insurance Need. Multiply for Time.)

Reviewing life insurance ought to be a painless and easy process, but to do the job right it is usually a fairly involved process. All of the reasons for buying life insurance in the first place must be considered each time. The persons being protected, the policy particulars, the state of health of the insured, the financial condition of all involved, the availability of new types of products, and the state of the economy should all be considered. If you include this housekeeping task among your regular financial overhauls, it can be less painful, for much of the pertinent date will be fresh and easily found. Be sure to include it on the rehash list of things to review if anything of note takes place in your financial-responsibility picture.

Unfortunately, with today's rapidly changing marketing and legal situations, price isn't the only important consideration when shopping for insurance. The overall low-priced life companies are not in most cases the low-priced ones in terms of the newer universal and market-share policies. So you must decide what *type* of policy you want before you shop, too! In addition, premium price is just one cost factor. Others include dividends (in mutual whole life policies and annuities), cash-value accrual in whole life, and prevailing interest rates in the economy. However, mutual companies (selling participating or "par" policies) are rarely cost-competitive on an annualized basis because they cost you the interest on overpayment of premiums. This way they let you take a share of the "net" proceeds, but take almost all the earned interest beforehand. Thus non-par policies are generally more cost-competitive.

Cash value pertains only to non-term policies. Some of the newest products provide a much higher rate of return than did the whole life policies of the past, but they are as yet paltry compared to prevailing available interest rates. It is technically possible that some universal and market-share-type policies with floating rates could pay out as much as money-market rates temporarily in periods of declining interest rates, but this is unlikely and leaves them at a disadvantage compared to straight term.

While company and policy shopping, always keep in mind that life insurance is really *death* insurance, and what you are really after is the death benefit (policy payout) rather than the life benefit (added features meant to sell the product or make money for the insurance company at the policyholder's expense). The insurance companies have been called "the hidden bankers" because of the vast funds they control. Let them do their own banking, and buy only insurance from them. Your banker can offer you better and safer havens for your extra monies at better rates, and he'll let you have your money back when you ask. The insurance company won't.

CALCULATING MORE INSURANCE NEEDS

If you ask the average life insurance agent to calculate how much insurance you need, he'll gladly whip out an impressive-looking chart which purports to illustrate what amount of coverage is recommended by the industry for various circumstances. Go through the process with him and you'll get a final figure that is two or more times what an impartial financial planner would come up with. The calculations behind the company charts are based upon two criteria: safety needs (which are so subjective only you can decide what they are anyway) and ability to pay (which the insurance company views as an opportunity while you should see it as a limitation).

Safety needs are the main criteria for all of us, yet we're encouraged to meet them through the back door. We're presented with insurance and asked to look at our lives to see whether it sounds appealing. Rather we should examine our needs, identify risk, and then shop for the most cost-effecient available policies that help us to cover or eliminate our risk exposure. Anything else is bunk, salesmanship, or both.

A billionaire buys life insurance only because he knows that his estate will require a lot of unencumbered money to survive the probate period. A $20,000-a-year worker with five children has the same need, plus the need to replace his earning power in the case of his demise, but he is constrained by the amount of premium he can afford. The billionaire's dilemma is to buy what makes sense as a courtesy; the worker's dilemma is to buy as much as he can afford to because he can't afford as much as he needs.

Given the chance to persuade, the average life agent will oversell to both. Even if the worker fails to keep up his payments, the agent gets his or her commission and the company gets to cancel with a clear profit. The rich can afford some excess, so any way you slice it, the agent is induced to oversell, despite his upstanding morals. Thus comes the cardinal rule to keep in mind when dealing with insurance agents: make your decision about how much insurance to buy in conjunction with someone other than the agent and in addition to your spouse. Your financial planner or other financial professional are good beginnings: Consumer guides are the cheapest route.

Easy to say but not so easy to do? Maybe so, but if it weren't often necessary, most states wouldn't have the "second-chance laws," as they do. These laws provide that if anyone buys insurance, he or she has a grace period (usually ten days or so) in which it's possible to recant and receive a full refund, no questions asked. The laws exist because they're needed, so don't feel bashful about following the precedent of the legislators.

EMERGENCY INSURANCE

You can't look up "Emergency Insurance" in the Yellow Pages, you won't find it listed in Best's Insurance Guides, and your agent won't recognize the term if you call him up and ask about it. But it exists, and for many of us it is very important at least once in our lives. Emergency insurance is protection that short-term coverage of very specific risk which you buy because long-term coverage is unavailable or inappropriate. Some typical examples of when emergency insurance is needed include: the person who is suddenly laid off the job where he has enjoyed group insurance and suddenly has a grace period of a few days to find new coverage for himself and his family; the person whose insurance company goes belly up and no one knows what if any coverage still exists or for how long; the person whose insurance company suddenly sends a notice that in a few days the policy will terminate due to corporate decisions, and there will be no new renewal or conversion to other coverage; a widow, widower, or divorcée whose spouse had been carrying health, auto, and other insurance through a group plan that disavows the unfortunate survivor as ineligible to continue as part of the group. The examples go on and on.

Many people in these situations let themselves slide without insurance, but these are the times when they need protection most. In most states and under many plans, there is a courtesy period during which coverage must extend, but the periods vary, so you have to check right away. Also, in certain states and in certain plans the individual can *convert* group coverage to individual coverage to personal coverage for a limited period (usually up to a year) or permanently, but at a different premium scale. The insured does this by paying the portion of the group plan previously paid by the employer in addition to the contribution which had been coming out of the paycheck or benefits plan. The trouble with this is that group plans are structured to take advantage of corporate tax breaks, and the total premium fee turns out to be very much more expensive—often twice as high—as comparable coverage obtained through an open group plan. Nevertheless, if you find yourself in such a position, the peace of mind can well justify the high price for a limited time. Presumably when you get a new job or otherwise find a new insurer you can drop the old plan in favor of the new cost-effective one. Of course you can't just bail out of old plans, you have to let it lapse, even for getting out of a plan which doesn't want you. Fortunately, some states are adopting "guaranteed convertibility laws" to handle these very problems, so check with your agent or your state insurance commission office.

Another option for households with two or more workers is for the newly uninsured person to join the spouse's group-insurance plan as a dependent. Some companies will allow this designation and coverage to persist even after a laid-off spouse takes on a full-time job. But even if the company insists upon dropping the coverage later, it can be an excellent interim protection plan.

The simplest alternative for someone suddenly caught without health insurance but wise enough to insist upon having some is to buy some short-term protection, which many insurors have begun marketing in the past few years. Most of these plans are major medical coverage for families and individuals, with higher than average premiums. In essence the companies let their actuaries set up a separate group and assign a high risk factor to it, allowing few restrictions in return for a high premium rate.

As with regular health, short-term health comes in a wide variety of packages. The most important variables are the deductible, the daily hospital rate, and maximum allowance per illness or injury. If you can afford to self-insure for the first $1000 and get a policy with an average ceiling, you may get away with very reasonable rates. If you can only find plans with no deductible, high maximums per illness, and offering $1 million or more in lifetime benefits, the price can be heftier. You can console yourself that it is only temporary until you can shop around for a permanent plan or join a group with a full-featured, cost-effective plan.

Short-term coverage is usually sold in blocks of from thirty days to one year and is often renewable just once or twice. Exclusions and other features may be less attractive than those in the average policy, but the entry requirements will usually be more lax as well. Knowing about emergency insurance and having thought out how to use it is insurance in itself, for it is a difficult thing to discover and deal with while you are in the midst of a personal crisis.

Specialty companies usually offer short-term insurance. The best-known type is probably the one-day life insurance you can buy from vending machines at the airports. These companies may also call themselves "assigned risk" specialists, although this most commonly refers to auto and business insurance carriers. The most famous is Lloyd's of London. Most are more difficult to locate, and each must be investigated individually for products offered, premium rates, and strength.

MANAGING YOUR ASSETS

Surprisingly, one of an insuror's biggest expenses is the customer who keeps his policies and coverage meticulously up to date. It's true that the direct consequence of updating insurance is usually an increase in premiums from expanded coverage, adding riders and attachments of different kinds, but the added cost is assumed only after evaluating the risk and deciding that the added insurance is needed. It is a prudent, voluntary choice. On the other hand, the policyholder who makes a claim on an outdated and inadequate policy loses big in the protection he receives, and the insurance company saves big.

In all kinds of insurance, the odds, otherwise known as the actuarial tables, are figured on the basis of a lackadaisical public. The industry makes billions of dollars off people who let their policies lapse, who fail to review their limitations in their policies, and especially those who fail to update policies to meet new circumstances in their lives and in the economy. All these people receive very little payment from their insurors when they need it, and it's all *their* responsibility.

The following example perfectly exemplifies the problem with out-of-date insurance. The average homeowner's insurance policy contains property, liability, and limited medical coverage, with real property being the focus of the coverage. Typically the agent and homeowner sit down right after the home is bought or the lease is signed and figure out how much insurance is needed in case of major catastrophe, such as fire or a falling airliner. This is great, and if everyone is satisfied, the policy goes into a drawer and is not seen again for years.

Well, it may come to pass that Mr. Doe's house does burn down, so he retrieves the policy, or a copy from his agent, and sets up a meeting with the agent. He feels kindly toward the agent because he hasn't bothered Mr. Doe, and the company has hardly raised the rates over the years compared to other expenses. Now he wants to replace his house and everything in it that was burned up.

"Sorry," is the agent's first word. It seems that the coverage hadn't been updated since the house was bought and there are some problems. He starts with the small ones: Even though the Does claim they refurnished the house with fine heirloom antiques and expensive collectibles, they do not have certified appraisals or receipts to prove it, so in accordance with the standard policy provision and standard industry practice, the company elects to pay them for the average price of all furniture calculated from standardized tables and depreciated for several years' of wear.

"Wear!" screams Doe. "My furniture was worth more yesterday than when we bought it—it appreciated in value!" But without proof, the company is obligated to pay him or her for the average cost of replacing average American used furniture. It's a tiny fraction of the actual cost of the beautiful pieces he and his family had worked hard to collect.

More bad news—his $2000 stamp collection was specifically excluded—he would have had to pay for a special rider to protect it. The same goes for his wife's gold jewelery inherited from Aunt Bessie—the standard policy restricted the family to $500 worth in the house at the time. And as for her mink coat and Ming Dynasty vases, forget it without both the appraisals and the riders.

As soon as he recovered from catalepsy, Doe asked the agent about the house. Even if they had to live in furniture from the Goodwill store and could only reminisce about their lost treasures, at least they could live in a reconstructed version of their old house, right? "Wrong," sympathized the agent. "Why didn't you tell me that things had changed so at your house?" As with most homeowner's policies, the Does' required that they maintain coverage equal to at least 80 percent of the actual *current* replacement cost. Doe had boasted with pleasure how much his house had appreciated and how "houses just aren't built that way anymore." How true.

The face value of the policy would only cover a third of the estimated rebuilding costs, but the company didn't even have to pay that. Because Doe hadn't met the 80 percent requirement, they were also allowed to reduce the payout according to a depreciation scale, in effect paying him the price it would have cost to build the house ten years ago minus ten years' worth of wear and tear. The final figure would rebuild the garage quite nicely, figured Doe, but the house, forget it.

All policies and state laws differ, but the Does' experience is not uncommon. Take the hint: *Insurance policies must be reviewed each year plus every time something happens to affect their coverage or qualifications.* Doe's tragedy was with a homeowner's policy, but similar disasters can occur in other coverage as well. The same is true in health insurance, which was designed ten years ago (the cost of health care rose over 300 percent in the decade 1970 to 1980 and remains the fastest-rising personal expense, according to government statistics), or life insurance, which was written to protect a small estate, three dependents and according to the law ten years ago, but now ignores the new baby, Grandpa, hasn't been adjusted for inflation, and conflicts with the new probate laws, not to mention the new will. Auto insurance when a new member of the family begins driving, when the new car is transformed into a heap, when you quit smoking, or when you stop commuting every weekday and now use your chariot only for a few trips to the market and a trip now and again. When something changes in your life, odds are your insurance needs change as well, and either you need to increase your coverage or you may be eligible to drop excess coverage and save yourself some unnecessary premiums.

For those of us who keep insurance up to date, the laziness of those who don't is a blessing, for it reduces the cost of our insurance and keeps rates down. If so many people weren't so careless, insurance companies would have to pay out considerably more, would be considerably less efficient, and the premiums would inevitably rise. So praise be to all those who let their insurance policies lapse and deteriorate, but please don't be among them!

Beyond the standard forms of insurance most of us indulge in when they make sense for us, there are many special kinds we are presented with or that we seek out to protect our interests. Mortgage, vacation, legal, maternity, motorcycle, and other special insurance must be approached with the same risk-management analysis you apply to your other insurance considerations.

Policies offered at the site of the activity or which in some other way come to you instead of you seeking them out are usually among the most expensive available. A disproportionately large number of insurance-commission complaints trace back to these kinds of insurance buys. If there is a possibility that you will need special insurance, call your agent to see if he offers any. Whether he does or not, he may well be able to give you advice about how to compare policies against each other and against your needs. And then there is always my favorite source—the consumer magazines. Magazines covering special interests are often advertising targets for specialty companies, and the magazines often feature articles about the special insurance.

As are the other financial services, the insurance companies are diversifying as widely and as quickly as they can. Companies that were very narrow in focus a few years ago may have coverage available in a large number of specialty areas. That doesn't mean they have a policy with good features, or, that if they do, that it is priced competitively, but it is encouraging to know that finding insurance is getting easier all the time.

One type of special insurance deserves special mention—the so-called Social Security and Medicare supplementals. Whether it is meant to fill the gap between monthly fixed expenses or your maintenance medical expenses, the shopping process can become rather complicated if you want to ensure that you are getting a good deal. Naturally you do, for if you are a person who requires the insurance, you cannot afford to toss unneeded premiums out the window. The fact is that many, perhaps a majority, of the companies offering such coverage do not have cost-effective plans.

First, you must find and define the gap in protection in living or medical expenses left open. The government agencies can help you do this; just call the local office and ask. Many consumer and advocacy groups also have counselors and offer worksheets and guides to help. The idea is to provide coverage in risk not covered by Medicare, to provide additional coverage when the amount provided by Medicare is inadequate, and to make sure that none of the additional coverage being bought duplicates protection provided by the Medicare coverage.

The biggest rip-off artists in the industry are many of the mail order insurance companies that use scare tactics and deceptive advertising to urge people to buy coverage that duplicates existing coverage, thereby lowering their payouts, making the insurance almost useless, and cheating all the policyholders. Other plans provide protection in addition to existing coverage, but only if you lose coverage you already have—an extremely unlikely possibility. So if you shop for "Medi-Gap" insurance, make all the comparisons you can identify and be extra careful.

Remember that insurance is not the kind of contract you can put into a drawer and forget. It changes with every change in your life, with changes in the economy, in the laws, in the industry. If you want good, efficient protection you must do a certain amount of insurance policy maintenance. That maintenance is a sort of insurance that you carry on yourself, ensuring that you are getting your money's worth and what you deserve.

When shopping for both an agent and a policy, there is no equivalent to the APR standard as we have for bank accounts, but it is possible to see an interest-adjusted cost index for the coverage you are interested in. If the insurance office doesn't have this information, they can easily get it from their home office, and you can sometimes find condensed versions in consumer magazines or insurance trade journals, easily found in the library. The reason this standard is so important is that among the top companies—those with a Best's rating of B+ or better—the American Institute for Economic Research has found that for equivalent coverage the per-decade cost can vary by a factor of two to one. In other words, some policies are twice as expensive as others for essentially the same coverage. That's about the best argument I've heard for price shopping. Only some thirty states require that interest-adjusted cost figures be shown to all prospective customers, but that doesn't stop the prudent shopper from asking for them.

HOW TO READ AND COMPARE INSURANCE POLICIES

It is an unwritten rule that whatever is written in large type in an insurance policy is relatively unimportant. That is an overstatement, but the point is valid, for the information that is most critical is usually listed in small type in sections with such titles as "Exclusions," "Conditions," or "Limitations." This is where the real parameters of the policies are defined. When comparing policies, then, list the limitations on your worksheet right along with the premium amounts, guaranteed payouts, and grandiose claims.

Most consumer-protection laws relating to insurance are meant to guarantee that the policy shopper has guideposts to follow in the hunting process. Although there is no equivalent of the "annual percentage rate" most states impose upon banks advertising interest rates, insurors are required to be honest and responsibile in answering questions. Any bona fide insurance office knows the average premium, average payout for a standard claim, and other basic information. This is a part of the information agents receive from the companies to aid them in understanding the claims process and also to help them sell more efficiently. If the agent won't give this information, then he or she can get it. If he won't get it, or at least some of it, he's lazy or malicious.

Comparing a number of policies requires reading the contracts and compiling a worksheet. This needn't be excessively tedious. You will find the sections of the policies with the important data rather quickly, and learn to hurry through the pat paragraphs in every policy to satisfy legal requirements. You can also use the recommendations of special-interest groups that compare policies. Some auto clubs do this, as do a number of consumer magazines. Realize, however, that policies can change drastically in a short period of time, so that a relatively good policy in January may be completely outmoded by September. The only safeguard, clearly, is to compare the available policies yourself at the time you need the coverage.

WHERE TO FIND INSURANCE INFORMATION

The details of buying homeowner's, property and liability, auto, and specialty insurance share many of the problems inherent in buying life insurance. The sources of information are essentially the same, and just as necessary. The Yellow Pages will connect you with companies, but only checking can tell you the Best's rating of a company, the comparative price of its policies, and the actual protection provided by the policy features. You'll find that interested nonprofit sources are excellent places to find helpful shopping information. Auto clubs, real estate commissions, insurance commissions, trade and special-interest associations are often very helpful in providing local insurance shopping information.

With all kinds of insurance, it is necessary to close the "facts gap" between what you assume is covered and what is actually covered. When you get down to a policy or two in the shopping process, make a list of all the features actually stated in the policy. Then make a list of all the circumstances in which the insurance is voided (and every policy has a long list of them). Ask your agent for a disclosure statement of the state laws that apply to the type of policy and add the problems stated on it to your list of negatives.

Before leaving the topic of insurance, I must mention annuities sold by the insurance companies. The purpose of an annuity is to give the insurance company a sum of money, and based on your age and thus the number of years you are likely to live, they guarantee to pay you a monthly stipend, beginning at a given age, for the rest of your life. The yield is based on the payout.

Historically, annuities have been very poor investments, even the tax-deferred and variable-rate versions. They were very popular when tax rates went to 70 percent, but are less popular now, although they can be of use to those in high tax brackets who wish to diversify their tax and savings plans and are willing to accept slightly lower than competitive rates in return for the security and tax relief. Annuities based on currencies, gold, money-market rates, and other changing instruments provide a more exciting form, but annuities remain a relatively low-yield investment vehicle and must be used and selected with that in mind. They are almost exclusively useful to those who need substantial tax deferral.

INSURANCE POLICY COMPARISON WORKSHEET

Policy Covers	Amounts	Does Not Cover	Amounts	Voided by

INSURANCE POLICY CHECKLIST

type of policy	physical location	broker/ phone #	gross coverage	date when to review	events which say "review!"	premium date/amount

ONCE YOU HAVE YOUR POLICY

The law stipulates that the insurance company must provide each policyholder with a complete disclosure statement of legal restrictions relating to the type of insurance being purchased and other legal parameters relating to the policy, in addition to the policy contract itself. In some states you get this automatically and in some you must ask for the extra information. Even if it bores you to death, read it all once.

As you read the policies, make a list of notable provisions and things you don't understand. Send or call in the list of things you don't understand to your agent. Keep the list of notable provisions with your insurance records or home financial records, or wherever you will be able to refer to it readily. You may be surprised at the number of things you did not know, but which can make all the difference in whether your insurance works the way you need it to.

For example, most auto insurance policies require that any defects existing in a newly insured car be listed in detail. Failing to do so may entirely void your policy! Similarly, most policies require the policyholder to make a report to the company every time there is damage or a policy-related repair to the insured car or equipment, even if an insurance claim is not sought. Some people may fear that their insurance rates might rise and try to hide the results of an accident from the insurance company, or may have a small repair expense that could be covered by the policy, but they don't want to go to the trouble. In both situations they may be giving the insurance company the right to cancel the policy or to refuse to honor coverage in the future!

Life insurance policies often restrict the allowable wording in naming beneficiaries, and there is no guarantee that the agent will take the trouble to double-check everything. A child born after the policy is written may have to be protected by adding a codicil, or a simple notification to the company may be sufficient. But failing to do either may leave the child entirely unprotected. In short, the complications are limitless and must be forestalled by reading the policy and making sure that you stay within its restrictions.

INSURANCE POLICY REMINDERS

Life Policy
    Company   _____
    Key dates   _____
    Dates for review   _____
    Policy does *not* cover   _____
    Review policy if: _____
        _____
        _____

Automobile Policy
  Company   _____
  Key dates   _____
  Dates for review   _____
  _____

Liability
  Policy does *not* cover   _____
  Review policy if: _____
  _____

Collision
  Policy does *not* cover   _____
  Review policy if: _____
  _____
  _____

Homeowner's Policy
  Company   _____
  Key dates   _____
  Dates for review   _____
  _____

  Policy does *not* cover   _____
  Review policy if: _____
  _____
  _____

Liability Policy
  Company   _____
  Key dates   _____
  Dates for review   _____
  _____

  Policy does *not* cover   _____
  Review policy if: _____
  _____
  _____

_____ Policy
  Company   _____
  Key dates   _____
  Dates for review   _____

  Policy does *not* cover   _____
  Review policy if   _____
  _____
  _____

7

Agents of Risk

AGENTS AND HOW TO PICK THEM
BEFORE THEY PICK YOU

EVERY AGENT DEVOTES a certain amount of time to selling, and if you ask for reasonable information, he'll be glad to give it to you. (And there is no reason not to ask for detailed quotes from several companies at once.) An addendum could be, "If an agent won't give you reasonable information you need to compare policies, you have found a good agent to avoid." Often a phone call is all it takes to get an agent to serve you as a potential customer. If the agent insists on a personal meeting, just say that you want to look at a sample policy first, but that afterward you'll be glad to talk and review typical and average premiums and benefits. There's nothing unreasonable about *your* being the person who decides when to meet, but there *is* something wrong with the agent who insists upon his or her convenience over yours.

A shortcut with tradeoffs is to locate a few independent agents who handle a number of companies. On the other hand, the policy that suits you best may be handled by a one-company agent. Nevertheless, odds are high that the independent agent will be able to provide more cost-effective coverage for you than one who is stuck with one company's products. If you get a good agent, he or she will be able to give you suggestions as to which company's policy may best suit your needs. Of course there's no guarantee that the agent isn't steering you toward the policy that pays the fattest commission or the one that has the best sales contest running currently. But most agents are more conscientious than that, for they know that a satisfied customer is a repeat customer and a good source of referrals.

If you take on the task of shopping among companies yourself, the company agent is more likely to be conversant with the details of the few

141

products he carries, as opposed to an independent who might not have the time to familiarize himself with a dozen different policies in each category. So you can see that both types of agents have their pluses and minuses. Truly fine agents will even point out which features to compare in each policy. As a concerned customer you can get that information ahead of time from consumer magazines, your state or local insurance commission or consumer office, insurance company promotions, and from insurance industry literature.

As do all salespeople who deal with high-ticket items, successful insurance agents do everything they can to broaden their careers and solidify their knowledge of their business, especially things that will help them and the world know that they are serious about their job and good at it. Insurance agents need only have a license from the state in order to operate legally, but good ones belong to clubs and professional organizations and associations that help further their education and act as spokesmen for their profession.

Professional prizes, awards, degrees, diplomas, and the like are not usually fluff window-dressing. They're one sign that the agent is dedicated to his or her career. To us that means he's probably more knowledgeable than a less dedicated competitor, and you can probably expect him to be in business next year and five years down the line. (The washout rate for agents is approximately 90 percent in the first three years.)

The next criterion for selecting an agent is whether the two of you click. For some people, personality is never a problem—they are capable of separating the business end from the emotional side. Great, if you are that type and find a similarly inclined agent. Usually, however, the way the agent handles you is important, for if and when you take out policies through him and eventually enter a claim, you want him on your side, and you need to have confidence in him.

To many insurance offices, the manager is the person who can put you together with the most appropriate agent. In the first place, this is one of the manager's traditional functions, and in the second, if you ask, the manager is likely to understand the needs and capabilities of his agents. He'll know which one is adroitly sophisticated, or is comfortable with street jive, or is chatty and personable, or who gets down to brass tacks without socializing or delay. In short, the manager can help you find the right agent much more quickly. The result is more sales for him, and better, smoother service for the customer. Speaking to the manager first cannot do any harm, and it eliminates those situations where you end up talking to whoever happens to be in the office or whoever lays claim to the incoming calls that day.

As a shopping prospect, it's something to keep in mind. In many offices, it will be you and not the manager who has to take the initiative in making sure you're matched with the best agent for *your* needs. Later on, it may be of use to go back to the office manager and remind him that he referred you to the agent who subsequently gave you poor service or a hard time, or who served you beautifully.

There is always the question of how to spot the undesirable agent right off the bat. Unfortunately, it's often a matter of judgment, but these clues may help:

Life insurance is inherently a soft-sell product. The professional sales seminars pound this message home constantly. As soon as you sense the hard sell from an agent, you should be suspicious that something is awry. For all kinds of insurance, the honest agent suggests what will meet your needs rather than simply selling you on what he or she has.

Any competent agent knows that in the long run it is more profitable to sell the appropriate product to each prospect than it is to try to oversell. The business comes back to him or her in new sales and referrals. When you meet an agent who is trying to sell you policies that don't suit your circumstances, you probably have an agent who won't be in business very long, or one who moves from agency to agency as he uses up the suckers and goodwill in each location and reaps the wrath of bitter customers and indignant managers.

What are the positives to look for in an agent? There is nothing necessarily wrong with a beginner, but a track record is worth looking for. You want someone who will maintain your policy and communicate with you on a regular basis, so ask if these are standard policy. You also want someone who is familiar with your circumstances and understands your needs, so someone in your age group or social circle may have insights that help him or her relate to your needs. The best agent will go to bat for you against the insurance company in case something goes wrong or there is a dispute, and only references from other customers can tell you that.

The professional designation for life insurance agents is the Certified Life Underwriter, or CLU. There are similar earned designations for other insurance specialties. The CLU means the agent has gone to school with the American College of Life Insurance and studied a fair amount of law, insurance, and salesmanship, as well as professional ethics. A CLU or other designation is no guarantee, but it is a good indication of a minimum level of competence and dedication. While it's not a legal requirement, as is membership in the bar for lawyers or the state medical society for doctors, the CLU makes sense as the first thing to look for in your life insurance agent. Non-CLUs should have another kind of track record to prove their mettle.

You find an agent's credentials through him and/or through the office manager. No professional agent with a solid background is going to object to you finding out how great he or she is. He knows that it only draws attention to his good record from both his company and his customers.

Only someone with something to hide will object, so if one does, look upon it as a favor. He or she saved you from finding out the bad news in some other way, perhaps the hard way.

Why look for an agent who is in or near your age bracket? In the first place, he or she is likely to have analyzed insurance from your own point of view and have an understanding of your motives, feelings, and outlook. Secondly, assuming you have found an agent you decide to stay with, you are assured that you'll have someone who's familiar with your needs when you or (perish the thought) your beneficiaries call. If you are in your twenties, there is little point in seeking out an agent who is a couple of years away from retirement when you can probably find a good one who is closer to thirty and has a stable career. That same young agent might well be less useful to someone twenty years his senior who approaches his insurance needs from experiences and perspectives steeped in a different time. Likewise, the average freshman agent is not going to be able to adequately serve the client who needs to know if the latest tax law will provide incentives for business-related policies or breaks for deferred annuities.

KNOW YOUR AGENT'S NEEDS, TOO

One insurance agent joked to me that that many people sign up for the package their life agent recommends and then for the rest of their lives they're sorry they lived! Well it's no secret that most people don't buy insurance; they're sold. So it's a good defense to know something of your adversary and ally—the agent. A teaching text for agents used by one of the largest companies tells the agent that there are three reasons people buy life insurance: love, fear, and greed. Notice that "need" isn't there. Obviously you don't need to insure against your own death. You could buy out of greed, especially if you are buying insurance not on yourself but on your spouse. But if you do, you will almost surely vastly overbuy, or commit fraud, or both, which will get you into trouble later. That leaves love, the good and best reason, and fear, the dangerous reason to buy life insurance.

Most of the reasons insurance agents present to convince you to buy insurance exploit the fear motive, especially if your agent possesses a thin book of moral character. A quick education in this regard is to locate a few copies of the insurance sales trade magazines, which are filled with "surefire" sales pitches. Usually they make life in the United States sound as dangerous as a freshly laid minefield. Sample approaches include: "When you die and your wife, poor thing, finds that she's incapable of earning a living in this dog-eat-dog world, she'll be so grateful that you bought enough insurance to enable her to live without lifting a finger." And, "When you are gone, they won't be able to handle money as well as you do. Given any less than you have coming in now, why, they'll let the mortgage lapse, squander all the savings, and be reduced to welfare! So you'd better be smart and protect their incompetence with this larger policy—after all, you love them, don't you?"

It is true that owing to legal precedent, it is safer in most states not to take out life insurance on yourself or to pay the premiums on your own policy. Thus, husband and wife should take out policies *on each other*. The husband pays for the policy on the wife and vice versa, even if they share other financial activities. In certain circumstances, paying your own insurance premiums can cause the insurance payments to become part of the after-death estate and part of probate proceedings, and therefore unavailable to the beneficiaries to use just when they need cash the most. The IRS and the states sometimes try to levy estate taxes on life insurance proceeds that were paid for by the decedent. Often people are advised to buy much larger policies than is necessary, the rationale being that when one spouse dies, the other is suddenly saddled with children and grief and rendered incompetent and unemployable. Watch the logic of why you are buying at all times.

The list of ploys used by hard-sell agents is endless, but these examples should give you an idea of what to guard against. The same guidelines apply to other forms of insurance.

FIRST, CALL YOUR AGENT

When a change in risk occurs in your family or business life, call and write your agent. Why write when you already called? If you write he won't forget. (If he forgets, the insurance company probably won't be impressed with your argument about who's to blame.) If you miss a deadline, that's tough, so make sure in writing. Insurance companies become very concerned about legal requirements when claims are settled. Without a written record of correspondence, you are limited to your own memory, the writing on your policies, and the laws of your state. Written correspondence is vital if you decide to protest an agent's conduct, the settlement of a policy claim, or lodge a complaint with the state insurance commission or any other body. Without written proof it is just your word against a roomful of high-powered insurance company lawyers. Take your pick.

Questions to Ask Prospective Insurance Agents

1. How long have you been an agent; how long have you been with your agency?
2. May I talk to you briefly about your experience as an agent? What are your plans for the future?
3. What is your experience selling this type of policy?
4. How many policyholders do you have in my income range and with my general insurance needs?
5. Do you have any special qualifications in selling this type of coverage? Any professional designations? Any special training?
6. How many companies do you represent? How much of your business time is spent working with the type of policy I am shopping for?
7. How would you rate your knowledge of the available coverage in this area?
8. Whom can you refer to if I have questions you cannot answer?
9. What hours during the week are available, and what happens if I need information or help when you are not in the office?
10. How will my claims be handled when you are out of town, for instance, or if you should, for whatever reason, have to give my policy to another agent?
11. What is your experience in situations where this company disagrees with the policyholder in claims matters? When this happens, what is your responsibility to the company? To the policyholder?
12. Are you involved in or eligible for prizes, contests, or bonuses connected with the sale of this policy? If so, what are they?
13. Do you have any standardized figures, such as interest-rate tables or policy payout records that compare this company's record with those of other companies?

8
Lawyers, the Law, and You

IN OUR SOCIETY, most lawyers are hired to work on financial problems. Lawsuits are usually stated and resolved on the basis of monetary definitions, and even criminal codes specify monetary fines. The system calls for money with which to pay the best attorneys. For most of us, the law is a financial problem, and attorneys help us solve financial problems. To stay on top of personal finances, then, eventually requires using a lawyer and successfully maneuvering within the confines of the law. Just as with banking, investing, and budgeting, it's something you need to be acquainted with to be financially secure and independent.

The promoters and the incompetents in the legal profession depend for their livings upon the fact that most people don't look for a lawyer until long after they need one. Many people also fail to connect their need for a lawyer with their financial affairs. Correctly drawn wills, trusts, and estate plans allow loved ones to get your money without waiting the months or years it can take to get a date in probate court. A friendly lawyer can keep crooked or lazy real estate agents, accountants, brokers, and contractual partners in line and out of your pocket. Legal advice guards your money. It's also important to realize that you get to decide how much to pay for legal services only as long as you partake of them in advance. Once you have to go to court, the hourly rate is entirely in their hands.

REMEMBER, THE CLIENT PAYS THE LAWYER

Back when the founding fathers laid out the country's ground rules, they took an interesting departure from the British model which they followed. Just as they had liberalized the kingship/prime ministerial roles and replaced them with an elected, accountable presidency, and similarly replaced the House of Lords and Commons with the Senate and House of Representatives, they liberalized the legal system by making lawyers *optional*. As with their stances on religion, free speech, publishing, and other radical moves toward freedom, they took this great and innovative step to ensure that no one group absorbed too much power. It means that in this country, in most situations, lawyers are hired hands, and we can shop for them just as we shop for any other service.

The greatest demonstration of pure American law in action can be seen in most cities in small claims courts. In the majority of cases lawyers are specifically excluded, and the cases are heard by judges simply on the merit of the law and the facts presented. In a way, that is antithetical to everything lawyers are taught when they seek to serve at the bar. It is no mistake that the small claims courts are, as their name implies, primarily arenas for monetary disputes and are among the few places where lawyers can't get in the way of the law or the truth.

LEGALESE COSTS NONLAWYERS

The first problem in the legal system, from a practical cost point of view, is that all the laws at every level were written by lawyers in legalese. By this device the barristers have been able to ensconce their own cultish views of justice and moral practice, and, as we all know, subvert the English language. It's pathetic that normal, intelligent people go to college, then law school, studying thousands of hours in order to learn a language that makes the simplest thoughts incomprehensible and that excludes the normal man in the street from understanding the very laws that govern him. But as you may realize, that last point is not accidental at all.

When the English legal system, upon which our own is based, was organized over the course of several hundred years, there were several logistical problems the barristers had to overcome. First, the English language was not yet a stable system as it is today. Thus, in order to communicate effectively between dialects and through time, the barristers mixed a good measure of Latin into their speech and writing. Back in the sixteenth century this made perfect sense, for all educated people in Europe at the time spoke and read Latin. Most books were written in it, and this convention allowed those of different native tongues to understand one another. It was the international language of its day, as French was to become later, and English is today.

The vestiges of that heritage are with us today in the form of countless legal terms that are revered and engraved in Latin. Sadly, even a Latin scholar who has mastered this dead language often cannot decipher the legal terminology, for the words often don't carry their traditional meaning, but refer to some long-forgotten idiom or event. A good example of this is the word "client," which means plebeian, a second-class citizen in Rome, or it may mean "indentured servant," a servant under financial obligation to a patrician. Under no circumstances would a plebeian or a servant in Rome "hire" a patrician, much less be in a position to fire one, now would a patrician offer to serve either of the two. Lawyers apparently liked the position of personal authority the word inferred, however, and adopted the term "client" to describe the people who hire them. Now the term has stuck, along with many other legalese misnomers.

The result of the lawyer's education in obfuscation is that the average citizen usually needs a lawyer (or thinks he does) to handle any legal maneuver, meaning money out of the bank and into the lawyer's purse. Back in the 1970s, when Supreme Court Justice Warren Burger outraged the legal community by proclaiming through the nation's press that at least half of all lawyers who practice in the courts are incompetent to adequately serve their clients' needs or cases, the issue of whether lawyers are worth the money they charge was briefly raised. In an unintentionally humorous act of attempted one-upmanship, the American Bar Association took the matter under advisement, conducted its own study, and issued an angry rebuttal: Only 20 percent of the practicing lawyers are incompetent, they declared!

So, depending upon whether you believe a Supreme Court justice or the predominant lawyers' advocacy group, at least two, possibly as many as five, practicing lawyers out of every ten are incompetent. This all serves to demonstrate the first rule of dealing with lawyers: *If you think you need one, shop around until you find one who will serve your needs in a way that makes you feel confident.*

YOU SHOP FOR A REFRIGERATOR — YOU SHOULD SHOP FOR A LAWYER

Steve Meyers, the lawyer who, with his partner Len Jacoby, opened the nation's first advertising law-offices and also the first large storefront clinics, found in a survey among his company's clients that when they decided they needed a lawyer, nearly all of them retained the first one they encountered. This is crazy. Lawyers charge very high hourly fees compared to the average person's income. If a person is willing to shop around for a refrigerator or a car, he or she should be willing to shop around for a lawyer.

What makes the law clinics and advertising so successful is that most people do not know how to shop for a lawyer. If you need one, not shopping is not only financially irresponsible, it may be dangerous if you end up with a crook or an incompetent!

BE SURE YOU NEED A LAWYER

That brings up the first real question: Do you really need a lawyer? Small claims court is one do-it-yourself alternative if the amount of money involved is small. But, as lawyers will often tell you, the cheapest way to avoid using a lawyer is to *think things out clearly and then communicate*. The fact is that half of all litigants have never discussed the problem they want to file suit over before going to a lawyer. Credit collectors found out long ago that an ultimatum, if reasonable and believable, often works wonders when there is a disagreement. A confrontation is resolved, and there is really no reason in most cases why the two sides can't use a friend or a business associate to arbitrate as effectively as two lawyers. Going to the lawyers first is just a convention, and not a very valid one at that. Too many people are too willing to hire a couple of overpriced lawyers to stand between them and do the haggling they are not willing to do themselves.

Here's one example of how alternatives can be found: Until a few years ago, virtually every person who wanted to form a corporation to shelter his taxes or protect his business hired a lawyer to do the paperwork. Then, along came a guy named Ted Nichols, who pointed out to anyone who would listen that anybody can form a corporation in the state of Delaware, by mail, for under $50, without a lawyer. Hundreds of thousands followed his advice, saving millions in legal fees. Doubtlessly, for most of them it was a sound decision. Today you can find do-it-yourself incorporation kits that work in most states.

Likewise, divorces used to bring to mind the tedious, agonizing misery of divorce court—they even made a tasteless TV show out of it—or else a nasty trip to Las Vegas or New Jersey. Typically, two lawyers quibbled over legal points that the man and woman didn't understand and that the judge obviously considered superfluous, but that always lengthened the proceedings and thereby fattened the legal fees substantially. Then, along came a rash of best-selling books telling how couples can handle their own divorces in almost every state—often for under $25. To the dismay of thousands of lawyers, millions have dissolved their marriages in private, almost cost-free ways.

The point is not just that these people saved money, but that they also saved themselves the wretchedness of having lawyers turn an already painful situation into a war zone. But bear in mind that the laws are actually structured so that lawyers feel compelled to act that way.

It's true that conscientious lawyers don't have to aggravate the process, and a number of them do not. But consider that they are cutting their own fees if they make every case as brief as possible. If all else fails and you must use a lawyer, shop for one who has a history of solving cases amicably, not one who turns divorces into battles, with the counselor one of the well-paid mercenaries.

ADVERSARIES DON'T SOLVE PROBLEMS

Of course it is not always the lawyer's fault that courts intensify problems, for the tendency is naturally built into our legal system. In another holdover from our English heritage, modern jurisprudence is based on the concept of adversary relationships. Lawyers speak of "adversary" and "nonadversary" proceedings, but if there are two lawyers and a judge in between, there is going to be an adversarial role played out. The lawyer's job is to whip the other guy. That is swell, but it isn't the same thing as solving the client's real-life problem in the best, most expeditious manner. From a financial point of view, that is what you're after. If you are after blood, well, that's another story.

The adversarial role dates back to the era in English history, just about the time when burning witches became really popular, when legal disputes could be settled by combat as legally as by a judge's decision. If the king, governor, or judge felt the urge, the principals in personal, property, or monetary disputes had to "prove" their cases by combat. This made great sense to those in authority, for "the good Lord chooseth the truthful man over the liar, for to believe otherwise would be blasphemy." After a spell, the resourceful authorities allowed that the principals didn't have to fight *personally*, but could appoint or hire seconds to wield the swords and suffer the wounds. Later, the combat was phased out, but the posture of the two sides facing one another in preordained hostility remains. Thus, lawyers are mercenaries trained to wage special battle in the legal arena.

ARBITRATION COSTS LESS

Another terrific alternative to hiring your own legal soldier is to consider out-of-court arbitration. This almost always works just as well without lawyers as it does with them. Either way it saves money, and very often yields results acceptable to everyone involved. The biggest rallying point for this approach are the organizations connected with thousands of churches and synagogues. Sometimes pressure in the community comes to bear, and the two principals are prevailed upon to settle their dispute in an amicable way. More and more, the arbitrators are sought out by the partners involved. Businesses use arbitrators because they're a bargain compared to the legal alternative. The same is true for many private-party suits.

There are professional arbitrators readily available in most cities. The main clientele consists of businesses that don't want the delay, hassle, and expense of court delays. But many arbitrators also handle personal arbitration for a reasonable fee, certainly much less than legal fees and court costs. Take a hint from professional sports teams and labor organizers, who use arbitrators all the time. They could go to court, but the delays and the fees are not worth it, and a good arbitrator won't let anyone be destroyed.

Arbitration is not a way to get revenge or to nail the person you are mad at; it's a way to solve a dispute that can't easily be handled by the parties involved, and to handle the problem with the least damage to all concerned. Often, if you lose a lawsuit, you spend the rest of your life feeling that you've been cheated. In arbitration, even if you don't come out as well as you had hoped, you usually end up in reasonable shape. Knowing that you were treated fairly is easier to live with than knowing that you risked a court battle and were clobbered, either justly or unjustly.

Businesses can get referrals from the American Arbitration Association for both arbitration and mediation. Individuals can try them, too. Also, try the Yellow Pages, your local church or synagogue council, the local Better Business Bureau, chamber of commerce, your banker, or your insurance commission for names and advice for finding arbitrators in your area.

FALSE COMPLICATIONS

What is it about the law that makes lawyers believe they are so indispensable? It's not just the complexity of the written laws, for if it were, the problem could be solved with a good index or even a computerized reference. It is another nagging legal heritage from our British forebears, that of revering established precedence. It was long ago decided that if the law were to have any stabilizing effect upon the populace, there must be some thread of continuity connecting similar legal decisions. Basically, it means that if the first judge to make the determination decides that declaring a vacation home as an auxillary office violates the tax code, then every lawyer thereafter will point to that decision and say, "See, there is a precedent that interprets the law this way. Well, judge, you don't want to rock the boat under four hundred years of legal tradition and scandalize the legal profession, so you'll have to base your decisions on this precedent." Since the judges are all lawyers who believe in the system, they accede to the demands. Between you and me, as citizens, one man's interpretation is as valid as the next, but we see that this is not so with the law. This creates a vital need for lawyers who understand the traditions. They've memorized the traditions, the Latin, the legalese, and the economics, and they work to stack a higher pile of precedents before the judge than their opponent: Highest pile wins. But this doesn't mean that the law, justice, or the client is necessarily served by having a lawyer in charge.

AN AMERICAN TRADITION: I CAN DO IT BETTER MYSELF

A few years ago judges were automatically upset to find individuals in their courts representing themselves. It almost surely meant that here was a nut who would eventually cause the case to be thrown out as the result of some kind of shenanigan, or else it was an indigent criminal who had been burned by an incompetent public defender and figured he or she could do no worse. Often, the cases were delayed while the judge lectured the person on what to do next, or what not to do. Today, in contrast, as the lawyers avow, most judges will bend over backward to help these *pro se* (legal Latin for "in one's own behalf") advocates. This isn't just because they have to if they want to get the case on its way, it is because these days, most *pro se* cases are well prepared and the individuals take the care to be aware of how to act and perform in court.

On the civil side, the *pro se* tradition has grown up around necessity and poverty. In the sixties, tenants' rights blossomed in a big way, but not enough lawyers donated their time to handle all the irate tenants and those who wanted to fight evictions and code violations in court. This led to the formation of hundreds of tenants' rights groups, most of which advise tenants how to battle effectively on their own in local courts. A good many of these persistent people have gone on to win their cases and appeals in the high courts as well.

Here are some of the kinds of legal tasks do-it-yourselfers have been pursuing: incorporations, name changes, amicable divorces, contested evictions and civil suits outside small claims court, and also wills. Few of these people are going the *pro se* route because they are too poor to afford a good lawyer: The vast majority are middle-class. They seem to fall into two categories. One group is made up of those types who like to do everything for themselves. They'll be the knitting, home canning, workshop, handyman-weekend folks who have problems and want to do it themselves if possible. The other group likes to seek out alternatives, fight against injustice, and participate directly in the system. They believe there's a better way and that they can control their own lives through their own actions. And there are those who have "just heard that it's possible," and plunge in out of curiosity, thriftiness, or passion. By the way, statistically they are successful in their cases just as often as are lawyers.

There are many reasons why *pro se* can be effective, and these concepts can be applied to lower legal fees and improve your odds if you ever do use an attorney. One is that lawyers tend to be very busy people, and they may charge as much per hour as many Americans earn in a day. Thus they either spend the minimum amount of time that a case requires and end up doing a mediocre job, or they spend extra time doing a bang-up job and the fee goes through the roof. Or they devote little time and still charge exorbitantly, but then you have a case against them.

Seen from inside, the law office scenario can be even more frustrating for the client. He may find that the lawyer whose expertise he is counting upon has merely delegated the task at hand to a legal secretary who fills in the blanks on a pre-printed legal form (and these days he/she probably does it automatically with a computerized word processor), and presto, you have a pile of documents that may or may not be what you need. (In simple matters, you may well find the equivalent legal forms at your local stationery store. If so, a notary seal and a witness may be the biggest part of your legal fees.) He may have asked you all the right questions, but even if he did, will he remember them at the right moment in court or when he's haggling with the opposition attorney? If there is any investigative footwork to be done, the lawyer hires someone to do it who has no personal insight or interest in the case, and then he charges you his lawyer's hourly fee for the gumshoe's time. In the end you may well get a case that is presented in a pat manner with inadequate research and investigation, by a preoccupied lawyer who is trying to save you money by not spending time on your case.

The *pro se* advocate, in contrast, can get all the specific information he needs about how cases such as his are typically handled in the local courts by doing all or part of his own investigation. Then he can spend unlimited time in the law library (all large cities and many small ones have ones open to the public) looking up all the precedents and legal tidbits he feels are necessary. Then he can spend as much time as he wants doing the footwork—all on his own free time. He can go to the various government agencies and look up records, and, unlike the dispassionate gumshoe, he can probe into related evidence and inquire about obscure references. And it it takes three trips, the three trips get made. He won't quit because it happens to be lunchtime; he won't forget to look up that last document, provided he has taken time to learn how to resarch properly.

Another deadly expense that can occur as soon as two lawyers set sights on each other rears its head as they present "discoveries." This is a process wherein one lawyer at a time presents a pile of vaguely relevant facts in order to delay things (more fees) and to intimidate the other side into rebutting all the points, lest one of them be the keystone to the courtroom drama. The *pro se* advocate, usually with the sympathy of the court, which has suffered the boredom caused by hearing discoveries too many times, takes all the time he needs to eliminate the discovery items one by one. Later, when presenting evidence, entering testimony and affidavits, etcetera, the do-it-yourselfer doesn't get his case mixed up with a half a dozen others, doesn't worry about his caseload, and doesn't forget the important points at hand. What he lacks in experience and training can often be more than compensated for by homework, footwork, and more work.

If you hire an attorney anyway, the same principles used by *pro se* advocates still apply. The things you would do to prepare your case if you act as your own attorney can be done to (1) save yourself a large portion of the fees your attorney would otherwise charge, and, (2) ensure that your attorney will have superior, conscientiously compiled preparation for your case. You save money and get better representation from your lawyer—what better deal can you get, if you can afford the time? (If this is questionable, just ask yourself if you can afford to lose the case.) And, by educating yourself enough to do a good job of investigation, you have performed your own legal consultation, familiarized yourself with the details of your case, and demonstrated to your lawyer that you are going to be active in preparing one of his or her cases. The squeaky wheel gets more grease, and the involved client gets better service for the dollar.

Unless you earn more than the average lawyer (formula: Take the legal minimum wage and multiply by 10 to 50), your active participation in the legal process will save you money and aggravation. As they say, "The most expensive lawyers are those who charge a large fee to lose a case that probably had no chance, or those who charge anything to lose a case that should have been won."

FINDING YOUR CHAMPION

Referrals, they say, are a good starting place and the most common method of finding lawyers. As with any professional, don't take a pig in a poke, for, like MDs, LLbs come in a variety of flavors—general practitioners and specialists.

Without a friend who can provide that referral, where do you look? The court of last resort is the local bar association referral service. Many of the best individuals and firms take a certain number of cases from the bar service as a matter of public appearance, so if you're willing to interview them, it can be a viable source. Your banker should either be able to give you a direct referral or should be able to plug you into one. The same often goes for a good accountant, the local newspaper legal reporter, and many of the nonprofit public service organizations (which depend for survival on their knowledge of the local legal community). Somewhere there is the right referral for you, regardless of your need.

Find a prospective lawyer and you're stuck with the decision of whether to use him or her or not. If he has accumulated a track record or is with a reputable or large firm, you'll find him listed in the law directories in every libarary. (Martindale Hubbell is the oldest and biggest, but there are others as well.) They are graded from AA+ to C, a system that is no more fair than the grading used in your school days. An AA+ is no guarantee of a conscientious counsel, but is an argument in the right direction. A C lawyer may be an idiot or a fine attorney on his or her way up the ladder of success. The most valuable entries are danger signals that appear as notes in the better directories. Assuming a clean bill of health by the directories, call the local bar association (state or local) and ask for the person's standing. Again, the idea is to unearth any major complaints outstanding. Finally, you have to confront the lawyer himself, so get out your list of questions and shoot until you shoot him down or he fields them all successfully.

Questions to Ask a Prospective Lawyer

- Do you charge for this meeting or an initial consultation? If so, how much and why?
- Here is my problem. Are you a good choice as a lawyer for me? Why?
- Do I really need a lawyer to resolve this satisfactorily?
- How long have you been a member of the local bar?
- How long have you specialized in this area of the law?
- What are your credentials?
- May I speak to a half dozen of your current or past clients about their experience with you?
- Have you been censured by the bar associations or been banned from practicing in any jurisdictions, or have you been convicted of any crimes?
- How do you intend to charge for services such as the ones we're discussing?
- What is included in your billing agreement?

- What happens if we initially agree to work together but one of us subsequently decides to terminate our agreement? What if the other person terminates?
- How often and in what ways will you communicate with me about your work?
- Do you charge for brief phone calls?
- Will you object if I do some of the investigative work involved?
- Under what circumstances would you stop working on this case and suggest that I seek the counsel of another lawyer with special expertise?
- Do we get along and are you genuinely interested in performing this work for me?
- Other questions you think may be important.

OTHER SOURCES

If you have failed to find an acceptable attorney by other means, you might try contacting the quality law schools in your area. They often have clinic programs operated by experienced attorneys and staffed by eager beginners anxious to prove their mettle. Some require that you be indigent to take advantage of their services, but many don't care. If this doesn't fit your needs, ask for the names of professors who teach in the area of law that covers your problem. Their research and moonlighting income often bring them into contact with the best (as opposed to the richest or most notorious) practitioners in that specialty. Also, if you're not too embarrassed, try asking the company lawyer where you work. If you don't end up with a direct referral, your company attorney should be able to work through the legal-community grapevine to find a good one for you.

For many people, a terrific way to find lawyers which didn't even exist a few years ago, and many people dismiss offhand, is through advertisements. Why? Because advertising lawyers are under close scrutiny in most states. The bar will have a large file to leaf through, and you can insist upon a list of ex-clients to call for reports of their experiences. In fact, no matter how you find a lawyer, you must still go through the interview process to ensure that you are getting the person who will do what you want and will do it well.

Doctors have to compete against other MDs, osteopaths (who are often as well educated as MDs and have learned chiropractic besides), physical therapists, and a whole host of medical specialists. Lawyers compete only against other lawyers. Happily, there are too many of them for their own good, and you can usually shop with impunity, knowing that there is always another *LL.B.* around the next corner. Someday this surplus of lawyers may drive down prices, too, but until it does, we must all protect ourselves vigorously at that critical moment of confrontation between the lawyer and his or her client—the fee and bill agreement negotiation.

INSIST UPON YOUR MONEY'S WORTH

In most states a contractor, whether a builder or an auto mechanic, must give you a written or oral estimate of how much his job will cost, and he is limited by standard codes. Unfortunately, lawyers never got around to writing such laws for themselves, but the principle is nonetheless a sound one. Instead, they offer written contracts which guarantee that the client pays, but are very vague when it comes to the performance end. Since it is a two-sided agreement, it is your prerogative and your responsibility to insist that the agreement also contain an estimate, broken down into components, of what he or she thinks it will cost to bring your case to conclusion.

Most critical to an estimate is a projection of how long it will take to wrap things up. Comparing the situation to a few previous cases might be a good way to start, but the idea must be clear to you. Obviously, there also has to be a contingency allowance, but that is for the protection of both of you. You want to know that if the case takes longer than the two of you anticipated, the agreement stipulates that you sit down together and talk things over before another dime is spent. Like the mechanic who used to be able to take your car, replace everything that moved, and hold it as ransom until you paid the fee, a lawyer retained without an agreement with an expected completion date or maximum expected fee can soak you for undeserved fees. Really, it's only fair: If he wants you to guarantee the fee, he should be able to guarantee that the fee will be reasonable.

Along the same lines, you must ask how closely the lawyer will want to work with you and how you will be charged. Is he going to charge you every time you say hello on the phone? Is he going to agree to let you lower his potential fee by doing some legwork yourself? And is he interested enough in your case to do a good job on it? If not, no fee will be worth his time.

Agree to nothing without finding out what happens if the two of you come to a parting of ways. Will he slap you with a trumped-up bill or will he minimize his bill to compensate for the ill will? Even the bar association considers it fair pool to add a phrase to the fee agreement allowing you to submit any disagreement disputes to mutually satisfactory arbitrators. Those words are your best insurance.

In short, you want to ensure that you will be treated fairly when your bill is compiled. Two policies recommended by lawyers are (1) insist upon a monthly or more frequent statement (itemized—any well-run office itemizes it for their records, so don't let them charge you extra for that), and (2) insist that you be notified of any significant actions in your behalf and that you receive a copy or record of all communications made in your behalf within, say, a week or two. Not only do you keep tabs on what's going on, you are more apt to catch some expensive mistakes before they take root and grow. You know that no lawyer would think of dealing otherwise with his big, important accounts, so demand the same respect, if not quite the same service, because your money is as important to you as theirs is to them. Maybe more so.

Here's a summary of some things to ask for when the lawyer asks you to sign his or her fee agreement:

- Monthly (or oftener) itemized billing statement
- Notification of all actions on your behalf (they cost!)
- Agreement to submit billing to arbitration if asked
- Prompt notification of any unusual or large bill items
- A written definition of how fees are to be charged, and when
- A written, signed statement of the agreement
- An explanation of what happens if you fire him or he quits
- Whatever else you feel strongly about

I don't believe you can stop a person from padding your bill if he is bent upon it, but asking for an itemized bill and expressing your intense interest in the subject certainly establishes the proper attitude. Too often, people are so carried away by the emotion of the moment that they forget that a dispassionate professional, whether malicious or simply susceptible to human weakness, sees the opportunity to submit a large bill with little chance of protest.

CONTINGENCIES SHOULD BE SHARED IN VICTORY OR DEFEAT

In contingency-fee arrangements, the lawyer will usually try to get you to sign an agreement that his or her fee and the court expenses come out of *your* share of the spoils. Some lawyers will admit on the side that this can be negotiated. Often, attorneys will split the expenses when an award or settlement is obtained. Some balk at the idea, but you just have to do your best at persuasion. All indications are that it will get easier to bargain on all kinds of attorney employment contracts as the vast numbers of lawyers in law schools in the 1980s comes to bear on the professional marketplace.

Unfortunately, many of the things you want to know about a lawyer's operating procedures and ethics, which will ultimately be reflected in your bill, are difficult to ascertain. A lawyer who has a reputation for being a heavy "bomber"—one who is unmercifully relentless in pursuing his cases and in exploring every avenue toward beating the other side— may sound like the one to have on your side when you are in the heat of anger and anxious to lash out at someone or something. As many a lawyer will attest, the bombers in the courtroom are often bombers in their offices as well. And, worse for you, bombers when it comes to hammering out fee agreements or in deciding what approach to take when judgment calls are needed.

Often a good lawyer will suggest that noncriminal problems be settled out of court or may offer alternative solutions that will expedite things. This isn't entirely selfless, for as with most businesspeople, a good lawyer can make more money by handling a larger volume of cases that pay out more in the first hours of involvement than do long drawn-out affairs.

IT'S THE CLIENT'S RESPONSIBILITY

We the clients can be the first to set precedent in this regard. It is our responsibility as clients to tell the lawyer that we will consider arbitration, or will do investigation, or whatever it takes to get better results and a lower bill.

IMPROVING THE LAW AND THE LAWYERS

Back in 1977 a group of lawyers in Washington decided that they would advocate legal reform from within the system. They formed HALT, an organization of lawyers and nonlawyers that actively supports legal reform on both the professional and legislative fronts. They promote the idea of citizens doing their own legal work when possible, and they publish manuals that tell how to get started, how to stay out of trouble, and, if you desire, how to shop for the best lawyer for your needs. They are champions of the movement nationwide to simplify the language of the law, and in their most radical stance, point out that the national, state, and local bar associations are protective trade associations, pure and simple. They promote consumer protection through participation in attorneys' grievance committees in the ABA—the backbone behind any official enforcement of lawyers' ethics in this country. Best of all, they publish do-it-yourself guides and books on topics such as how to use a legal library and how to find and select an attorney.

ON LEGAL FEES AND THE FUTURE

Since there is no "legal commission" as there is an insurance or a banking commission in each state, nor is there Blue Cross–Blue Shield for legal assistance, there is no standard for legal fees. The rule is to charge what the traffic and the reputation will bear. For a while, back in the 1970s, when legal clinics were new, most of them could be counted upon to render fairly competent service for a very competitive rate. Back when the ABA was angrily trying to prohibit advertising of clinics, indeed of all lawyers, the ABA Journal did an investigative article about the biggest clinic—the Legal Clinic of Jacoby and Meyers—then a small neighborhood business. The researchers found that despite significantly lower rates for virtually all services, the work performed and the success rates at the clinics were as good or better than those at the average traditional legal-partnership-style firms. Since then other clinics have gone franchise, aligning themselves with department store chains, insurance companies, and just about any other avenue to fast, efficient business expansion.

Now that there are numerous nationwide chains, the rumor in the legal press is that the firms tend to don the cloaks of convention as soon as they become successful, and rates rise accordingly until they match or nearly match those of traditional firms in the area. To my knowledge, no one has done a survey of the overall services available from the fees charged by the giant legal clinic chains, but as with other franchise operations, quality control must be a terrific problem when the entire staff consists of hired guns. Put that together with the trend toward higher, less competitive prices, and it appears that the advantages initially offered by clinics may be fading with time. It brings us back to the old truism: No matter what, you have to shop around for your lawyer.

ASSURE YOUR LEGAL GOOD HEALTH

Following the lead of the medical profession, the legal community is seeing a rise in the number of general practitioners—lawyers who are able to handle all the ordinary hassles in a family's or a small business's life, but who can bring in a specialist when the complications exceed his or her purview. Again, following the lead of those medical experts who advise that we *not* have a physical exam every year, but only every three or five years, or when something raises the alarms, the bar associations advise that the average person sit down with a GP every two to five years and review the family legal status. Naturally, if any major event comes to pass and you have to call upon him or her anyway, that is a good time to go through the list of legal protections. A major event in this case is anything that changes any legal responsibility or liability, such as birth, a death, a child coming of age, a divorce, a sudden windfall of wealth, a sudden loss of assets, serious health problems, etc. A good GP will offer you more services than you actually need, and by elimination you are assured of covering all the legal bases. This is the part of the basic strategy of heading off any legal problems before they arise, because it's always cheaper and easier that way.

THE LONE ALTERNATIVE

The new alternative to shopping for a lawyer, and in some instances to taking the initiative in defining services needed, is the prepaid legal service. This fairly new invention, conceived in the perquisites office of some Wall Street conglomerate, is spreading rapidly. Available in most major cities and through many large companies in the fashion of company insurance plans, they afford the subscriber limited access to the services of a law partnership or legal clinic in return for an annual or other periodic fee. Typically you get a certain amount of consultation time and a fixed amount of telephone time each year, and some predetermined services. In addition you are guaranteed preferred rates for a wide range of services, from will drafting and estate planning to contract renewal, alimony disputes, and perhaps criminal defense.

Most of the prepaid plans I have seen have earned mixed reviews from the legal press, with the general consensus being that they provide generally good but limited services while substantially saving the members who use the services. Unfortunately there are no guarantees, and like individual lawyers and clinics, they must be investigated and weighed against your specific needs. Even if they are available, you may find that you need more personalized service, or you might wish to use them, especially if you get the fee as a salary fringe benefit, and supplement them with occasional visits to other specialists. As long as they are available, consider them, for they can save most people money.

THE BEST WAY TO USE YOUR LAWYER

Once you find a lawyer, you must use his or her expertise to do yourself good. Legal disputes are becoming as common as visits by the milkman, and legal pitfalls mount even higher as the laws and regulations constricting our lives grow in number and complexity. The bargain service of the average family lawyer is when you ask about precautionary measures regarding things in everyday life. What should you be aware of before you invest in the limited partnership your broker is advising? Is the insurance on your new vacation home adequate? What are your liabilities if the new maid, the caterer, a babysitter, or a construction worker is hurt on your property? What precautions need you take as the new swimming pool is installed? The list can grow as long as you think of potential legal problems. Each one may cost you a small consultation fee, but if you are careful and protect yourself with the lawyer's knowledge, none of them will cost you a fortune.

LEGAL ALTERNATIVES

HALT

A nonprofit legal-reform advocacy group that also provides advice to the layman through extensive literature and periodicals available to members.
201 Massachusetts Avenue, NE
Suite 319
Washington, DC 20002

Legal Action Workshop

A school, bookstore, lawyer-referral service and legal-advice center (not nonprofit) that provides information and help to those who want to be their own lawyers.
4515 Van Nuys Blvd.
Sherman Oaks, California 91403

The People's Law School

Primarily gives classes to tenants who want to face landlords' lawyers on many fronts, but also provides some literature. Asks for donations and is nonprofit.
558 Capp Street
San Francisco, California 94115

The National Lawyer's Guild

Provides information on common actions, such as facing eviction without a lawyer, fighting traffic court, etc. As of this date provides half-hour consultations for $10.
1255 Post Street
San Francisco, California

The Nolo Press/Folk Law

The first and largest publisher of literature on self-help law. Has a long list of hardback and softcover books on everything from how to win in small claims court to do-it-yourself bankruptcy to *Legal Care for Your Software*, a book about computer copyright law for programmers. Subscribe to their quarterly journal, *Nolo News*, by sending $5 to:

950 Parker Street
Berkeley, California 94710

Your Local Bar Association Referral Service
See your telephone directory.

Your Business Association, Chamber of Commerce, Other Bodies that Draw Professionals Together.

The Overseas Citizens Service
Part of the government, this office finds lawyers for U.S. citizens who are out of the country.
Department of State
Washington, DC 20520

State or Local Agencies
In some cases, the government may have powers that make hiring a lawyer unnecessary, especially when you are involved in a group action that the government wishes to pursue.

Advocacy Groups, National or Local
Not only good sources for lawyers with special skills and knowledge, they often know of alternative solutions to problems so that you can stay out of court.

Trade Associations
These groups often have influence over their members and in many cases can give advice and information if not direct assistance. May also know of specialist lawyers.

Arbitrators
Our courts are overcrowded partly because people ask judges to act as arbitrators. If possible, save money, time, and trouble by using an arbitration agreement. You might even hire a lawyer to draw up the agreement. Church councils, better business bureaus, state business councils, and business consultants know where to find good arbitrators.

HOME LEGAL CHECKLIST

- Family lawyer's name and his/her various phone numbers
- Specialty lawyers who have been referred to you
- Location and status of family wills (including all those that may involve *you* when the author dies)

- Include your complete estate plan to help you when you revised wills, etc., and to help others in case you die
- A reminder (included in your personal financial calendar) of when your will needs review and what events might creat a need for revisions or codicils (additions)
- A reminder to be included on your calendar of important legal dates, such as contract renewals, payment due dates, referral dates, etc.
- Location and status of all legally binding contracts and agreements. Mortgages, partnerships, debts, lawsuits or other actions pending, etc. Also all securities, etc.
- List of legal alternatives. Phone numbers of legal-help organizations, information sources, business lawyers, and anything or anyone else you run across that you want to save for future reference

FINANCIAL QUESTIONS FOR THE FAMILY LAWYER

Most legal questions and needs are not the result of disasters or emergencies. They are simple financial "housekeeping" tasks that require knowledge of the current judicial environment, recent legislation, and access to information that lawyers typically keep track of.

- How much life insurance is adequate for your family?
- How much other insurance coverage is prudent for your situation? Auto, homeowner's, liability, business, special coverage, travel, etc.
- Are the provisions of the policies complete and adequate from the policyowner's point of view?
- When should insurance policies be updated?
- What type of will should be written, and when should it be updated? This includes attention to new laws, new situations in life, and changing financial needs.
- Should trusts be considered and established? If so, what needs to be considered? If not now, when?
- Review details of major purchases and sales, especially real estate and business transactions.
- Review the terms of any contract with significant potential value.
- Are your other financial counselors giving you sound advice?
- Referrals to other legal and financial professionals.
- Ask when else you should seek advice.

LEGAL-COST WORKSHEET

First get your lawyer to make an estimate of the average hours needed to resolve cases such as yours. Multiply the hourly rate times that figure. If your lawyer charges for phone calls, forms, and other detail items, figure in those costs as best you can. Compare that to an estimate of the cost of not using the legal channels and see if the cost is justified. Note the maximum you expect to spend and specify in the payment that no fees are to paid beyond that amount until you agree to the services rendered. Compare those figures against what you want to spend and what you figure you could spend in a worst-case scenario.

If there is a potential financial gain involved, compare the lawyer's probable share to the number of hours estimated, times the average hourly fee in your area. The answer should be an approximation of how much work to expect from your lawyer. You may have particular circumstances that will affect the ultimate bill from your lawyer. Don't forget that there can be other costs, too, such as situations that force you to miss work, the possibility that you will lose your case, that your lawyer may be a bumbler or intentionally prolongs cases or pads his bills, etc.

LEGAL SERVICES SOURCES

- Your current lawyer(s)
- Your other financial advisers who can make referrals
- Family and business associates
- The local bar association service
- Local law school intern programs and experts
- Advocacy groups, whether profit or nonprofit
- Your state or local agencies may have enforcement powers that make your hiring of a lawyer unnecessary.

See all the entries in the list of "Legal Alternatives." You may find that you have another solution to your legal problems.

LEGAL DIRECTORIES

Martindale Hubbell Law Directory
The original. It's the biggest, but some feel that while it has the largest listings, the descriptions are sometimes disappointing.

American Lawyer Guide to Leading Law Firms
This was the first of the directories to attempt truly honest descriptions.

National Law Journal Directory
Details specialists and is primarily business-oriented, even more so than the others.

Law & Business Directory
Has only a few hundred entries, and lets the firms describe themselves along with brief newsy articles. Similar to the two above.

9

Taxes and Accountants

WHEN IT COMES TO TAXES, there are only two possible issues—how do I get it done with the least hassle and how do I minimize what I have to pay the government? Whether you are concerned with income taxes, tax shelters, or death taxes, the mechanics and strategy must be different for every person and family, so I'll try to tell you some of the "hows" and give you some frequently overlooked possibilities and suggestions to draw from when you plan your taxes.

The basic formula for income taxes is:

	gross income
minus	standard deductions
equals	adjusted income
minus	itemized deductions and exemptions
equals	taxable income
times	tax rate
equals	gross basic tax
minus	credits
equals	total tax due

That ought to be complicated enough, but as we all know, it is less than the tip of the iceberg. Clearly, to arrive at the total tax, you have to assemble all the components of the equation, and if you want to minimize the total, you must manipulate the variables, namely, all the *minus entries*. Standard and itemized deductions, exemptions, and credits can all be maximized within the law. Theoretically, gross income should be an invariable amount, and when it is not, this usually constitutes creative bookkeeping, which the IRS may interpret as fraud.

Nevertheless, gross income is the first thing we can manipulate in the tax equation. To minimize it legitimately, you can either lower the dollar amount (hey, I didn't say to, I just said you could) or you can adjust the

169

type of income so that subsequent taxes will be minimized. This is what tax shelters are all about, and there are other strategies as well. For instance, if you are in a tax bracket higher than the 20 percent rate, then you can save money by making investments that yield income which can be classified as capital gain, and especially if the gain is long term. Assume that your tax rate is 35 percent and you invest $10,000 in a bank certificate at 10 percent. Your income will clearly be $1000 and the nominal tax $350. However, if you can find another investment, say a stock that yields capital gains dividends and happens to also yield 10 percent, assuming you keep the stock for the period qualifying it for long-term capital gains, the tax rate would be 20 percent, and your tax would be just $200. On the first deal your net yield is 6.5 percent ($1000 − 350 = 650 = .065). On the second, net yield is 8 percent. So, by choosing an investment that allows a different tax rate, you can save on taxes. Pretty common stuff, but easy to forget when you are eyeballing various investment opportunities.

It is important to know your actual tax rate, for the rate indicated by your gross income usually won't be your actual rate. And the fact that your gross income goes up or down doesn't necessarily mean that your bracket will climb or fall. Sorry to say it, but the only way to figure your tax bracket is to estimate your gross income and go through the beginning calculations on the 1040 tax form and work up an estimated adjusted income. Then match that to the current tax tables. If you have a personal-finance computer program with "what if?" programming capability, you are just about set. But the rest of you will have to put together your own worksheet if this year's return is going to be significantly different from last year's. If your income and expenses have changed little, you may estimate fairly accurately from last year's return. Of course, barring unforeseen changes in your position, one worksheet can be used for every investment and analysis decision all year long.

Marginal Tax Rate Worksheet

1. Current income
2. Current marginal tax rate (get this from last year's 1040 instruction book or form)
3. Next marginal tax rate
4. Amount I can declare before I reach next marginal rate (#3 minus #2)
5. Amount of anticipated added income
6. Percentage of taxable income (taxable income divided by total income)
7. Multiply #6 by #5
8. Is #7 greater or less than #3?

(If greater, you're ahead; if less than, then you are giving everything to the government and you had better consider tax shelters, converting some of your income to capital gains by investing differently, or other alternatives.)

Well that sounds easy, but again, sometimes it's not. You may find as you go that there are more than one, and possibly several tax rates, that apply to you. Just as you minimized total taxes by opting for long-term capital-gain income, your marginal tax rate (the tax rate you would be charged on your next $1000 of income) may be combined with other rates, usually the excess rates. The excess rates are shown in the tax tables as separate columns, showing that if your income in a particular area, say, your "net long-term capital gains" exceeds a given level set by the tax law, you pay a higher tax rate. So, as an example, you might pay 20 percent on the first $50,000 of income from capital gains, but you pay half your nominal tax rate after that—if you are in the 50 percent bracket, you pay 25 percent on the excess (all of it over $50,000). If you are not in that league, don't be put off by the size of the figures, there are plenty of duplicate tax rates down the scale, too.

Another common way of reducing adjusted income is to invest in nontaxable income instruments such as municipal bonds. Unfortunately, this is very inefficient for anyone below about the 40 percent tax bracket. If you are not at that level, or close, ask your accountant what kinds of investments will give better after-tax yield. There are always many.

An added strategy includes arranging cash-equivalent income that is not within the tax code purview, such as employee benefits paid by the employer and not you, the employee: insurance, business expenses, and the like. (A good exercise in learning the value of employee benefits is to take a look at the *Forbes* list of the top 400 executives in America. While they are all earning six-figure incomes and up, you'll notice that almost all of them earn more in benefits than they do in salary. Otherwise, they would be saddled with huge taxes. Instead they enjoy *effective* salaries that are often twice as high as their stated salary if not higher. Most of the nation's auto workers are also doing the same thing. In 1980 the average hourly wage was supplemented company-paid benefits to such a level that a self-employed worker would have had to earn $26 an hour to enjoy the same standard of living, assuming that he could buy all the services at the same rate the auto worker gets them, which, because the auto companies buy worker benefit services in quantity discounts, which they could not.)

An increasingly popular method of tax reduction for those who invest in business ventures and equities is to save all failing investments for tax-reduction purposes. For instance, if the $10,000 investment we mentioned earlier were in a stock that *lost* 10 percent in value, and it seemed certain that the stock would not recover any time soon, then it might be a good idea to take the loss and reinvest the remaining $9000 in something that would produce positive income. However, if you do sell the stock and realize the $1000 loss, that is considered a capital loss (opposite from capital gain) and is either long-term or short-term. The long- and short-term gains and losses are segregated on the tax forms so that short-term losses can reduce your taxable income by the amount of the loss, but long-term losses can reduce your income by a fraction of the loss. So, if you bought and sold the stock within the year, the loss reduces your taxable income by the full $1000. At the 30 percent bracket we mentioned, that means you save $300 in taxes and so the actual out-of-pocket loss is only $700. Assuming that the long-term capital-loss discount rate were 50 percent, the tax saved would be half of $300, or $150, for a net loss of $850 instead of $1000. It is interesting to note that the higher the tax bracket, the bigger the savings in nearly all tax-reduction strategies.

It doesn't take much imagination to see that paper losses, as in tax shelters, can add up to significant tax savings when your marginal tax rate climbs into the higher brackets. There are often cases where intentionally losing money and taking the deductions will keep a person from moving into a higher tax bracket in which all the tax rates would be higher, and thus the good accountant will advise the client to intentionally take a loss in order to effect a net savings through lower overall taxes. This is quite common, and you can often get tables from your banker, accountant, and broker that show approximately how the system works and how you can estimate your position and whether you should attempt such a move or other similar strategies, such as stock exchanging, real estate trading, or taking once-in-a-lifetime deductions. A good accountant can figure these things out fairly rapidly if he's familiar with your affairs. If you are contemplating so major a plan, take the effort to go through a complete tax-form rehearsal to make sure what you are doing yields enough tax savings to be worth the effort and expense.

The point is that you should get a start on defining your tax-preferred items and your tax-penalty items as soon as you can. The ideal time is the January before your taxes (that's fifteen months' lead time). If you understand the tax preparation in your bracket, you can work up your own list of preferred and penalty items along with worksheets for figuring out the dollar amounts. Otherwise I suggest that you pay your accountant extra to go over your last year's tax return and to discuss the new things in your financial position, and have him or her put together the list and the worksheets. Either way, you have something tangible to base your investment and other financial decisions on—lower taxes.

MOST OF US PAY TO SAVE MONEY

Your accountant is going to be able to make more involved decisions that can affect your adjusted income level—as in deciding whether or not to use income averaging. Unless you have a very simple tax structure, you are probably not going to save as much doing your own taxes as you would by paying a good accountant to advise you on possible tax-savings strategies.

On the other hand, if you have fairly simple taxes, the benefits of doing your own tax preparation (even if you get some advice from an accountant or tax preparer) are valuable. Going through the process keeps you familiar with the items on the tax form and which categories you must keep records on through the year. It may save you the tax preparer's fee, but only if you know all the correct decisions to make or if you have a very simple tax situation. Remember, even if you hire a preparer, you still must invest time double-checking all his entries on your form and looking for mistakes before you sign them and give them to the IRS and the state.

Reducing your tax load by maximizing the number and size of deductions, exemptions, and credits can also be ungodly complicated if you let it, but even so it can be well worth the trouble. Aside from going over *last year's* deductions with your accountant, you can put together a list of desirable and probable deductions to look for and to accumulate during the year. That way you aren't spending all year calculating whether an item is worthy of your effort; you just compare it against your checklist, assuming that your finances and the economy haven't undergone dramatic reversals recently.

DEDUCTIONS PLANNING CHECKLIST

Last year's marginal tax rate　　　　　　　　　_____
Last year's itemized deductions
    dependents　　　　　　　　　　　　_____
    medical　　　　　　　　　　　　　　_____
    travel and entertainment　　　　　　_____
    depreciated assets　　　　　　　　　_____
    business expenses　　　　　　　　　_____

This year's probable tax rate   _____
Need more deductions? _____ If so,
   deductions to be continued   _____
   possible new deductibles & investments   _____
                                                     _____
                                                     _____
                                                     _____

STARTING FROM "ZERO"

Did last year's deductibles exceed the "zero-bracket" (standard deduction given to everybody—see the 1040 form for the current amount) figure? If so, be sure to use the long form and take the deductions.

Be sure you save the records and receipts for the deductible items, and keep your list handy to help make decisions during the year, as the deductibility affects the true cost of the items to you. Keep in mind that the savings are only as great as your marginal tax rate.

IS THAT TAX DEDUCTION WORTH THE TROUBLE?

true cost = total price (including tax) × (1 − your tax rate)
Example: if your tax rate is 35%, and the deductible item cost $1000.
Formula: $1000 × (1 − .35 = .65) = $650 (true cost)

If you can afford the time, too, you might want to rank the importance of each type of deduction according to the potential savings. At any rate, after you do that with your accountant, or variously decide to forego that with your accountant, ask your banker, broker, and insurance agent for literature about tax savings. As a part of their sales literature, all the financial-service businesses produce lists of deductions obtainable through them or related to their services. Very often you can adapt one of those lists, and better, even if you start with a good list of your own, you may well find possibilities you hadn't considered. This is especially true of new products and laws that come along and are difficult for the average person to learn about, much less understand. Check out the forms at the end of the chapter for ideas.

So far we've discussed ways of reducing tax loads by reduction of taxable income directly. There are virtually endless variations on that theme. However, there is another approach that shares the same effect but is really a process of *shifting* the tax burden to others so that the effective tax rate is lower.

USING PRE-TAX VERSUS POST-TAX DOLLARS

If you can spend pre-tax dollars, you can often part with less wealth than if you spent the same number of post-tax dollars. One way to do this, if you are giving charitable contributions to needy organizations, is to donate your investment assets instead of cash. This can often have the effect of giving the charity as much or more value than you would have in cash, but with the result that you end up with lower taxable income. The reason is that if you liquidate an investment, you must pay tax on the capital gain and the earned income, which must be subtracted from the selling price to give you the true yield from the sale. If you give the exact same security to a charity, they can sell it at the same gross price, but they do not pay taxes. Thus you donate more to the charity and it costs you less, and everybody wins, even the IRS, for it is contributing to the support of nonprofit organizations.

Another way to transfer tax liability is to make sizable gifts within your family (check methods carefully). There are limits to the annual rate (raised from $3000 per recipient to $10,000) but the principle is sound. Basically, if a father is going to pay his kid's way through college, for instance, he typically does so with dollars on which he has already paid income taxes. If he has a security which has appreciated in value, how-ever, he can give that to his child, transferring the appreciated value of the security without having to pay the capital gains or earned-income taxes. That way, by the father giving less, the child receives more. In 99 percent of cases, the child is in a very low tax bracket when college rolls around, so when he sells the security to finance college, he pays the capital-gains tax on the basis of his very low bracket, and there is a considerable savings. Good sources for specific methods and information about these types of arrangements are bank trust departments, college placement offices (even if your kid is in diapers), and your broker's office.

The Uniform Gift to Minors Act provides a means for giving relatively small amounts of money to kids every year with tax savings, and is especially handy at banks, thrifts, and brokerages where they have forms and automatic accounts set up to take advantage of the law with a minimum of hassle. In a few states the name is different, but the general rules are the same. UGMA trusts used to be even more attractive, but naturally the government stepped in and changed things so that the minor has to pay larger taxes on the proceeds from the trust than was once the case.

The main catch with the two strategies I've just outlined is that for them to work legally, the gift to the minor must be "irrevocable." That is one of the few five-syllable words that means the same in legalese as it does in English.

A second hitch is that all these irrevocable trusts immediately become sole property of the minor and are solely under his or her control at age of majority (legal adulthood). There is an alternative to this if you are queasy about the idea of your child gaining full control of the money at age eighteen or twenty-one, as is the case with all the trusts save one type. These are the "reversionary trusts," the most popular of which are the Clifford trusts and certain types of "no-interest and callable" loans within the family.

These are great not only for children, but all dependents, such as elderly, infirm, or disabled relatives who need financial help. The basic idea is that you place your income-earning assets in the trust for a predetermined period of time, and the income goes to the beneficiary (the dependent). You thus are able to avoid taxes on the income by temporarily lending the assets to the dependent. The dependent is presumably in a lower tax bracket and thus enjoys a larger gift than if you had kept the assets, paid taxes on the profits, and then given the remainder. At the end of the term the ownership of the assets reverts (thus the name "reversionary") to you. You have saved taxes, the beneficiary gets a bigger gift, and it's all legal. The only drawback is that the minor's bookkeeping is complicated by a number of forms and you both need to fill out the long form at tax time. Also, the IRS is always fighting to get this type of tax reduction changed, so you must watch the laws carefully.

WITH INFLATION, A PENNY DEFERRED IS A PENNY EARNED

Your accountant, lawyer, and broker can point you in the direction of other ways to shift the tax burden off the shoulders of the high tax rate carried by the main income earners in a family. One, which also relates to tax shelters, is deferral of tax payments. Postponing taxes is the major tax-saving strategy in most corporations, and it accounts for over half of all the international and offshore banking by businesses, if the Bahamian bankers can be believed. Back when interest rates were *regularly* single digit, the standard saying was "A tax deferred ten years is a tax saved." With higher interest rates the number of years shrinks, and the annual tax savings grows.

The logic behind tax deferral is that the money which is not paid in taxes itself can be put to work to earn money, and through the magic of compounding interest, this begins to add up quickly after a few years. Secondly, because of inflation, every year that taxes are deferred means that the dollars that are paid are worth less. Thus, one thousand 1985 dollars will be worth more than one thousand 1990 dollars. Assuming you are to defer paying until 1990 the tax that you'll be asked to pay in 1985, you will be giving up less monetary value, although the number of dollars paid is the same. Preserve the value of your assets, and you will be money ahead, yet legally correct.

Also, you may be in a lower tax bracket in later years, and, we hope, in a stronger position financially. The benefits of tax deferral have to be weighed carefully, however, for some tax-postponing products are as good as they sound. For instance, tax-deferred annuities issued by insurance companies have historically yielded less tax savings than could be gained by investing the money and paying taxes, unless you happen to be in a high tax bracket. If you are not in the high bracket, the annuities are a silly investment at best, and you could do better elsewhere. If you are in a position to benefit from them, however, they may be a great way to diversify your investments and simplify estate planning.

But there are a multitude of other devices that are often very useful: IRA and Keogh (HR-10) plans are the most common; tax-qualifying pension plans; employee profit-sharing plans; employee stock-purchase plans; employee saving plans; postponing the sale of securities; and a variety of methods of selling stocks and bonds to move taxation into the succeeding year, plus many more. Life insurance salesmen will tell you to use the cash value of your life insurance for this purpose, but it is not cost-effective, and won't be until inflation hits 4 or 5 percent again. (Liquidate it instead and invest it.)

You can also use the favored device of about two-thirds of the nation's manufacturing and sales corporations by converting your securities inventory accounting from a FIFO to a LIFO system. FIFO (first thing acquired or "First In" is the first thing sold "First Out") is the concept the IRS uses when figuring your capital gains. If you bought stocks using a flat-rate averaging system, you would have many shares of a given stock which cost different prices, because you bought them on different dates. Thus, if you sell ten shares of AT&T for the first time, you must figure the capital gain or loss against the price of the first ten shares that you bought. Usually. If you choose, and you can identify the shares by serial number, you can select which shares to sell. For maximum tax advantage, you sell the most recently purchased shares first, thus LIFO (the most recently purchased "Last In," are sold first (First Out). This can save you money just as it does General Motors. (To do this effectively, you must take possession of stock shares when you purchase them in order to have actual certificates. If you simply trade shares through your broker's account, you do not actually own specific shares, you cannot identify the serial numbers of the stock certificates, and the plan can't be used.)

TAX SHELTERS CAN PROTECT OR BURY YOU

As soon as you have a tax system that even a few people construe as being confiscatory, you are going to have a lot of bright minds figuring ways to get around it. Some of the ideas are going to be legal, some will skirt the limits of the law, and some will be patently prosecutable. If you are interested in any of them, the difference can be very important.

If you are going to pay for the services of a professional tax avoider, be sure you have just that—a professional. Many of the tax-shelter schemes investigated by the SEC and others every year are being sold by people who have state or federal "cease and desist" orders outstanding against them! Professionals have references, answers to all questions, and they have easily confirmable backgrounds.

Tax shelters that are beneficial are not just plans which avoid income taxes. They may simply change the type of tax that is paid, they may postpone the date on which a tax is due, they may alter the rate at which a tax is calculated, they may change the legal entity to which a tax is payable. You can see that these options, which are only a few of the most used, exploit the entire range of tax-law variables to benefit the taxpayer. A good professional tax consultant will be able to discuss many options with you and will know which ones suit your financial circumstances. If your consultant or salesman cannot discuss these kinds of decisions with you, there is someone else out there who can. That person is valuable to you and may save you in sheltered taxes as well as in safer investments.

A big problem with tax-saving schemes is that they often are confusing and funky. A swirl of promotion surrounds them, and before you know it, that incredible tax shelter you bought into is disallowed by the IRS, the investment falls apart, and instead of a 5-to-1 write-off you have lost a bundle. The other common problem is that it is easy to get caught up in the magic of the idea of tax savings and find in the end that the effort was not worth the savings. If the savings aren't appropriate to your circumstances, it doesn't make any sense. If you are a young, single career climber, you may be better off using your assets to further your career, for a strong business career will ultimately bring you more income over the length of a lifetime than will some tax deferrals, all other things being equal. You must keep in mind that the bottom line for you usually does not appear on the salesman's worksheet. For you, the goals are either spendable income or savings for a future date, and the road between a given transaction and those goals can be a long and incredibly complicated one.

TAXING MORALITY

Discussion of the nature and size of the underground or subterranean economy has become popular recently, along with acceptance by many that avoidance of taxes is considered more or less acceptable. This doesn't seem to clash with the notion that tax evasion is still considered by many an underhanded act, and is in fact a crime at any level. But increasingly we, society, seem to be accepting legal tax avoidance and illegal evasion (disputable middle ground having been coined "evoision" in Britain) as increasingly legitimate practices in the face of rising tax rates and punitive inflation.

Obviously the black market has existed in every country since the notion of taxation was put into effect over three thousand years ago. The only thing remarkable about it, as far as I can tell, is that governments persist in pretending that it might somehow be overcome or that ignoring it will make it go away. The fact is that underground economies become stronger and more pervasive as the tax systems and prevailing economies corrode the true earning power and the respect of the population. Thus, fifty years ago when tax rates were barely double digit at any level, the American honor system of tax collection—still unique in all the world— was much more efficient than it is today, despite today's vastly larger tax-collection agency and the assistance of computerized tax forms and tax-reporting systems.

It's ironic that recent administrations, which rode to power on a wave of conservatism and individualism, have brought in the tax bill that makes the collection system more automatic and oppressive than any of the Democratic administrations which preceded it, save one, and that was urged on by the money demands of a world war. The effect is to broaden the base and scope of the black market in this country.

As the economists and social scientists who have studied it will attest, the underground economy is a natural counterpart to the official economy of any nation, and the United States is no exception. What has made news in recent years is that people openly declare that the tax system has become so repressive (rhymes with "progressive") that tax evasion as well as avoidance have become for many, perhaps most, Americans a morally acceptable alternative. What used to be the concern of the few rich has become the pastime of the masses. Ann D. Witte and Carl P. Simon note in their 1982 landmark work on the underground economy, *Beating the System*, that there are many reasons why honest taxpayers choose to turn coat and skirt the law, but all the rationales boil down to economic hardship on the one hand and a distrust or disrespect for the existing government on the other. Neither alone seems to be enough to precipitate an outfalling of new tax evaders, while the public's perception that both are growing worse is getting more distinct and certain.

As the history of failing governments tells us, the public's tolerance for accepting illegality is a one-way expansion factor. Once a family or individual has taken part in the illegal act, the human tendency to justify and accept succeeding similar acts takes over, and a pattern of self-justified lawbreaking is laid. The mores change, societal norms readjust, and the efficiency of tax collection is irreversibly lowered a sizable notch. The tendency, then, is for the government to impose higher taxes, new taxes, or to devise stricter enforcement of the tax codes. Thus, the underground economy is contrapuntal to the regular economic system, providing both relief from taxation for those who need it or want it, and also producing a burden on the remaining taxpayers and ensuring that future taxes will be more numerous and repressive. The biggest inequity of the black market economy is that not everyone can take part in it, and in that respect it is as evil as any punitive tax code.

The question for the average American is whether and where to earn or spend underground. For most Americans who do, the chief activity is moonlighting while reporting less than the full income or none at all. Others participate in unreported or illegal activity full time. Another large category consists of those whose zeal in seeking to avoid taxes through various investment devices is so great that they willingly slip across the line between legal and illegal tax shelters. The question isn't merely one of morality, "yes" or "no," but also of dollars and cents and year-end assets. What follows is the advice a willing accountant gives for adventurous clients.

If you do decide to skirt the law, take the example of most small businesses and keep just one set of books or totally separate books with no commonality at all. The problem with duplicate bookkeeping is that in the event of an audit, or just a casual error, things can get mixed up and incriminating very easily. The government has made it easy for big businesses to keep duplicate books legally, but almost impossible for the small business, which helps explain why small businesses often choose to operate off the books. It is imperative to have a strategy and stick to it so that there is no paper trail for an auditor to follow. The basis of an IRS audit is twofold—one, to find funds that appear or disappear without explanation, and, second, to uncover improper accounting. That means that the two sides of the books don't balance when the auditor recalculates, and you can be sure he won't post figures the same way you do. Most audits which end up in prosecutions uncover only some of the creative bookkeeping that actually takes place in the business or by the person.

Most tax-preparation firms never knowingly work on any tax return that doesn't comply with the letter of the law. All the preparers and accountants can do is use their best judgment with the information the clients give them. This is important to remember, for it reminds us that tax evasion is the taxpayer's responsibility—you sign the tax return and you take the risks.

You might infer from what I've said so far that I encourage or approve of tax evasion. But I do not. In fact I strongly discourage it because, after all, it raises my tax bill and encourages my government to be nastier about the whole tax issue.

Several things have transpired to change the nature of financial morality in this country, but the two most potent catalysts were probably war and modern taxation. When income taxes were first initiated to help pay for the Civil War, they were seen as a temporary solution to the insatiable appetite of a morally justified war machine. It was phased out for a couple of decades, but was brought back by Congress ostensibly for a temporary cash transfusion, and besides, the rate was so paltry it barely affected the wealthy, much less the average working man. Succeeding war and the cost of the Depression encouraged the government to forget that income tax was temporary and to escalate the base rate beyond reason. Inevitably the progressive tax structure drove the rich underground first, followed by the direly poor.

Today middle-class Americans are likely to feel safe and morally justified in describing their tax-evasion tactics on national television interviews, as indeed they have. Today the government is in some ways emulating the worst intent and spirit of other governments that have widely despised tax systems. In countries where compulsory tax returns, prepayment of taxes, and other highly oppressive methods are the order of the day, violating tax laws is much more prolific than it is here.

This "tough-tax-collector" attitude is the same climate that in England makes it standard fare for anyone with money to have an offshore bank account, or in Italy for two out of three adults to have a second job on which no taxes are paid at all. If there is not some effective effort made to reestablish the morality of paying our taxes and realigning the tax rate to the real ability of people to pay, then there is little doubt that the U.S. will follow in the footstep of these other countries where tax rates are insanely oppressive specifically to counter the effect of the underground economy and the overt tax evasion. It's a cycle we can avoid.

One of the most irrefutable causes of disrespect for the tax laws is the plight of the elderly who dare to honestly report gainful employment. The cutoff point changes yearly, but in 1981, if the Social Security recipient earned just $5500, he would have lost half of his Social Security payment for the year—which was typically in the $5000 range. The net effect is that if they work and earn enough to improve their lifestyle, but don't earn enough to support themselves in any kind of dignity, then they are punished for their industriousness and productivity. The example cited above would be the equivalent of putting a $10,500 per year worker into the 50 percent tax bracket and denying any deductions. If the elderly refuse to work, or if they choose to lie to the government, then they are substantially rewarded. Sadly, that is the New American Way.

The United States remains the only nation where income tax payment is voluntary, depending upon the honor system for just over 98 percent of all returns, despite increasing computerization. Unless things change, many economists predict, we will see more and more respectable citizens retreat into the underground economy. Then the burden on those of us who follow the straight and narrow line of legality will be even weightier. A direct correlation here is the offshore banking system located principally in the Caribbean, where a vast Eurodollar black market launders money going in and out of the country, money which the government considers either illegal or taxable. In both cases, the return to our country is principally pride, and the loss is in bank revenues, lower tax revenues, a less stable money supply, and a stifled economy.

Let's take an aside here and probe how you find these experts in offshore tax relief. If you have an income that is large enough and a good CPA to match, he or she may have the connections to put you in touch with an attorney specializing in offshore banking. Certainly any of the largest international accounting firms have either branches that specialize in offshore banking or have staff experts, or retain independent experts. The ones you will want to start with and probably finish with are the experts in international banking with heavy experience with U.S. monetary policy and law. The handful I have been able to talk with require more than a nifty recommendation before they will accept you as a client: you must provide a financial résumé and provide some proof of your actual worth in *addition* to having references. What they are pleased to say is that you need a tremendous cash flow, usually in the high five figures at least, annually, to make the venture worthwhile. Forgetting special fees, which can be outrageous, these lawyers charge hundreds of dollars per hour for services, and a substantial number of hours can quickly be tallied with international phone calls and bookkeeping arrangements, which are necessarily not relegated to the firm's regular clerks.

Tax Haven Information Sources

Tax Management International Journal
    Tax Management, Inc.
    The Bureau of National Affairs, Inc.
    943 Key West Ave.
    Rockville, MD 20850

Practical International Tax Planning
(formerly *How to Use Foreign Tax Havens*)
By Marshall J. Langer LL.B.
From The Practicing Law Institute
    810 Seventh Avenue
    New York City 10019

Also visit the nearest large legal library. Most have the above and other up-to-date related publications.

Above all, if you consider any creative tax planning, discuss the underground economy with every prospective lawyer, accountant, financial planner, or broker, and mention practices that you feel should be off limits and those you are interested in. If the other person doesn't accept your attitude, then the sooner you find out the better. "Be explicit," is an excellent rule here. Inferences and raised eyebrows can be interpreted in many different ways. No one is going to sic the IRS on you if you tell them that you cheated on last year's tax return, but they and you will be thankful that you avoided a misunderstanding on such a sticky topic. More to the point, you'll probably regret it if you end up hiring a professional who refuses to do your bidding, or, as in my case, goes ahead and acts without your approval. (Yes, it happens. I hired a CPA to prepare my tax return and found that he added a dozen deductions that were not only false, but were not legal. I had to completely redo my tax forms to correct his bungling. More proof that you must be your own guardian.)

MEET ALLIES EARLY

Few things are more frustrating than hunting for a tax accountant between January 1 and April 15. They are all busy, harassed by their clients, and grumpy about the incredible amount of work they are temporarily involved in. That leaves you eight months of the year when it is a good time to shop for a new tax preparer. Please don't wait until New Year's.

If you have been preparing your own returns, you have to decide what kind of service you need. If you are salaried and use the short form, you may just be after the convenience, and any of the large, reputable commercial services will be just fine. They have generally competent staffs, are up to date, and specialize in just your situation. They will be able to guard you against the most common errors and oversights for a reasonable fee.

PICK THE ACCOUNTANT WHO IS
COMFORTABLE IN YOUR NEIGHBORHOOD

If you must use the long form and have complex variables in attached forms, and especially if you are in any but the lower tax brackets, most accountants, financial planners, and other professionals agree you can probably save a significant amount of tax money by hiring a good CPA. There are two tiers that the professionals speak of. First, the general CPA firms that do general business accounting throughout the year and do taxes only during the season. Second are the firms that specialize in income tax preparation year 'round.

The general accounting firms must be given the once over, too. Do they hire overload help during the tax season, and if so, who will do your return? If it's one of the associates, you definitely want one of the principals to review the service and advice you are given. You want to be sure that the person who works on your return has most of his clients in your general financial position and income level, for his knowledge of the details and strategies will be stronger in certain areas. If you are the smallest client of the firm, you may not be worth taking extra trouble for. If you are the largest, the preparer will not be intimate with your kinds of problems, but will be busy looking them up—not investigating the approach you want.

Some accountants will charge for an introductory consultation. This can be a reasonable charge if you get some advice and the accountant takes the time to give your history and your story a close examination. If you have unusual circumstances in past years, as for instance income averaging, large changes in tax or income from one year to the next, or any other oddity, expect a good accountant to ask about them. Ask about audits. A good accountant is involved with a certain number of audits; overly conservative ones rarely are; dishonest ones frequently are—be sure you are both on the same wavelength here. The IRS audits clients of preparers on its famous list of "Problem Preparers" much more frequently than it does the general population of returns, so unless you like to share your bookwork with the IRS, don't take the possibility lightly. You can ask a prospective CPA how many times he's paid preparer-negligence fines to the IRS, and why. Accountants who are creative and will be able to explain their logic to the IRS auditors satisfactorily should be able to completely convince a mere client, and the experts suggest that you have him do so. It's one test worth giving. Overly conservative CPAs have a reputation for being lazy and unresponsive to their clients' more complex needs, claim some CPAs. Deserved or not, it's an allegation worth pondering.

These days one of the key jobs of a tax preparer is structuring your return to avoid setting off alarms in the IRS screening and computer processes. The IRS has admitted that certain professions are audited much more frequently than others. Certain kinds of investments trigger a closer look at your return. Gray areas where the IRS can force hard to prove documentation, such as in business expenses or alimony, are favorites as well.

A class act in the CPA's office may be a rephrasing of the title of your occupation, or knowledge of alternative ways to declare certain expenses so that the totals on page one are proper, yet more innocuously labeled or less specific. This is just one area where the average person doing his own returns has no chance of matching a very alert CPA in avoiding tax trouble, even avoiding an audit, or, if an audit is held, avoiding embarrassing entries yet conforming to the tax code in every way.

Considering that about 2 percent of all returns are audited every year, it seems likely that a large proportion of those must be returns picked on the basis of the IRS problem lists and computerized callouts. Actually, less than 10 percent of the audited returns are selected purely by random, and just over three quarters are chosen by the computer callouts. Therefore it's reasonable to assume that avoiding "problem areas" must reduce a person's chances of being audited tremendously. Remember, if you are audited and substantial errors are found, or if you are stuck with a penalty, you are likely to be audited again very soon. This sounds like a good club not to join.

Many people contest their returns and even audits every year and win. The common appeals are heard in cities around the country within weeks after April 15 or the receipt of the taxpayer complaint. The most common outcome is not a "win or lose," but a compromise, assuming a reasonable argument on your part. If your claim is denied there, you must pay the tax and possibly a fine, and then sue the IRS in tax court. Naturally that means a lawyer, legal fees, and possibly years of delays. If you decide to go this route, you must file a "note of deficiency" within a month after your return is sent back to you. After that, your accountant, lawyer, or the local IRS office can tell you how to file a petition in court. If you blow the petition process they throw your complaint out, so be sure to follow all the rules and meet all the deadlines. Once you get there, win one for the Gipper and all your fellow taxpayers who have been wronged and never avenged. If you lose, well, the taxes mostly go for a good cause.

SHELTER FROM WHAT?

This next topic straddles the areas of taxes and investments in the form of tax shelters. They're the homeland of more investor fraud than any other scam, measured in numbers of victims or dollars heisted. They're increasingly popular because of the way inflation has accelerated tax-bracket creep. Auto workers are often in the mid-30s brackets! (When income taxes were reintroduced in 1913, opponents blasted that the new taxes would end up stealing 15 percent from hardworking American families. Supporters won their cause, in part, by branding these unbelievable declarations as inflammatory lies, ridiculous on their face. No one laughed.) While you shouldn't buy tax shelters through your CPA, you *should* consult with him or her before you seriously consider any plan.

Not only are many of the hot-selling plans disallowed by the IRS, sometimes years later, and involving punishing fines, but the loss of the actual investments by fraud is growing by leaps and bounds. The SEC guidelines, as I outlined in the chapter on investing, work around the same principle that all financial experts give for individual investors: If it isn't first a sound investment, it isn't going to be a sound shelter. That isn't to say that many people won't get away with some 8-to-1 write-offs, *or* that laws won't lend preferential treatment to certain investments as tax shelters. Surely both will come to pass every year, but these are both a matter of luck and special knowledge. If you don't have the latter, you have to depend upon the former. Please don't.

Basic Tax-Shelter Checklist

1. Can I afford the investment involved?
2. Forgetting the tax angle, is this an acceptably safe investment on its own?
3. If the investment produces no tax shelter, can I expect to get all or nearly all of my investment back within a reasonable time?
4. If this is not a government or major corporation, have I investigated the company and the principals to see if they are under investigation or have records of fraud? (See text for details.)
5. Assuming an acceptable level of safety, am I in a tax bracket that makes this type of risk/shelter a better deal than paying taxes and putting money in another investment at available rates?
   Formula =
   Shelter
   probable cash return + tax savings = total value "a"

   Alternative Investment
   (cash investment × available interest) − tax = total value "b"

   All other considerations aside, if a is greater than b, then the shelter holds promise. If b is greater than a, then other investments will be a better choice
6. Have I checked with my accountant or financial counsel for added information to decide whether this shelter meets my true needs?

7. Do I have the time and inclination to investigate, monitor, and work through this shelter/investment?

If you cannot answer "yes" to every single question in the checklist, you had better search very hard for a reason to consider the shelter any further. Avoiding taxes with an intriguing tax shelter makes sense only if the total savings at the end of the investment life is actually greater than you could achieve through careful investing. About half of all tax-shelter investments do not yield profits.

See the detailed Tax-Shelter Worksheet on pages 189–190.

Income-Tax Checklist

- Dates for preparing and paying annual, quarterly, and other taxes fixed into calendar and set for action
- Plan for upcoming year's tax minimization made and ready to implement. Includes notes to look for special investments, recommended tax shelters, to keep all medical receipts, to organize all itemized entries, etc.
- Dates for contacting your CPA, tax preparer, broker, etc., for advice on how to take advantage of new laws, to change plans if financial conditions change significantly, etc.
- Review of filing status, exemptions, expected withholding, adjustments to income, itemized deductions

TAX RECORDS

Keep tax returns for the last seven years (that's as far back as an audit can go, barring unusual circumstances) unless you have declared bankruptcy or had other major financial difficulties, in which case save for ten years.

Review items from last year's taxes that must be carried forward or excluded, such as income averaging, depreciation schedules, once-only deductions, losses or gains that are limited by the number of years they may be claimed, etc.

All receipts and records of items that *might* be legal deductions or proof of taxable status. (Be sure to keep note of the purpose of each one if it is not evident.) These include all forms sent by the banks, by companies you have invested in, and income records from your employment, and store and service receipts. It is better to save too many than to find that you have thrown out some you weren't sure could legally be used.

Records of all income or outlay that must be listed on your tax returns.

Remember this includes all records for every itemized deduction, all investment transactions relating to losses or gains, and anything else that must be proven if and when you are audited. If you assemble and organize this material as it arrives, you not only have saved yourself a big headache at tax time, you may also find opportunities to save taxes by planning ahead. If your accountant charges by the hour, you also save on the time he spends making sense out of your chaos.

Questions to Ask a Prospective CPA

- How long have you been a tax preparer?
- What kind of annual refresher course do you take?
- How else do you keep up to date on tax law, methods, etc?
- If you are not a CPA or are not the boss, who reviews your work with me?
- How many other clients in my general tax bracket do you have?
- Why are you a good choice for someone with my tax problems and needs?
- What are your fees and how are they calculated?
- When and how often should I contact you during the year, and for what reasons? (The answers should be compelling.)
- May I speak with, say, five of your clients to ask their experience with you?
- What kind of interview will you want to give me when we meet and what kind of information will you want me to bring? How well do you want to know my situation before you work on my taxes?
- Do you have experts in specialty tax areas whom you can consult if my planning or return involved decisions you are unsure about?
- How many times have you been called to attend audits in the past five years? How many times have you been fined?
- Have you been convicted of improper tax preparation? If so, what were the circumstances?
- Here is my attitude toward taxes; do you have any objections or suggestions?

You may well have other specific questions that will be important for you to ask. This is the time you want to find all the differences you might have with a tax preparer so that you don't make such a discovery in the midst of a particularly difficult tax problem on April 14.

Tax-Shelter Worksheet

- Initial cost
- Type of investment
- Expected chance of profit/loss
- If loss, estimated chance of IRS disallowance

- If disallowed, what tax bracket will you move into, what will be the estimated fines and late-payment penalties?
- If loss, expected first-year loss and deduction
- Unacceptable-loss level
- If gain, expected first-year tax increase
- If gain, what marginal tax bracket will you move into?
- Unacceptable-gain level
- Risk acceptability high/low
- Planned need for tax shelter high/low
- Types of acceptable or desired shelters based on your interests, your risk acceptance, your willingness to shop around, etc.
- Recommendation of advisers
- Last year's marginal tax bracket. (Look up in last year's 1040 return and booklet. For years, the standard breakoff point for reasonable use of tax shelters has been the 40 percent bracket, although those in lower brackets can benefit if the shelter is also a worthy investment.)
- Can you afford to move money out of more secure investments into a tax shelter large enough to help you?

Your Need For Tax-Sheltered Income

Investment-risk ratio: expected risk/expected return.
    Rate from 1 to 10 _____
    a. Expected tax-exempt yield available _____
    b. Expected tax rate _____
Multiply (a) times (b) = _____ (expected savings)
Acceptable yes/no _____

TAX-PLANNING WORKSHEET

Last year tax bracket _____
Expected current-year marginal tax rate _____

taxable capital gains
(realized this year
according to tax laws)

	asset	short-term	long-term
	_____	_____	_____
	_____	_____	_____
	_____	_____	_____
TOTALS	_____	_____	_____

realized capital losses

_____	_____	_____
_____	_____	_____
_____	_____	_____
_____	_____	_____

TOTAL
net gains/losses for year   _____   _____

Tax-Reducing Alternatives

- Income averaging
- Investing in a high-risk tax shelter
- Maximizing your allowable deductions
- Taking loss on securities and other investments that are down in relative value
- Moving investments into tax-favored investments such as government or municipal bonds, tax-deferred annuities, etc.
- Opening or increasing contribution to IRA or Keogh plan
- Adding optional amount to group pension plans
- Increasing portion of total actual work compensation to nontaxable benefits
- Professional incorporation
- Giving high-tax-liability investments to charities, etc.
- Transferring assets to other members of the family in lower tax brackets
- Transferring assets to trusts
- Other possibilities _____

Checklist for Reducing Income Taxes

- Choose the most advantageous filing status. Many, perhaps most, households qualify for more than one filing status, such as couples who may file jointly or separately. Depending upon credits, income, and business variables, one may be considerably cheaper than the other.
- Make sure you qualify for all dependents listed and list all that you are qualified for. The standards for exemptions change with every new tax law, so look for changes.
- Make sure that you list only taxable income and keep track of all withholdings. Some investments may be all or partially tax-exempt,

and some employers may withhold more or less than is necessary unless you request that they do otherwise.

- Discuss plans that may work for you with your tax preparer or accountant.

TAXABLE-INCOME CHECKLIST

	taxable	tax-exempt or prepaid
Earned income		
Business income		
Interest income		
Dividend income		
Capital gains		
Pensions, alimony, etc.		
Other income (rent, royalties, windfalls, etc.)		
TOTAL INCOME		

- Be sure to segregate out all of your capital gains and losses, and segregate all long-term (assets owned over one year, or the current legal holding period) and short-term gains and losses. Frequently overlooked items here are personal assets, such as property, which usually qualifies for gains, but not necessarily losses. Check with an accountant for details or check the state and federal tax tables.
- Pensions may be only partly taxable, depending upon the employer and the investments involved, so ask for a statement reflecting this. Same with annuities.
- Look into the rules regarding unusual income. Some examples of taxable special income are prizes, unemployment benefits in some instances, bonuses, gambling winnings, value of profit obtained through barter, fees collected from the government (like jury duty pittances), and the list goes on. Some of these are tax-free, as are many other kinds of income, depending upon the circumstances. Some are subject to special taxes. The only way to find out is to check.
- Be sure to enter all allowable adjustments to your income. *Examples*: IRA or Keogh contributions, business expenses, moving expenses (if related to income), alimony payouts, some penalties incurred in investments, and others.
- Check all your potential deductions to see whether they exceed the standard minimum deduction, which everyone gets. If they don't,

your tax preparation will be a breeze; if they do, you will save more in taxes by itemizing your deductions on the 1040 long form, using schedules.

• If you have any unusual change in income, always check to see whether you may be eligible for *income averaging*. This can offset the impact of steeply increasing or one-shot income and reduce taxes significantly.

• Be sure you have entered all credits in your favor. Examples: one-time home sale, over sixty-five, political contributions, solar, oil, and other energy credits, child and infirmity care, and others.

• Make sure you have deferred all income that can be taxed in later years. This may involve liquidating investments after the first of the year instead of just before, delaying pension or annuity payments, changing some investments to tax-sheltered categories, etc.

• Make sure you have made the most advantageous contribution to an IRA, Keogh, or qualifying pension. You may extend the date for allowable contributions beyond April 15 of the following year by applying for a filing extension. Only this contribution and not your tax-payment date is affected.

• Check with your accountant or tax preparer early in the year for ideas on how to plan for your next year's taxes, as plans for the future are much more successful than trying to find alternatives in what has already come to pass.

BASIC ESTATE-TAX CHECKLIST

Gross estate value (your net worth)
Deductible expenses and payments
Marital deduction (% times estate value)
Taxable disbursements to be made
Credits and exemptions (vary with familial status)
Estimated total tax
Estimated distributable estate

Minimizing Estate Taxes

• Write a carefully prepared will, keep it up to date, assign a capable and responsible executor, and include specific instructions for each person mentioned. If the executor is not a probate attorney, leave instructions for consulting an attorney and in what circumstances.

- Distributing gifts while living.
- Establishing trusts. Most tax-effective trusts are irrevocable, but there are a few kinds that are reversionary; that is, you do not necessarily lose control over the assets until you die, and taxes are still minimized. This not only requires an expert attorney, but you have to keep up with rapidly changing legal requirements.
- Buy life insurance. The trick is to buy it on each other, and have each person own and pay for the policies he may benefit from and not pay for the insurance on yourself. This usually removes the insurance claim from probate proceedings and eliminates almost any chance of tax liability on the insurance payment. Be sure to pursue this, as many life insurance salesmen do not suggest this in most cases since it creates more work for them and from their point of view increases the risk of lapsed policies.
- Buy annuities only if you can't find a better investment and if interest rates are artificially high.
- Make sure you have property owned in the format that minimizes tax liability and probate procedures in your state. Usually this means joint ownership rather than tenants in common, but this is not always the case. In fact, years ago, just the opposite was true, and a change in legislation can reverse the situation again, so . . .
- Keep up to date, either by checking every year with a probate attorney, a general practitioner who is conscientious about monitoring probate law, or do it yourself by following one of the law journals or other publications that follow such legislation and interpret it for their readers (this includes many finance magazines).
- Invest in tax-exempt federal securities. Inflation has reduced the desirability of using so called "flower bonds," but in the larger estates this may still be worth investigating.
- Check with an estate attorney to find strategies that are peculiar to your estate. In most states, state estate taxes are much larger than the federal ones.

WILL PREPARATION

Before going to an attorney to have a will written, or before creating your own (see format requirements for your state; the wrong format, believe it or not, can invalidate a will), assemble at least all of the following information. You'll probably have to collect it later anyway, but having it early on will expedite the process and allow you to consider other details.

Assets	est'd value	who gets it
Home & other real estate	_____	_____
Business interests	_____	_____
Debts owed you	_____	_____
Major personal property (cars, etc.)	_____	_____
Other personal property of value	_____	_____
	_____	_____
Items of sentimental value	_____	_____
Transferrable pensions, other income	_____	_____
Investments stocks	_____	_____
bonds	_____	_____
bank accounts	_____	_____
collectibles	_____	_____
partnerships, etc.	_____	_____
others	_____	_____
Other bequests		
Proceeds from life insurance policies	_____	_____
Name of first preferred trustee or executor	_____	
second	_____	
third	_____	

Desired responsibilities of trustee or executor _____

_____

_____

_____

Statement listing which debts and responsibilities should be paid first and in which order, especially if debts against the estate will likely exceed the probable value of the estate _____

(This is your priority list and may be superseded by statutes.)

Dates when minors reach age of majority (legal adulthood) _____

Beneficiaries, trustees, and expiration dates of testamentary trusts (those set up to activate when you die) _____

Beneficiaries, trustees, and expiration dates of living, *sine vivo* trusts (those that become active while you are living) _____

Extraordinary conditions of survivorship specified by you _____

Legal spouse, including means of contacting _____

Surviving children, including means of contacting _____

Closest living relatives, in order of legal proximity, including means of contacting

---

Identification and revocation of prior wills (this eliminates contests after you are gone) ———————————————————————————

Your will should accomplish several goals, depending upon your family, lifestyle, acquaintances, and so on. Among the most important common goals are:

- To ensure the continuation of the dependent survivors' lifestyle to the fullest extent possible
- To ensure that the after-tax assets are responsibly managed to meet the needs of dependent survivors
- To ensure that your property and assets are distributed to those you choose, insofar as the law allows
- To minimize taxation so that a maximum portion of the estate can go to the persons you choose, rather than to the government
  1. Direct estate taxes, federal and state
  2. Income taxes accrued by the estate and liable against it (they can grow between the time of death and the time the assets are distributed)
  3. Inheritance taxes paid by the beneficiaries named in the will or in probate

HOW OFTEN A NEW WILL?

Historically there is a significant legislative overhaul of federal estate taxes about every twenty years, but there are important changes at least every four. Then there are more changes that come unpredictably. This all means that a will must be at least perfunctorily reviewed every year.

This is doubly wise, for it not only guards against an out-of-date document that may be ineffective, it is also labor-saving. If each change can be addressed individually, the will can be amended with codicils very simply. If the whole thing must be revamped, you are in for another major session with the lawyer, a complete new will, and the expense and bother that acompany it.

10

Banking On Your Money

TODAY THE FUNCTIONS different banking institutions can play in a person's life are changing so rapidly that the traditional image of the financial community we once saw clearly and confidently is melting into a blurred, mixed bag—I call it "the banking mix." Banks are being forced to accept severe strictures on both incoming and outgoing interest rates. S&Ls, after almost collapsing because of inflation and government restrictions, are becoming less like home lenders and more like banks themselves, and have even tried to make the switch in their charters. Even the securities and money brokers have begun to offer services to the general public and the business community that mimic, duplicate, and even surpass the banking services of old. To bank effectively these days requires not only a trusted banker, but also an attentive ear to the latest-breaking news story. Wall Street America is keeping the banking mix as wild as a bartender's Mixmaster—in high gear and whipping up a real kick for those who dare to drink it up.

THE BANKING MIX

which institution	which service	what cost/return
federal bank	savings account	?
state bank	checking	?
federal S&L	loans, mortgages	?
state S&L	credit cards	?
credit union	financial counseling	?
stockbrokerage	sale of bonds	?
finance company	commercial paper	?

certificates of deposit	?
stocks	?
treasury bills	?
estate planning/services	?
trust services	?

Take any institution and you'll find that the mix of services it offers is becoming more diverse each year. The rates of return and cost of borrowing and of services are changing rapidly as well. The ideal institution for you depends upon what services you need, how the rates of return or cost compare, who will accept your business on your terms, and what is convenient for you. Complicated, yes, but the mix means better shopping for the customer, as well.

For us, the customers, this offers up a double-edged sword with which to slice off a hunk of profit or commit monetary suicide. It also demands an attentive ear to the marketplace in these new financial areas, and a willingness to be flexible. We have a rapidly expanding field of savings, investing, and borrowing choices at many levels to choose from, and the process of deciding what and how much goes where deserves serious attention.

So how can we keep abreast of banking changes without spending an inordinate amount of time studying disclosure statements and filling out mountains of little forms? The answer is by letting the laws of the marketplace do some of the work for us and by cultivating our bankers so that they'll work out as many of the details as possible for us. That is what businesses do, and any individual can do the same. The basic principle is to take advantage of all the services and opportunities that are obvious and try to improvise those which are not. Since 90 percent of the public does neither, you can be successful very often by default.

This is a great time for banking customers (and customers of all banklike service businesses). Back in the sixties and seventies they gave away toasters and microwave ovens, but today the emphasis is on providing just what bankers *should* offer—flexibility, variety of products and services, and competitive return on investment. It's almost as if the banks suddenly decided to serve the people, even if it wasn't their idea.

What all this opportunity means is that the inattentive, inactive banking customer will be left out in the cold and left behind in the race against inflation, devaluation, and depreciation. Clearly, if the banks are anxious to offer instruments that yield much higher rates than regular passbook savings accounts were allowed to pay until recently, then it must be for a reason. The reason is that customers leave the banks and S&Ls in droves every time interest rates climb above the passbook savings rate. The banks pleaded with the government for permission to fight against the black knight of the money-market funds, and they were granted the right to offer the now famous T-bill accounts, which yield approximately the same as government Treasury Bill notes. Now the banks and S&Ls have permission to offer a wider variety of interest-bearing accounts, (some have already arrived, but the rush is yet to come), yet a large number of customers won't benefit a bit, and most won't benefit nearly as much as they could.

Why? I prefer to think it is a form of future shock rather than laziness. After all, there have been more changes in the ways we bank and handle money in the past ten years than in the previous five hundred, and there is more novelty every year. It is a hassle to find out about all the new features your banks offers and then to implement the few that fit your needs, but it's worth it. During the early years of 1977 to 1982, a period of comparatively mild change, the average increase in available interest was over 2 percent—a 50 percent increase.

Two percent is appealing, but the argument becomes more persuasive as you add up the effect over a number of years. Two percent compounded for five years adds up to over 11 percent in accumulated interest missed by a bank customer who was eligible for the investment. Assuming a return of 10 percent per year for four years, that's the same as getting an entire year of interest free, just for spending a few extra hours filling out bank forms and making sure they are properly serviced and posted. Today, a 3 percent reward or better is often attainable. The difference between a 7 percent annual return and 10 percent return is 100 percent in just twelve years!

Taking advantage of the advertised services a bank offers is just one way to maximize your benefits (and one way to join the half of all customers who change their banking services for the better each *year*). Another important way is to do what every businessperson eventually learns to do—apply assertiveness to your banking.

I was recently in my bank in time to witness an amusing and very instructive incident. While waiting for my personal banker (ever ntoice how now that you have personal bankers, presumably to serve you better, you have to wait around for that individual to be available, whereas before, any officer on duty would do?), I was seated in one of those new open-style offices where the desks are cheek-by-jowl. Just behind me, another bank officer was busy explaining to a customer the procedure for buying into one of the bank's T-bill certificates. As you know, these are issued by the bank and carry a rate slightly lower than those issued directly by the government. It seemed that the banker had just about hooked his sale when a third banker brought his client to a nearby desk.

In a loud voice, the client asked whether the banker had the customer's Treasury Bill from the government auction the day before. Yes, the banker replied in an equally voluminous tone, and the bank was certainly pleased to offer this service, too. This did not pass by the first customer, who asked rather icily for the same service. The banker acceded and she got it, and the bank lost out on its slice of the pie, much to the banker's embarrassment.

Obviously there are banking services attainable that are not advertised, nor generally available, nor easily found. They are a symptom of the bank's willingness to bend and adapt in order to serve, and thereby retain, valuable customers. It's probable that the bank wouldn't agree to buy Treasury Bills for every customer who came in with $10,000 (the minimum bid), especially someone who generally kept only small sums at the branch. Doubtlessly, both the customers I described had substantial accounts and were valued customers, but the point is that they didn't receive equal service or opportunity. At least not until they asked for it.

It's no secret that at banks, or in most businesses, preferred customers get preferred treatment. You don't always have to be a millionaire to get this, but you do need a banker who is aware that the bank is making money from your deposits. Theoretically that could be as little as $1000, but that won't get you red-carpet treatment in McDonald's today, much less at the bank. You needn't be rich either. However, you do need tact.

My wife tested this theory just about a year ago when she decided to move one of her accounts to a new, more conveniently located bank. The new-accounts officer was delighted and acted certain that she had a new customer when my wife mentioned the possibility that she might transfer *all* her banking assets. Then she dropped the bomb and asked if it might be possible to waive some of the more troublesome fees attached to the new accounts. Certainly! was the reply, and before a minute had passed, she had erased about $15 per month in fees and in the process had greatly simplified the monthly account-balancing process, for those fees don't have to be figured each time. Incidentally, it is not mentioned in any of the bank's literature that the fees are negotiable, or that they are a matter of policy. But in banking, as in all business, most things are negotiable if you have an impressive enough hand. The only way to find out if your hand wins is to show it and call.

GOOD READING

Demanding particular services is usually at the far extreme of getting good banking services. A better first step, and one that banks constantly howl that people fail to do, is to obtain and read the literature. By law banks are required to provide understandable and complete explanations of their advertised services to all inquiring customers. Since nearly every new service is advertised these days, the only excuses for ignorance are neglect or not understanding the publications. When that happens to me,

I call my personal banker and ask what the heck the confusing document says. Occasionally she doesn't know, but she always eventually finds out and tells me so I can make a decision. The personal banker is only as useful as you make her or him.

Along the same lines, banks are spending more than ever on advertising in all forms, and printed customer-service literature is getting better and better as a result. Following the lead of Citibank, which started the diversification, many banks and other institutions offer literature on every aspect of finance, from personal financial planning courses to credit managment, securities trading, and a myriad of topics in addition to basic explanations of day-to-day banking services. Get the brochures that interest you—after all, they are free for the asking, and often tell you just what you need to know. Frequently you'll find what the advertising left out and perhaps what your personal banker forgot or decided not to tell you. My bank, for instance, just issued a booklet detailing how to evaluate real estate partnerships, and they aren't even in the business—but many of their customers are.

Probably little of what I've mentioned so far is news to anyone who has had extensive dealings with banks, but it all bears emphasizing because, as the president of one of California's major banks told me, "We make a lot of money off the people who don't cash in on what they are entitled to." In fact, banks make many millions of dollars each year from customer accounts that are out of date, are rolled over automatically, or are simply forgotten.

The courts have ruled that banks may declare accounts inactive if the customer doesn't make a transaction within a defined period of time, as short as only six months or a year. And with modern computerized record keeping, nary a fish slips through the nets, either. When an account is declared inactive, most states require that the bank attempt to notify the customer, and usually place the funds in a trustee account for a time. If the customer cannot be found, as in a new address without mail forwarding, or prolonged travel abroad, the bank may claim the money or the contents of a safety deposit box, though the time period and mechanics with the boxes is different. Or the money may go into a state fund, depending upon statutes. It can and it does.

If the customer comes along the day after the deed, that's too bad. He may get compensation and he may not. Moral: Don't fail to monitor and post even a single account, and don't forget to keep every account active by making transactions within the prescribed minimum period. Checking these should be a regular bookkeeping task. Put them on the calendar. The alternative is state-sanctioned confiscation.

All you can do is watch out. If you have one you can reprogram your personal financial-computing system to flag you when your accounts are approaching the danger dates. And if you're not at least considering the day when you'll computerize your finances, especially your banking, better open up your mind and accept the concept. The idea has been successfully tested and promises to spread rapidly over the next decade. It'll be another way to separate the customers who get the best service, and hence the best return on their money, from the stick-in-the-muds who accept the banks' minimum services and, in many instances, minimum interest payments.

THE REAL "FULL-SERVICE" BANKS

Although banks have been hopping mad over the incursion of securities brokerage firms into what have traditionally been exclusively banking services, banks and S&Ls have been moving in the opposite direction, too, as fast as the lawmakers will allow. Beginning in 1981, banks began joining forces with brokers, and now the legal barriers are falling fast. The promise is that we'll be able to do all our banking and investing at our truly full-service bank. The Glass-Steagall Act, which has kept the two businesses apart for over half a century, is finally being seen as an anachronism, meant to control the robber barons who ruled the financial skies at the turn of the century, not the tightly regulated industry we know today.

There is no guarantee that a stockbroker at a bank is any better or worse than a broker at a specialty house. That has always been a matter of individual performance, anyway. The move is a response to the banking services that some of the large brokerage firms now offer to their customers. So you see, it promises to be a battle among giants for the wee folk— we customers. The banks not only want new sources of revenue, they have to fight the appeal that the new cash-management accounts at Merrill Lynch, Dean Witter, and others have for the well-heeled customers. The CMAs grew out of the margin accounts at brokerage firms, which were in turn devised by the SEC as a safeguard against a repeat of the 1929 stock market crash.

Currently the government requires that individual traders who want to trade on margin (a bet on the future stock market with shares borrowed from the brokerage firm) put up 20 to 50 percent cash in a trust account as good-faith money. Back when interest rates hovered around 4 to 6 percent, that wasn't much of a problem, but when rates jumped into the double-digit range, that money sitting idle represented a hefty loss of earning power, and some margin traders were taking their "crazy money" elsewhere.

So, to keep margin accounts full, the brokers offered to treat them as if they were bank accounts. After a bit of fancy legal footwork, and after figuring out how to attach some snappy code names to the accounts and the money, they found a way that was acceptable to the regulators. Today money in many such accounts can collect interest in a variety of ways, often by having a daily or other periodic balance "swept" into a money-market fund account. The account holder can write drafts (checks) against all funds that are not currently being used as margin security, almost as if it were a checking account, and usually can move the money from function to function with just a telephone call. It hasn't yet replaced the convenience of a bank, but obviously the challenge is there and the banks know it.

Literally every week there is some new service available from one of the brokerage houses or S&Ls that fulfills a banking function. Soon, some critics warn, there won't be any distinction between the two camps from the consumer's point of view, and the banks, which obey different regulations, will suffer. That may be the fear, but there are many reasons why it will probably never happen. Chief among them is that the federal offices which regulate banks and securities brokers are competitive themselves and continue to insist upon autonomy among themselves. And they have the legal arguments to back up their policies. In the meantime, while the battle rages in the open market, we customers are being treated to a cornucopia of new services, many of which are terrific. The only price we pay is in the transience of the situation: Today's featured service or product may be next year's history.

Banking *today* is futuristic, and tomorrow we'll see services and methods we can't yet imagine. Among the possibilities being tested are automatic paycheck deposit and direct Social Security deposit and other federal transfers. Many large companies, and now even small ones, as long as they use computerized payroll, also offer automatic check deposits directly to the account of their choice, at many institutions. After the money arrives, you can have it split into parts to service more than one account or to have it service loan or credit accounts set up in advance.

On the other side of the personal ledger sheet, some institutions offer automatic bill paying for monthly, quarterly, and annual payments to companies, agencies, or other destinations with computerized funds-transfer capabilities. Add that to a major credit card and it's perfectly possible for anyone to lead a complicated and sophisticated financial life without ever using cash or depending upon the postal service for banking services.

The best automatic services of all actually manipulate your money for you. Once your money goes into the bank, whether or not you did it with your pen or let the computers do it, many banks will allow you to set up and authorize a mini money-management system. The example of old is the automatic savings plan, often christened the Christmas Club, in which the bank makes transfers from your checking or passbook into a time deposit. Now the savings and loans have usurped the lead and offer money-market rates combined with the NOW-style checking services. Where will it all end? It probably never will, and along the way the banking services seem to be getting better and better.

The why, if you don't already know, is computers. They make all the banking functions easy and quick compared to the days, not long ago, when deposits, withdrawals, and, most of all, transfers had to be posted by hand and all calculations were evoked from deafening, gear-whirling adding machines. Now the work of a thousand toiling clerks is performed by a few cents' worth of electricity, silently and ever more rapidly. Electronic funds-transfers are not only changing bank accounts, they're revolutionizing every part of banking.

Computers are also responsible for the banks wanting to eliminate paperwork, which costs more to process than electronic records. Slowly, inexorably, the banks will squeeze until paper receipts, returned checks, and frequent statements are a thing of the past. At many banks that already do this, you can request to receive the old-fashioned paper versions of record keeping.

Another area where EFT is zooming into the future is with credit cards. I say "credit cards" out of habit, but there are easily twenty different types of cards, with more on the way. Back in the seventies, pundits were predicting that EFT and credit cards would prove as important to our economy as paper money had been centuries before. Their vision of plastic money is the ultimate in EFT—with your card and your personal code number, you are identifiable in a funds-transfer system that spans the breadth of the free world. Your checking account in New York is automatically debited for the cash you draw out of an automated teller machine in Tokyo at 2 A.M. some Sunday morning. Meanwhile, if your checking account is low, the computer automatically transfers the extra funds needed out of a savings account. Automatic protection, they usually call it.

Here's the ultimate extension of what may happen: Let's suppose that you decide to extend your stay abroad and the expense exceeds the size of your bank account. The bank computer will automatically activate your previously obtained authorization to sell certain securities held in your name. The securities branch uses its power of attorney to liquidate the most likely securities in your portfolio, say, some stock on the London Stock Exchange. The proceeds less commission and fees are deposited into your account. The same arrangement could be set up for virtually all your assets, even including such items as second-trust deeds, which would become active when your account reached a predetermined bottom figure. Or you might trigger a prearranged line of actual credit similar to the overdraft protection we see in checking accounts today.

Years ago, when bankers suggested these ideas, they were laughed at, but of course, much of what they described has come true or is being set up now. You may recall that credit cards (I include all money cards in that description, including bank cards, debit cards, travel and entertainment cards and the rest) began as aluminum charge plates with numbers embossed on them. They were for preferred customers at department stores that wanted to captivate their clientele. Soon the banks that were carrying the credit saw the opportunity in the new invention, made the switch to plastic, and the franchised bank cards were born. The embossed writing is archaic now that magnetic computer tape on the back is what identifies your name and account number to a machine, which in turn is connected to either a credit verification system or the bank's EFT system. Right now the credit card companies are experimenting with cards that will contain enough computerized memory to hold an individual's entire financial status. In your wallet you could carry your complete updated bank statement covering all accounts, plus you could use it as an instant financial-disclosure statement whenever needed. You may even be able to plug the thing into your personal computer so that you can monitor and update the records and your accounts electronically. The credit card companies are looking for more innovations that will make their business more competitive and profitable, and every change will appear as a challenge and an opportunity for credit card users such as you and me.

BEWARE OF INNOVATIONS

Not all of the experiments have been successful. The "debit card" was supposed to be a great innovation that would eliminate the need for cash, but few people used them. The reasons were obvious: They gave great benefits to the banks by eliminating check processing and transferring all work to the computers, but the customer lost the great benefit he or she had in regular credit cards, namely the thirty-day grace period in which to pay. Debit cards cause the user's bank account to be debited within twenty-four hours, thus eliminating the "float" credit card users enjoy, and providing the banks with more cash flow. Used in place of a checking account, the debit card forced the user to collect piles of slips instead of using the handy check-register for account balancing. And then there are no canceled checks with which to verify expenditures, to back up a lost or faulty register, or to back up claims at tax time. More faulty products will come and go, but along with them, keep an eye out for the useful ones.

HOW YOU TALK TO THEM IS IMPORTANT

When banks compete for new business, most customers come from other banks, and a game of musical bank-accounts takes place. Understandably, bankers are on the lookout for people who habitually do this. Threatening to join this group is not likely to get the average customer anywhere. Try instead to convey the idea that you wish to stay with your bank, and encourage better service by suggesting that you will provide the bank with more business in the future or will create fewer problems than the average customer in your category as long as you are treated right.

NOT ALL GOOD GUYS

The government has traditionally been a co-conspirator with the banking industry in allaying the public's fears and suspicions about banks and bankers' motives. This is only natural, since nearly all of the government officials who hold appointed positions of power over the banking industry have themselves been bankers and will be bankers if and when they return to private life. It's yet another price we pay for shortsighted economic controls. Things are much better than they were through most of this century, to be sure. We have more economic-protection laws, and the structure of the new interest-bearing instruments that are being allowed by the government are admitting the small investor into the anteroom of higher interest rates, which used to be the exclusive club of the rich. But we have many a mile to go before banking treats the public with an unjaundiced eye and before the federal government gains the pride to slip the banking community out of bed.

Back in 1976 the House Commerce Committee determined that state banking committees, which are traditionally much more responsive to local lobbying efforts, were several times more likely to identify and act on violations of the Truth in Lending Act and other banking statutes than were their federal counterparts. The only conclusion that makes sense to me is that the federal examiners were not acting on behalf of the public, but the banks. It is this type of situation that provokes so many people to view banks with the old "it's them against me" attitude. One notable move against the grain has been the requirement that lenders state the cost of money in terms of APR, or annual percentage rate.

THE *STANDARD*

The APR rule is a wonderful argument for the theory that government can keep the bankers honest. It used to be that a banker, or a store sales agent, etc., would try to "sell" you a deal based on an interest rate that was only part of the final calculation of what you would pay back. One place would advertise an "add-on" percentage, another would advertise a rate that was then recalculated according to an amortization schedule, which made the true APR much higher. Now we have a standard reference all lenders must abide by, and in most cases, if they want to pay interest, they also advertise the APR now.

This is very close to the "true interest rate" which you, the individual, need to calculate when you choose either a lender or an interest-bearing instrument or account. The true interest rate is the original rate adjusted to the APR and then adjusted to your individual circumstances. There are several ways in which the true interest rate can differ from the APR, just as the APR can differ from, say, the monthly interest rate or the total monthly interest rate.

One factor is the length of the loan. The same APR on a ten-year loan doesn't yield the same true rate as on a twenty-year loan. The twenty-year loan obviously will cost more to pay back, as the interest is being paid longer. And because of the way amortization scales work, the payback interest will be more than twice as high (ten years as opposed to twenty) as for the ten-year loan, because the principal repayment constitutes a smaller proportion of the total payback.

Another factor is the expected interest-rate pattern. Now I'm not expecting anyone to be able to predict next month's interest rates, let alone next year's (but let me know if you can); the idea is to make a comparison between alternative loans or interest-paying accounts or instruments. If the expectation is that interest rates will rise, you can also expect that the current rate you lock in will cost less against the rate of inflation. If interest rates fall during the life of the loan or the interest-paying period, then the current rate you lock in will be worth more against the rate of inflation.

So, if the choice you are faced with is between two loans, both at the same APR, but one for ten years and one for twenty years, you know that the twenty-year loan will cost you fractionally more. The difference may be small enough not to bother you, but you may be taking out the loan at a time when interest rates seem to be at a low ebb. The twenty-year loan takes on a new shine because you know that against inflation, and therefore the money you can make from investments, it will appreciate in its value to you. On the other hand, if you are in a situation where you expect not to have investment funds available at all, the difference between the two loans diminishes, and the importance of the length of the commitment may be your central concern.

From another perspective, if your use of a loan is going to yield a payout, then the price of the loan cannot be calculated alone, but must be figured against the actual total return (the true rate). A common example of this is with whole life insurance policies. If you have a regular life-policy with cash value, you have the option of borrowing the cash value at a low rate of interest, usually between 2 and 5 percent APR. Assuming a current attainable interest of 9 percent and a payout of 5 percent, you come out with a yield on the deal of 4 percent. But wait, that is the current yield. You must remember that the insurance company charged you to use that money, and has likely been paying you one-third to one-half the going passbook savings rate for it every year you owned the policy. So, if you owned the policy for ten years and paid in $500 toward your cash value every year and you received 3 percent APR, you would have accumulated just $150 in interest, compared with an excess of $350 assuming a compound available rate of at least 6 percent in the open market. The insurance policy further meant that you don't get the money outright, but must borrow it or attach it to your premium. So all you are left with is the difference between the amount the company charges you to borrow your own money—the 5 percent and the 9 percent return—for a yield of 4 percent. Over the span of years the policy was in effect, to get the true annual yield you would have to subtract the years in which no cash value was utilized, thus further reducing the actual yield. If the period had been ten years and you managed to extract 4 percent for ten more years, your annual actual yield is just 2 percent. You must compare true yield, not just APR.

SHOPPING FOR MONEY

When you are seeking a loan for any purpose, plan on shopping for the best available rates, and plan on selling yourself and your borrowing. Shopping around may seem like an obvious necessity, but too often people stop looking as soon as they find a loan they can repay. Not only can you find significant differences in interest charges, repayment schedules, and payback restrictions between different kinds of institutions, as between commercial banks, private banks, and finance companies, but within each category all these factors will vary widely.

Different banks or other lenders go through periods when they need new money and times when they are flush with funds. Obviously you have to shop around to find the ones that need to make loans and are willing to offer competitive rates and inducements in the form of loan features. Common examples are: no penalty for early payment, or reduced payment for early retirement of the loan balance, or a reduced interest rate for early retirement.

The first step in shopping for any loan is to draw up a proposal. The proposal contains the reason for the loan, the size of the loan, an explanation of why it is needed, a net-worth statement, a description of your means of income, financial references, and a statement of your intention to honor the terms of the loan. Just like a business loan.

If you walk in with all these things prepared, you do two important things. One, you show the banker that you have thought out all the details, are serious about the venture, and understand the financial implications of the prospective loan. Two, you have cut down on the work the loan officer has to go through before you and he or she get down to the important discussions pertaining to the loan qualifications. In other words, you have made things easy for him, and he's much more likely to make things easy for you, and that improves your odds of getting the loan. If you go in without any one of these things, every single loan officer is going to have you fill out piles of forms with all of the very same information. If the loan is refused, you have wasted all that energy. Being prepared makes the shopping process relatively painless, much more efficient, and much more successful. Often, but not always, you can call the loan officer's office, explain that you are planning to request a loan, and they will let you have a sample loan application. If you are very lucky, they may have a guide for applying for the type of loan you are interested in.

Sample Personal Loan Proposal — Minimum Contents

- Reason for the loan
- Size of the loan
- Reason for seeking the loan
- Personal net-worth statement
- Description of means of income
- Financial references
- Statement of how and why you intend to honor the terms of the loan

A REFUSAL IS NOT A DEFEAT

Most loans are not approved on the first try. If a loan is refused, be sure to ask exactly why. It may be that a small detail or a misunderstanding has caused an impass. If not, at least you will have an insight into what is necessary to get a loan from the institution you are dealing with. Further, if you pursue the quest with another lender, you will have an idea of what to emphasize and what to work around. Occasionally you may find that your request or situation is not the problem at all. It may be a time when the bank is simply not lending, the day between accounting periods, or another situation that sinks your loan. Occasionally you may find that you can return at a later time or with a slightly modified proposal and find success.

PICKING A BANK

In most cases picking a bank is more complicated than just comparing features. For example, small banks and thrifts often offer the best rates in town to small depositors and lenders. Actually, they can ill afford to, for it weakens their base far more than a larger competitor's, but they do so to compete for your business. The inherent danger is that a small bank may be so weakened by its concessions to customer demand that it is in danger of folding when times are turbulent. As many as 350 banks have been on the Federal Reserve Board's danger list at once in recent years. Deciding whether the added risk is worth the edge in rates or service has to be a personal one, but is nothing to be taken lightly.

Major banks are not immune from danger either, for they make bad loans and bad business decisions that are proportionately larger. Selecting a bank or other financial institution requires some investigation besides comparison of the advertised interest rates in checking or savings accounts. Most business sections in major newspapers run reviews of local banks on a periodic basis; look yours up.

Compare the banking services you are after against those offered by the banks. You may find that by driving a little farther or investigating a name you are unfamiliar with, you can get more for your money. The bank that suits your needs as a single, cash-rich businessperson may get your attention by offering telephone transfers, banking by mail, aggressive competitive rates on savings accounts, and a well-lit automated teller machine. The head of a family moving in and out of cash-flow problems may need none of those features, but opt instead for the bank down the street that pays less interest but also charges less on loans, allows a bigger margin on the credit cards, does automatic depositing of the Social Security checks, and gives the family close attention because the personal banker knows that rich Uncle Charlie is also a depositor.

Shopping for services and return are the basic interests of the customer. But as customers, we should be aware of the conflicts of interest bankers are faced with: the diametrically opposed responsibilities of their fiduciary obligations to their shareholders, controlling bodies, and trust clients, and their responsibilities, as defined by banking regulations and tradition, to serve the public convenience and advantage within the marketplace. The lesson of history is that business interests will take precedence until public opinion is perceived to be creating a significant effect upon business. That is why banking-reform movements and consumer-advocacy groups are not so much a matter of moral fudgecake emotionalism as they are a needed counterbalance to the influence of the banking community, which is considerable owing to the fact that it is brought to bear on everyone, and of the banking lobby, which is one of the largest and most powerful afloat.

The reason I mention these things is that people often fail to use the influence and persuasion available to them. A friend of mine was having difficulty obtaining a loan to set up his small business not long ago, and was about to quit, having queried just about every bank in town and used up two weeks' of work time in the process. All it took to get the ball rolling was for a satisfied customer to provide one of the banks that had turned my friend down with a personal call and a letter describing his ability to make the business a likely success, and the loan came through—with a preferred rate to boot!

My friend often describes that experience as the best bit of education he obtained as a businessman and an individual. Even though he is not a name dropper by nature, he exchanges influence with everyone he trusts, and his banking services are on a par with other businesses with many times his net worth. There is no better form of "fair disclosure" than pooling your influence as a customer, client, or depositor. When the assets of any group reach a size that gains the attention of the bank officers, then positive influence is naturally brought to bear. The idea is that since other people do it, you fall behind if you fail to. That's no moral judgment, it's just an observation. And it's the American way.

An element of banking I haven't touched upon yet concerns the professional services that are usually, or at least traditionally, reserved for the larger depositors. Among them are trust services, professional referrals, financial brokering, estate planning, bill collecting, business analysis, and a few others, depending upon the institution. The thing to remember is that all these services are made available with the expectation of being able to make a profit, to ensure the well-being of outstanding loans, to retain important customers, and otherwise ensure the bank's business well-being. Thus, the trust department will often have a lawyer who can advise you on a myriad of trust functions from estate planning to tax reduction, but you can be sure that the instruments he will promote will be those carried by the bank and that bring home a fee, a profit, or control over assets. Thus, a bank's trust operations are often not nearly as competitive as those available through other independent fiduciary agents. Also, even when a bank is chosen as the fiduciary in a trust, an advantage to the beneficiaries can often be obtained by having the trust designed by an independent attorney rather than using the papers written up by the bank lawyers. This seems fairly obvious from the outside, but when you are shopping, often under pressure, these possibilities are easy to lose sight of.

The issue of which bank from which to obtain a business loan or even a personal loan can also be influenced by their reputation for helping borrowers. A bank which can offer you an introduction to an accounting service that is especially adept at successfully handling your type of business could well be worth a slightly more expensive business loan. You may get helpful information about banks from your chamber of commerce and other business organizations.

CREDIT—GETTING IT AND GETTING IT BACK

Establishing credit for the first time can be a fairly painless process, and one your bank can help you with. Banks, like other institutions, base their credit history of you on the information they already have and the information they can obtain from a credit rating service such as TRW. Your objective therefore is to fill their information sheets with positive facts. No information (having no credit history) is as crippling as bad information, for credit simply is not extended to what the moneylenders refer to as "nonentities."

These are the most common and effective ways of establishing credit through your bank:

- Obtain a letter of reference from a large depositor.
- Using a relative or friend as cosigner, obtain a small loan at the bank. Make sure you pay it off entirely with your own checks or make personal payments. Make early payments if you have to, but under no circumstances any late ones.
- Using your banker as a reference, obtain credit cards at local stores (they are the easiest to get). Use each one at least once a month and pay each bill well ahead of the due date. It doesn't matter how small the purchases are; only that you have a monthly balance and that it is paid on time.
- After six months' of successive billings and on-time payments, apply for a major credit card. If you have other credit information, ask your banker to provide that data with your application. Do this with as many credit cards as possible for a year, then throw all but one or two away.

- If you must make a major purchase such as a car or an expensive appliance, arrange to make time payments with a provision that you can pay the balance ahead of schedule with no penalty. Pay the monthly billing for six months and then pay off the balance. It may end up costing more than if you paid all at once, but then you are after a goal: a credit history, and this is one relatively inexpensive way to establish that.
- If you cannot get a line of credit at your bank, consider borrowing first from a credit union or finance company. Minimize the amount of the loan, since the interest will be higher. Later, the fact that you successfully repaid a loan is more important than the fact that you borrowed from a finance company, which is your prerogative and your business. Credit cards can also be obtained this way.
- Get verification of a reliable source of income, a steady job, or other assurances that you will be able to make payments in the future, and have that information included in all your credit applications, approvals, and other paperwork.
- Use your credit as it accumulates if you see a future need for having it. It is both ironic and logical that people who don't use credit can't get it, and people who use it, perhaps even to excess, can obtain it easily. Everyone needs some credit history, for credit is often the best insurance against misfortune and unexpected hard times.
- Develop your credit to larger and larger amounts. If you need a $10,000, $100,000, or $1,000,000 business loan in a few years, borrowers are not going to be impressed by the fact that you are always up to date with your VISA payments. But they will likely be affected by knowing that you have taken out five loans over the past ten years, each one larger than the one before, and each one paid off ahead of schedule. They see dollar signs in the prospect of a good credit risk *and* in a borrower who will be a repeat customer.

REESTABLISHING CREDIT

Credit-rating bureaus are allowed by law to keep records of damaging credit histories for a maximum of seven years and records of bankruptcy and a few other credit disasters for ten years. Thus, no matter how violent his or her borrowing history, anyone can eventually reestablish credit. A given lender, however, can obviously keep records as long as he chooses. Before and during the seven-year span, however, there are other steps that can be taken to get back onto the good-credit roster.

Under almost no circumstances should you go to a commercial bill-consolidation service to develop credit. If you need counseling, ask your banker for a referral, as he will steer you to honest counselors. Many bill consolidators are in the business of fleecing customers without benefiting them, while many credit counselors can help seemingly hopeless cases.

If you have been negligent or abusive of credit in the past, consider not using it in the near future, as this is the only cure for some, and life without credit need not be any more difficult than life one step ahead of the bill collector. Much of the time, all it requires is saving *before* the fact, rather than paying afterward, meaning it requires discipline and planning. If you feel you cannot trust yourself or your judgment, see a credit counselor or a financial planner. Credit counselors are available free of charge in just about every city, and financial planners are available for modest fees in almost every income range.

Locate the credit reports that have damaging information in them by contacting the bank or other lender who refuses your loan application. Contact the credit-reporting agency within seven days of receiving the loan denial and request to see your file. There may be a small charge if you wait; after thirty days your legal rights expire if you have done nothing. If you can find an error in the report, you may ask to have the data changed, and even if the company refuses, you can ask to have a statement from you inserted into the report. The cost is small, and if you intend applying for credit later on, you may want the lenders who look at the credit reports to see your side of the story. This is one way to get them to see your version.

See your banker. Establish that you are abandoning the course that got you into trouble in the first place and make it clear that you are determined to prove your trustworthiness. The first step is to set a schedule for retiring previous obligations. In many cases this is sufficient to establish a new satisfactory credit rating, if all the billing parties agree. Second, either retire all the debt outstanding or restrict further debt to necessities. Having successfully retired one cycle of debt obligations, you may find lenders welcome your credit, for they recognize that even under the worst circumstances you make good on your promises. It sounds crazy, but you will find it easier to get new credit than people who have never had it before. And, as is best for them, build your credit slowly, in increments, until you have established a line that fulfills your needs and can provide a cushion in case of financial emergencies.

WHAT YOU MUST KNOW

- The Truth in Lending Act says that a bank must explain the true cost of every loan in annual percentage rate. Ask for the APR and compare that figure when weighing a loan or credit.
- The Fair Credit Reporting Act says that you can see any report that

is used to deny you credit, and you can have the creators of such reports correct errors and acknowledge your protests, including insertion of a statement from you. The law puts a time limit on each provision, so act promptly.

- The Equal Credit Opportunity Act says that you may not be denied credit on the basis of race, sex, age or marital status.
- The Fair Debt Collection Practices Act prohibits debt collectors from using abusive or harassing tactics, especially false or misleading threats, unfair business practices, and unreasonable intrusion into your homelife.
- It is a good idea to ask for a statement about each of these laws, as legal lenders all have them, and this introduces the topic. If you feel you have been treated unfairly, politely contact your banker and then your state banking commission for help in your area.

APPROACHING YOUR BANK(ER)

Do's

- Make an appointment, even if you are just opening a small account. You establish your intent, make a favorable impression on the bank personnel, and guarantee yourself good service at least once.
- If possible get a personal referral from someone else who has accounts at the bank, and, naturally, the bigger the accounts the better. Remember, you are not asking for a recommendation, just an introduction, but the act of getting the referral tends to cause the courtesy reserved for known, preferred clients to carry over to new ones. You obligate your friend to nothing.
- Make it clear that you are willing to make a commitment to the banker to give him your business in as many ways as possible. Steady customers, whether large or small, are desirable for bankers because they cut down on the workload.
- Ask about all the services available to new customers. Many are available at the bank officer's discretion, and if the bank is in a period in which it is seeking new depositors, you may get much more than the average person.
- Tell about financial successes that you are experiencing. If your career is advancing, if you have just joined a new company, if you are attending school—anything that suggests you will be increasing your deposits as time goes by.
- Take whatever services are available, even if you don't need them right away. Sometimes you may find yourself paying charges for

services you don't need or use, but if you are establishing credit, are building a relationship at the bank, this can be a plus. Customers are rated by the banks into categories, with size of total deposits being only one criterion; often the services being used are another important influence in the way the bank treats the customer, unfair though that may seem.

Don'ts

- Don't walk in unannounced to open a new account, especially on a busy day. You give up your opportunity to be a face that stands out from the crowd, and the chances that you'll get the kind of treatment you desire, much less that you'll get extra services, is greatly diminished.
- Don't come unprepared. Have your bank numbers and account descriptions ready to process. Have your previous banker ready to accept a call with references for you, if that's at all possible. This is especially valuable if you are from out of town.
- Don't talk about how terrible your previous bank or banks have been, and especially don't say that you quit banks every time they make a mistake or have a disagreeable staff member. The banker will be hoping to find someone with whom he will have a long and profitable relationship. You can assert your expectations without alienating the bank personnel.
- Above all, don't be a problem; be an opportunity for the banker to get easy, profitable business. Don't be rushed for the next appointment, don't criticize the banking industry, and don't expect the banker opening your accounts to be a miracle worker. The new-accounts post is not a plum. These days, the new-accounts person is the one who introduces the new customer to the personal banker and other bank officers, so this is the proverbial first impression. Make the best of it.

WHEN TROUBLES ARISE

If you have a personal banker, he or she should be able to find a solution to most problems. If not, ask to see the supervising bank officer. Very often this person can make the decision your personal banker felt reluctant to make and can sidestep certain procedures. This person can also steer you to a more appropriate personal banker if need be. Next in charge is usually the vice president in charge of the branch or office. These people tend to be quick problem-solvers and in most cases will find a resolution to your situation. You may want to visit the president's office as a final resort, but in a multi-branch bank you will probably be referred to an underling. That's not necessarily bad, as this person may just what you need. If you find you are dealing with an unfair policy or some other problem that is not going to be solved within the bank itself, you have your state banking commission, which is responsive in some states and not in others. At the federal level you have:

The Federal Reserve System (for all banks chartered by it)
Director, Division of Consumer Affairs
Board of Governors
The Federal Reserve System
Washington, D.C. 20551

Federal Deposit Insurance Corporation (FDIC)
(for FDIC insured banks not chartered by the FED above)
FDIC
Office of Bank Consumer Affairs
Washington, D.C. 20429

Comptroller of the Currency
(for all "national" banks)
Comptroller of the Currency
Consumer Affairs Divison
Washington D.C. 20219

Federal Home Loan Bank Board
(for federally chartered savings and loans)
Federal Home Loan Bank Board
Washington, D.C. 20552

Federal Credit Union Administration
(for federally chartered credit unions)
Federal Credit Union Administration
Division of Consumer Affairs
Washington, D.C. 20456

Federal Trade Commission
(for stores, companies, or other lenders with interstate networks)
Federal Trade Commission
Washington, D.C.
regional offices are in:

Atlanta	Cleveland	New York
Boston	Denver	San Francisco
Chicago	Los Angeles	Seattle

Every state also has an office that oversees intrastate credit traffic. If you are dealing with a company that only operates within your state, contact your state office of consumer affairs for a referral to the proper authorities. If you don't get the proper referral, call the consumer affairs office of the closest federal office anyway, and they will often be able to refer you to the appropriate and most effective office in your state or region.

Also, don't be afraid to contact these offices just because you're not sure they are the best ones to solve your case, for they routinely deal with thousands of complaints and are used to citizens who are nervous and unsure. Even if your complaint is not within their purview, they may well have literature, a referral, or a helpful suggestion that will solve your dilemma, whatever it might be.

MAKE A RECORD OF IT

Now that banks are almost entirely computerized, it's tempting to assume they'll never make a mistake, and let your home record-keeping go lax. Well, even if the bank doesn't make a mistake, your home records are vital. If you are killed, injured, caught traveling overseas, or perchance your bank books are lost or burned, then your records may be the only place one can locate that lost deposit, that unused account which was never closed, or other financial facts that must be proven in your favor.

Your Bank Account Checklist

- List of all accounts, including institution, type of account, balances required, date when account must be used to remain active, conditions that must be met to maintain account, next maturity date (if applicable), specific banker who manages the account (if applicable), purpose of the account, tax status of the account, etc.
- Tax forms that should arrive for each account either quarterly and/ or at year's end.
- Comparison of interest rates offered by competitive banks and other savings institutions in your area.
- Comparison of services and types of accounts available from competitive institutions and the corresponding advantages/disadvantages.
- Ease of access and handling of accounts and institutions.

Banking Calendar
(also useful for tax records)

- Dates accounts are opened or closed
- Dates when bankers were contacted
- Dates when statements/records *should* arrive
- Dates when each account must be balanced/reviewed
- Dates when accounts must be used to remain active
- Dates when tax records must be reviewed/recorded
- Dates when new tax rules or new laws will change usefulness or profitableness of accounts

If you have special accounts or special uses for your accounts, such as trusteeships, business partnerships, or separation of tax liability, you may have other reasons to keep track of dates. The important thing to remember is that dates and scheduling are often the key to making your accounts more profitable to you, and that, combined with security, is the very reason for using banks and their cousin institutions.

ABOUT BANK STATEMENTS

Bank statements will never be exciting, but as long as the banks keep sending them to us, they remain a vital means of communication. (The banks would rather not send statements because they cost money to produce. We still have them at most banks because they are a sacred tradition. Now we are being asked to accept electronic substitutes, and that benefits the banks, not the customers.)

Whether paper or electronic, they constitute the means by which we ensure that what transpired with your money is understood by both you and the bank. They are also a tradition that refuses to die. If you have a problem or complaint, your bank will expect you to refer to your statements to solve it, and if you do so, it will be solved much quicker. Like computers, banks do make mistakes, and the statement is the only real way to discover them. In the case of trusts, for instance, if your bank makes an error in its favor, in some states you must report the error within a year or else the bank may not be required to correct it! Finally, reconciling statements is the best way to correct your mistakes and to get a month-by-month-perspective on what is happening with the money you have at the bank. They're so handy, it's a crime not to use them, and worse, if you don't, it can cost you cold cash in lost funds and misunderstandings.

11

Securities, Brokers, and Security

AS A FINANCIAL WRITER, I am constantly interviewing and comparing notes with people in the securities trading business. Brokers, investment managers, analysts, consultants, and the market operators alike seem to produce a Pandora's box of advice on every conceivable topic, a surprising amount of it confusing and contradictory. Yet when I ask them what counsel they would give to beginning investors and those who are discouraged, they return to echo the same advice over and over again. You'll find it below. I am struck by how they also drive home the point that many, many investors are having a terrible time simply because they somehow never learned, or choose to ignore, the basics of investing.

Most of the principles of investing are the same for those who buy one share at a time as for those who buy a fortune in securities. There are different strategies for every circumstance, but I'm talking about the many constants in the investment game.

First and foremost is one that most articles, talks, and books about the specialized schemes usually fail to demand—that the investor should operate from a *sound financial base*.

Second, they conveniently omit the caveat that any investor should operate from a broad *information* base as well. What are the safest investments for beginners, and why? What levels of reserves should stand behind your estimated risk? This chapter gives the basic tenets that investment counselors and financial planners often gloss over. These guidelines allow you to play the various investment markets with reasonable security and with your risk/security ratio tuned to your individual financial base and your personal panic level. Also covered is that delicate topic of how to find and select the securities broker, or brokers, who will do the most for your money and your future.

HISTORY IS A GOOD, BUT NOT GREAT, TEACHER

When people talk about "the good old days" in reference to the stock market, they are usually looking back to the late 1960s, when a bull market raged on for years, small investors were successfully and profitably brought into the trading picture for the first time on a broad scale, and a smart investor had to look no further than a list of blue chip stocks to find a profitable investment strategy. Portfolios bequeathed to widows and orphans were routinely invested in "the Nifty Fifty" stocks with the expectation of leaving them untouched for years.

Not only is all that past, but the stock market of today demands an attentive eye to values, prices, and trends as well as steady nerves in order to assure continued success, much less a return that beats investments through other devices. The pace is quicker, the rules wilder, and the competition more sophisticated every year. So to keep ahead, every investor must be all those things, too.

If there is any sure lesson to be learned from the history of the stock and other securities markets, it is that history seldom repeats itself. Strategies that worked well in the 1960s fell flat on their faces in the 1970s. Part of the problem in the recession of '74, we know in hindsight, was that the institutional wise guys were using threadbare game plans to invest in a changing market. Pension funds, mutual funds, banks, and others watched their profits drop out from under them as doomsayers, who were betting on bad news, soaked up the red ink and turned it into winnings. It wasn't long before the entire market got wise to what was happening. The trade papers tolled the demise of the Nifty Fifty, and "blue chip" stocks were relegated to the history books. Today's traders realize that the nature of the markets changes much more rapidly than ever before. As Alvin Toffler predicted in *Future Shock*, the *rate* of change is accelerating, too. That means that every year we have to know more about what is new just to keep up with the averages, much less to get ahead.

LEARNING CAN BE EASY

Learning all about investing can seem to be a prodigious task before you start, but if you systematize the process and go a step at a time, it can be quite manageable even for a busy person. The first question is where to obtain information. Fortunately there is a surplus of information available on all fronts.

If you are literally beginning, there are courses given by most small colleges, by school districts, and sometimes by companies. There are even correspondence courses. Look in the business and investment periodicals for ads. If you are already an experienced investor and are looking for insight into specific markets, strategies, or a new level of competence, you may be surprised to find that there are also classes and courses tailored to your needs. You are also the prime target audience of most of the books published by the financial press on every topic. So, if you are adept at learning from books, you have unlimited resources. *Forbes, The Wall Street Journal*, and *Business Week*, among others, offer their own mail-order, how-to-invest-in-the-markets courses, which are great refreshers as well as initiation exercises. The barrier for most people is that they don't stick with these once they buy them. That seems to be the case, based on reports from the mail order companies, which show that a minority of those who pay for correspondence courses actually complete them. Many people refuse to take classes, arguing that they haven't the time, whereas the truth is that when all is said and odne, a good class enables most of us to learn more in fewer hours than self-teaching ever could. The reason is that in areas such as investing, the teacher acts as the "information funnel" who screens out the extraneous data, points out the priorities, and passes along that invaluable resource, the wisdom of experience.

Sources of Investment News and Data

The Wall Street Journal (five days a week, all investment news)
Barron's (once per week, more technical than the WSJ)
Financial Daily (briefer than the WSJ, less newsy)
Commercial & Financial Chronicle (strictly business)
Standard & Poor's Outlook (technical reports & reviews of companies)
Money (the average person's financial magazine—monthly)
Forbes (the premier monthly investor's magazine)
Business Week (useful, but oriented to business per se)
Fortune (also useful, but again, slanted to business needs)
The Exchange (published by the New York Stock Exchange)
Outlook (published by Standard & Poor's, mildly technical)
Better Investing (Journal of the NAIC—superb for beginners)
AAII Journal (Amer. Assn. of Individual Investors—10 issues per year)
Standard & Poor's Corporation Guide (libraries have it—stock market
     reports & company reviews)
Moody's Reports (similar to S&P, but reports on bonds)
Your daily paper business section
Advisory services
Newsletters

Only you can judge what type of education is going to "take" for you, but the one form you can't do without is reading the regular periodicals. Checking on the financial news is similar to following the sports scores or a news story from day to day and week to week, for it's really the only way to keep up to date. As with sports, you can pick up tips on factors that affect your investment decisions by reading the articles and editorials in the financial press. You can't be at all the stables in the country and can't handicap every horse in every race; and you can't follow all the financial happenings, so you count on the financial press to summarize the noteworthy news for you.

Reading the financial pages of your newspaper, *The Wall Street Journal*, or the analysis sections of the weekly or monthly press is no more complicated than you make it. You begin by checking the prices of particular stocks and bonds. Follow companies you have interest in and compare their performance against what you know and against the rest of the market. After you're comfortable doing that much, move on to the other data: market summaries; the year's average prices and highs and lows; the bids and asking prices; the dividend yields; the bond yields both past and present; the futures prices and volumes; the earnings briefs. As a list they are overwhelming, but one at a time they are important and interesting clues to the overall picture of how your investments may be faring.

Osmosis really is a fairly good method of learning about investing for many people. I don't mean that you stick a week's worth of the *Financial Times* under your pillow and hope for divine providence to prevail, but if you read the articles in the financial pages of the newspapers, you soon pick up the jargon and the basic concepts. You get a sense of what the financial experts feel are the important concerns in the various markets. You will also find that the writers in most of the daily newspapers, including *The Wall Street Journal*, have a habit of explaining the terms and principles that pertain to the market they are describing. There is a very good reason for this. The editors at newspapers compromise and write to anyone who has about an eighth-grade reading level. The occasional erudite piece slips through, especially in the editorials or a hastily written report of a technical story, but most financial news is readable after a short breaking-in period. This is great when you are learning, and not objectionable later on.

You can work your way through the financial periodicals by subscribing to the ones that match your current level of interest and education. *The Wall Street Journal* is easier to read than *Barron's*; *Business Week* easier than *Forbes*; *Forbes* easier than *Fortune*; and *Fortune* easier than *The Economist* or the other more specialized journals. Follow *The Wall Street Journal* assiduously for a year, or complete a beginner's text or course in investing, and you'll have the concepts and the vocabulary to work your way through any of them.

Just ask and you'll find that your stockbroker's firm, your banks, and other financial-service businesses are terrific sources of educational information. Merrill Lynch's *How to Read a Financial Report* is unsurpassed in explaining the vocabulary and mechanics of that mysterious beast, the financial report, and the booklet is free to all customers and even most noncustomers. If you own any stocks, you know that every stockholder gets a financial report and prospectus, and you know that analysts draw major conclusions from them right away. But few people know how to interpret all the signals in them, and 90 percent of the basic know-how is in this one publication. Merrill Lynch and all the financial-service companies also publish a veritable cascade of literature on all finance topics because they know that educated clients use more of their services, and that means more business. Ask your broker for as much educational literature as his or her firm publishes. Or, it it's a large outfit, contact the public relations office or even the publications office, if they have one, and get a list of all publications available. Researchers at Paine, Webber, Mitchell and Hutchins offices generate over 26,000 pages of information every year, and about half of that is available to individual clients. You read 13,000 pages of financial news and analysis and you are bound to get a handle on the workings of the financial mind! And that is just one of the many such company publication offices.

Years ago Citibank began offering a literal library of publications and mail-order courses to all their clients, and set off a wave of in-house publishing that hasn't stopped yet. They and many other major banks and S&Ls also have terrific lists to choose from. Many of the large publications from these sources can be ordered through your local bookstore. *Fortune* books can be ordered through Time-Life distributors, *The Wall Street Journal* books are put out by the companion Dow subsidiary, Dow Jones, Irwin, Publishers. McGraw-Hill and a few other major publishers also have their own lines of business publications which they promote, and a good many of their selections are tutorials or texts commissioned by financial companies or consultants for courses at individual companies or through associations and are now widely available.

A LIBRARY THAT PAYS

Since you can't know everything, and you certainly can't cram as much as the average person needs to know about finances into a single volume, you will want to set up at least a small set of reference books, if not a home financial library. Why not have some books that pay their way?

Many excellent publications describing economics and finances for the individual investor are available from the U.S. Government Printing Office. The federal publicatons are either ridiculously cheap by publishing standards, or, if they are so large as to be expensive, they are likely to be found in most libraries. Some of them are periodicals you can actually subscribe to, such as the *Federal Reserve Bulletin*, put out, of course, by the Federal Reserve Board. The Department of Labor, especially the Bureau of Labor Statistics, dispenses a slew of bulletins and data on everything from population to the the use of toothpaste in the average household. They don't have a subscription list, but you can get on their list of names for receiving their list of latest publications, which you can then order. If you are a devotee of mail-order catalogues you'll go wild over the publications list from the Government Printing Office in Pueblo, Colorado. It's usually a few months out of date, but you'll still find hundreds of educational and great reference texts therein. Many are free. Other great sources are the Department of Commerce, especially the Office of Business Economics, which churns out reports for Congress and governmental agencies by the wheelbarrow load. A good many can be real aids if you are following a certain industry or other narrow field of interest. The U.S. Chamber of Commerce has a good many useful publications especially pertaining to such things as recent legislation affecting industries and international trade. If you are not part of business yourself, the Small Business Administration has many guides designed for entrepreneurs that give insight into business psychology.

There are many kinds of investment services, but the most common by far are the newsletters, all promising advice second to none. There are somewhere over 200 popular ones, which gives you an idea of how varied they are: conservative, gold bug, retiree, patriot, daring gambler, whatever. There are specialized ones just for you, just about regardless of what your psychological or financial makeup. And for the true skeptics, or pure devotees, there is a newsletter that reviews the newsletters, giving statistical success and failure rates for the top ones on a monthly basis:

> Hulbert Financial Digest
> 409 First Street
> Washington, D.C. 20003

The idea, they say, is to always keep yourself subscribed to the newsletters that are having winning streaks. Do that with several, and the consensus among them may be the gospel; it sounds like a possibility. The financial press generally gives the newsletters rather poor marks for performance. Most seem to be winners for a while, then they lose their contact with genius and lose for a while. You can see from the comparison charts in *Money* and *Forbes* annual money-market reports which funds are doing well now and which have strong track records.

HIRING INVESTMENT SAVVY

Personal investment services are more formal, requiring you to appear in their offices or to hand them a portfolio of a minimum size, which they then manipulate to their own heart's content, and report to you regularly. Generally, if you have enough assets to take advantage of these, you have been approached several times already, or your accountant will have put you in touch. You won't find these in the Yellow Pages, and you do plenty of background checking. I have run into two such outfits that promise their clients "competitive yields," which usually means that they earn about the same as a good money-market fund, or, in a mild bull market, a good stock-fund.

The other sources of information are commonly known, but they are very valuable and too underused by nearly everyone. Most libraries have a pretty good business section because the local small businessmen like to have a good, free, reference library nearby, as it cuts down on office overhead, what with the prices of directories, catalogues, and the like. The investment manuals such as *Standard & Poor's, Moody's,* and their regular updates are invaluable when you are looking into a complicated or important possibility. They will also have many of those odd references you would never think of, like the *Oil and Gas Report, Banker's Monthly,* and other gems that often have just the tidbit of information you need to decide whether that stock tip was a gold mine or a blast of hot air. If your library has a staff librarian who is trained in business reference, you are really in clover, and I suggest that you visit that person as often as possible until you know all the common references. You'll know your way around finances as well as anyone in town!

GO STRAIGHT TO THE HORSE'S MOUTH

Another underused resource is the corporations themselves. Every publicly owned business has to provide prospectuses, annual reports, and periodic statements to all prospective and current stockholders. Some will give you only the standard stockholders' reports, but most will also give you the 10K Report, which is what they file with the SEC and is more detailed than the stockholders' version. You just get the corporate address from the library, your broker's office, from the stock, bond, or whatever exchange it is listed on, or elsewhere, then write a note requesting the items, and they will send them to you. Usually you address the note to the corporate secretary if you don't have a more definite direction to follow. Bigger corporations have toll-free 800 telephone numbers with operators who will take your request, saving you the effort of writing a note and the expense of a stamp. Most are listed with the 800 information service, but some are unlisted, and those you again can often get from your broker's office or from the exchanges.

Most corporate reports are painfully boring, although some resort to including nice graphics and photographs to break the monotony and distract you from the important stuff. There is always a letter from the chief executive officer which you should read (you can get satisfaction from finding out how arcane or effete he sounds), and this is usually where you find hints about whatever is important that may be going on.

If he or she says that things are "great, great, great," that's terrific. If things are great despite X, Y, and Z, then you know you have to check into all three. Mostly the numbers are repetitive, and if you have the time you can go through them using the Merrill Lynch booklet as a guide, but stop when you get to the summary statement. That's the big one that tells the story, and most elements of intrigue are found in the column identified "Changes From Last Year." In other words, did things get better or worse? If there's a problem, you may be able to isolate it here. You may have to review all the other numbers in the report and read all the boring text. But if everything checks out, then go back and read the footnotes, for that is where bad news is sometimes buried. You see, all the text and the figures in the tables and balance sheets have to be done according to "accepted accounting principles." That may sound vague, but what it really means is that it will be done according to the SEC formats. If anything is to be camouflaged, they deviate from the form and compensate with a footnote. Thus the old saw on Wall Street: "Read the footnotes first, then look for the small print."

THE FUNDS

Mutual funds are often recommended as the ideal first investment in the stock, bond, and money markets. A few of their advantages for the new investor are:

- Most of them require a comparatively small investment
- They are easy to move in and out of
- They provide regular statements that are easy to understand
- And if selected with some care, they reduce risk to a minimum
- Almost all of them are well diversified within their categories

The funds are a microcosm within the trading markets, for the variety of funds copies the popular markets: the money market, stocks, industrial specialists, ecology specialists, tax-free, municipal bond funds, and many others that narrowly limit their portfolios. Rather than risk your neck on the actual marketplace floor, you have the professional managers make the investment choices, mostly conservative ones at that, and you let them take a small cut—much smaller than the commission your stockbroker would take.

Most of them can be entered about as easily as opening a savings account. They are usually very liquid (you can get your money out quickly). Most of them allow telephone or check withdrawals, and they can be used with essentially the same planning as savings accounts at a bank. The no-load funds incorporate the management fee into the return, so you never have to calculate your "real" return, and as they have yielded returns equal to the load funds, which charge a management fee after the fact, there is really no logical reason not to use them, unless you need to use a particular fund for some reason.

The "family funds," which combine a number of different types of funds with different investment vehicles under one management plan, allow the investor to diversify without going through the logistics hassle of understanding and buying into different markets. One family may have a money-market fund that invests in short- and medium-term money-market instruments, a bond fund that trades corporate and government bonds, a tax-free fund that handles municipal and federal bonds exclusively, a stock fund that plays the open stock-market, and perhaps an ecology fund that invests only in companies promoting ecological technology or implementation. So the variety can be quite wide, yet the ability to diversify provides safety as before. Rather than an intimate knowledge of each market and each investment opportunity, the investor can safely switch between markets, basing his or her decisions on comparatively gross observations on the state of the economy, interest rates, and more easily understood parameters than are reasonable to use if you investing directly in many markets. Some of the specialized funds have performed spectacularly in the past, sporting double-digit gains in a matter of weeks, but none do so regularly, obviously. The prospect of finding the market that is earning the most at the moment makes trading among the funds exciting for those who pursue it.

SHOPPING FOR FUNDS

Both the *Money* (in the spring) and *Forbes* (in the fall) annual summaries of the mutual funds industry break the funds down into money-market, equity (stock), debt (bond), and tax-free funds, among other categories. They also rank them by the last year's, the past five year's, and lifetime performance. You just can't do better than to review the latest of both these special issues to help you select a fund to buy. These special issues also invariably have accompanying articles about the special conditions existing in the economy or the fund industry, which should be of interest to investors. They are an inexpensive alternative to *Hulbert* (see page 226) and have almost as good a track record, if you simply pick the current top performers (which is not reliable for the future, by the way). The fees charged by the load funds are compared, as are average maturities of bond funds, money-market funds, and breakdowns of investments in diversified funds.

DOING IT ON YOUR OWN

Moving beyond the funds for investment vehicles calls for a more sophisticated plan, beginning with an even more solid overall personal financial picture. It sounds as though it should be intuitively obvious, but you need to know in advance how much you can afford to invest and with what liquidity.

The financial world speaks in terms of "cash reserves" and "investment pool," but the concepts are simpler: How much money you feel you can afford to have in an inaccessible investment with some risk and how much you feel you need to have in a secure position with the added protection of immediate (read "twenty-four hours or Monday morning") accessibility (liquidity). If you deal with a financial planner, he'll tell you that the current economic conditons call for, say, a 30 percent cash reserve for the average person, or 20 percent, or 5 percent if there's a raging bull market. You have to evaluate your needs based on your financial health, the economy, your opinion of the outlook for the short-term and long-term future, and the state of the investment market you are considering.

PRE-STOCK INVESTMENT WORKSHEET

I need to retain _____% of my assets in property
_____% of my assets in cash
_____% of my assets in savings
_____% of my assets in preselected investments

That leaves _____% of my assets I want to invest in securities and other market investments.

This year, that involves approximately $ _____

I will allocate $ _____ to low-risk
$ _____ to medium-risk
$ _____ to high-risk investments

If you begin investing, or if you feel doubtful about investing, your safety reserves should be near to 100 percent of your investment funds. If you take the usual first plunge, you may move part of your safety fund into mutual funds. Then, as you feel confident, you move, say, 5 percent into stocks. Your position might be 70 percent safety reserves, 25 percent in mutual stock funds and 5 percent in stocks. If you are a seasoned investor you may have 5 percent cash reserves, 25 percent in funds, and 70 percent in direct investments, or another combination of investments. But either way you should have a solid idea of *how much* money you have in each category, and *what proportion* of your total investment fund is involved in each. If you were a businessman controlling a company's investment program, you wouldn't think of not listing such information, and so it is important, too, with your own money, for it allows you to gauge what you are doing against the backdrop of fluctuating markets and a changing economy.

As you may have guessed, *planning* and *allocating* are two of the areas individual investors routinely fail in. Without monitoring records, you may find that don't have funds *where* you need them *when* you need them. It's easy to deplete your cash reserves when buying a house or an expensive car and forget to adjust your investments. Up comes an investment opportunity or a sudden expense and there is a crisis.

Although I as well as others have used the metaphor of gambling in connection with the stock and bond markets, investing really requires a different mind-set. It combines the adventure of gambling with the systematization of business. Investing is an analytical process, not an emotional one, yet it can be difficult to separate the two. When an investment turns sour, it's *hard* to take your losses at the "stop level" (the price at which you decided in advance to cut your losses by selling). When you hit a hot streak, it's difficult to keep in mind that it was partly fate that brought you insight, and not your personal power, and you must wait for opportunity to come your way again. If you know that you let your emotions run your life, either stay out of the markets or enlist the aid of a friend or a counselor to steer you in those moments of weakness. Nobody's perfect, but those who are not, yet succeed, find ways to compensate for their weaknesses.

You can do it, for many others do. Louis Rukeyser, who has hosted *Wall Street Week*, the only national TV show devoted to the stock market, regularly receives mail not only from around the country but also from around the world from individual investors who literally buy one share of stock at a time and make a good profit. They are proof that the stock market is a workable investment choice for the average American. Remember: The $15,000-per-year janitor in the Midwest who left $1 million to his favorite charity when he died in his early sixties made his fortune by conservative investing in the stock market. There are no guarantees, of course, but there is an element of intrigue that appeals irresistibly to many Americans, and that is the prospect of making money, with money, by using your wits. It generates a certain sort of satisfaction that many people (and probably the average salaried worker is the perfect example) can get no other way simply because there isn't time.

WHERE TO BEGIN

Ten Quick Questions to Ask About a Stock

1. Is it high quality in its industry?
2. Does it have a solid earning record?
3. Does it have a record of steady or cyclical growth?
4. Has anything extraordinary recently affected its growth potential?
5. Does it carry excessive debt compared to its industry?
6. Does it pay dividends (good for income, poor for growth potential, given other good signs)?
7. Does it have a steady record of profits?
8. Is its price justified or is it inflated by fad interest?
9. Is its income tied to government regulations or contracts?
10. Does it meet your investment criteria and goals?

Technical analysis of the trading markets is both a personal process that can be cut short or carried to any length, and also a service you can buy, either for a pittance or at a premium. To buy it successfully, however, you must understand it first, which usually means at least a brief period in which you try your hand at it a bit. Technical analysis has a reputation for being drier than sand at high noon, but if you can delay gratification, you'll profit from it.

The following are indices most analysts look for first:

> volume of trading
> breadth
> segregated highs
> segregated lows
> number of advances
> of declines
> and identification of key groups

Volume means the number of items traded, as in shares. *Breadth* refers to who is trading. If only individuals are buying, that is "narrow"; if institutions, companies, funds, and foreigners are also buying, that is "broad." *Highs* and *lows* come in varieties: periodic, as daily, annual, etc.; and grouped, as when you join all the peaks or valleys on a chart, and these are usually the declining or ascending tops and bottoms you hear about, depending upon which way the line tilts after the peaks and valleys are joined. The number of *advances* and *declines* is self-explanatory; it's who lost and who won money. The *key groups* are usually the categories that analysts cast securities and debt into. They usually segregate stock by industry, bonds by type and rating, futures by lifespan and type, and debt instruments by the kind of source. These might include utilities, transportations, etc.

There are dozens of other technical indices, and more are being invented all the time, but these basic ones can steer the average investor in and out of many pending trades because they indicate *important, market-pervasive influences*. If you are serious, get yourself a good stock-market primer, such as the one from Dow Jones–Irwin, the one from *Forbes* or *How to Make Money on Wall Street* by Louis Rukeyser, and study what these indicators mean. You quickly begin to incorporate them into your awareness of your holdings. That "utilities are up," or down, takes on new meaning when you have bought into a handful of them all at once in an effort to diversify. You find real interest in the dividends that can accrue to you from owning utility stocks. If you are a blue chip devotee, you'll be interested in the volumes and notices of whether the institutions, which trade heavily in the conservative blue chips, are on the march or not. If you have been waiting for an opportunity to buy or sell a particular item, you may have a real or mental chart in which the daily or weekly highs and lows will shed light or indicate whether you are approaching a sell or buy signal that you have set for yourself. So, although together these various statistics sound like a cacophony of details, when you assimilate the meaning of them one at a time, they make good sense and become important.

If a baseball player's ERA and RBI and TAB and errors seem like reasonable things to understand about the players on your favorite team, or a horse's record at the track makes a difference in how you bet, then the popular technical indices are corollary indicators of the company's records and abilities in the areas that are important from an investment point of view. As a good sports fan, however, you know that a given player has idiosyncrasies that affect both his performance and the excitement of the fans. The devoted fan can guess what will happen much more often than the casual observer. If the dedicated sports fans could know as much about his favorite team as he can find out about stocks, bonds, and other investments, he could make a fortune by outperforming Jimmy the Greek and all the odds-makers.

DO WHAT YOU KNOW, THEN LEARN MORE

Meanwhile, though, I don't want to give the impression that utilizing these tools for the first time or in a new way is a big step or out of the province of beginners. You can conquer one investment at a time and do very well as long as you follow the basics and lay down your money only when you understand what you are doing and what the risks and opportunities are.

Lately the more sophisticated stock and bond traders are getting their feet wet in the comparatively new investment arena of liberalized futures and options trading. Suddenly, just being totally up to date on the stock market or stock and bond markets makes you a dinosaur among the sophisticated traders, for the hot strategy today is to guard against loss and increase the chances for profit on many investments that a few years ago would have been considered brave speculation. They do it the way institutions have for years, by hedging against possible losses with purchases of call and put options (contracts to buy and sell at specific prices at a future date) in opposition to the actual purchase. The problems of the past, mainly margin requirements, which limited the value of the futures contract, have been reduced with the new instruments, which are nowadays being used mostly for conservative investment strategies rather than for speculation.

In the first year the Chicago Board of Options Exchange was open, only a few hundred traders seemed to understand the principles, but it is becoming obvious that competitive investors will have to be fully conversant with the options-trading process in order to be effective stock, bond, or commodities traders. Primers on options trading are available from the CBOE, the American Stock Exchange, the Philadelphia Stock Exchange, the Pacific Stock Exchange (the markets where listed stock options are traded), and the Options Clearing Corporation in Chicago.

Don't feel awkward if you find the new mechanisms intimidating and difficult to adjust to. Merrill Lynch had to install a completely new computer system to handle the new options systems, ensuring that even customers of The Bull occasionally have to face the world on their own, if only for limited periods. The best primer to the system is to first review how standard futures contracts have worked, for the basic principles are the same. Options are merely another way to play the stock marekt, as long as you are careful.

Summary of Investment Self-Education

Reviewing or establishing amount of net worth devoted to investments

Establishing portfolio requirements:
   Evaluating acceptable risk

Dividing investment fund into high- and low-risk categories or further
  subdividing it
Assessing tax, income, safety, growth needs

Choosing investments vehicles:

Bonds: *Wall Street Journal,* other dailies
        Standard & Poor's Weekly Bond Outlook
        Moody's Weekly Bond Survey
        Bond Buyer; the yearbook
        Census Report on Government Debt in the U.S.
        Federal Reserve Bulletin
        Broker's stock description sheets
        Commercial bankers' reports

Stocks: *Wall Street Journal,* other dailies
         Weekly, biweekly, monthly journals
         Brokers' newsletters & pink sheets, S&P sheets, Value Line
         sheets,
            other sources at broker's
         Standard & Poor's guides:
            Industry Surveys
            Stock Guide
         Moody's rating manuals:
            Industrial
            Public Utility
            Banking
            Finance
         Advisory newsletters
         Investment services

Funds: *Wall Street Journal* or other dailies and weeklies
        Forbes annual survey (usually in early fall issue)
        Money magazine annual survey (usually in spring issue)
        S & P *Investment Survey of Investment Funds*
           (available in most large libraries)
        Wiesenberger's *Investment Company* guide
           (available in most large libraries)

PICKING YOUR BROKER(S)

Stockbrokers seem to agree that most people are much more expert at
getting rid of their brokers than they are at finding them. After all, when
they dump the account executive, they usually do so for a very specific
reason. They know how the broker handles people and how he handles
his business, they know whether his or her style fits with their own
personal style, and they know, above all, what his or her deficiencies are.
"If only they selected their broker with the same ammunition, then we'd
all be way ahead," lamented the manager of a local E. F. Hutton branch.

Okay, that's good advice, but what are the criteria by which you select a broker?

First, you have to decide what your investment goals are, so you have to do a bit of homework before you can expect to discern the difference between an appropriate broker and an inappropriate one. Are you going to be building a conservative growth plan to serve you years hence when you retire? Perhaps you are the adventurous type and want a rapid growth plan for which you are willing to allow some risk investments. Or perhaps you are on the verge of retirement, disabled, or for some other reason want to invest in income-producing securities. Or is it a college fund you are building as well as a retirement nest egg? Well, figure it out and write it down, because the decision will affect your selection of a broker.

You are going to investigate the brokers you consider and interview them. Yes, believe me, you want to interview them to find out whether they have the qualities you are looking for. For instance, you may ask rich Uncle Harvey to introduce you to his broker, and since you are Harve's relative, the guy may take you on as an account. And then, because he makes a mint off Uncle Harve and his cronies, he'll never give you another thought unless you call him, in which he'll try to rush you. So you see, the perfect broker for one person isn't necessarily even okay for another.

Is the broker going to give you the kind of service you personally need? Uncle Harve's pal isn't going to do a beginning investor much good, but knowing that is a very valuable thing. The beginner can explain his position to the broker and ask, "Do you like to handle new, small accounts? Can you give me advice and help along the way if I need it? Can you help me educate myself as we go along?" And, most importantly, "Do you have other clients in my same position, and can I talk to a couple of them about your service?" I have had brokers tell me to shove off, but then office managers and vice presidents at the big chain brokerages have told me that this is a reasonable thing to ask, no matter what your financial status. So I feel it's legitimate.

Talking to the office manager first thing is a good policy, regardless of whatever other criteria you employ. The manager is usually responsible for hiring the people in his or her office, and is certainly intimately familiar with how they work and handle their customers. If you have no other leads, the manager may be the first person you talk to. You relate your needs and situation to him, and he will know which brokers in his office will probably serve you well.

He'll know that a certain older broker may spend 70 percent of his time servicing income-producing investment opportunities, and has many retirees and preretirees among his clients, as well as being vitally interested in his own imminent retirement. Perhaps he has cut his workload, too, and is given to small talk.

Independent brokers are renowned for their personalized service, which is attractive to many, and their ability to vanish overnight, which is less a comfort. If you insist on chummy business relationships and don't plan to play options or short stocks that have to be traded on a moment's notice, an independent brokerage office may suit you perfectly. Most independents build their businesses on service and personal contact.

Merrill Lynch, E. F. Hutton, and the other Wall Street giants survive on retail business, but offer different advantages to small investors than do independents. They cannot afford to provide time-consuming personalized service. However, this does not mean you can't find a broker who will do wonders for your portfolio—some of the best ones work in the big houses—but don't expect them to hang on the phone all day.

Consider these recommendations for using one of the big firms: They are all registered with the SEC and subject to SEC rules; they are all New York Stock Exchange (NYSE) members, liable under NYSE rules; they belong to the National Association of Securities Dealers, which has stricter rules still; and they are publicly owned, with huge capital foundations, sure to endure major market-quakes.

Research is much touted by the larger firms, but a good broker can be better than any amount of research, which is very often confusing anyway. For many investors, the best thing about the major firms is the fact that each broker has many experts he or she can call for advice, plus the added convenience of being able to trade on the exchange as fast as anyone.

Small brokerage houses share advantages and faults with independents and major companies. They often can provide personalized service, but there's no guarantee. And, like independents, they do not deal directly on the exchanges, but instead clear all transactions through one of the larger companies for a small fee. When using a broker from a small company it is wise to review with them the time and service delay and for you to judge if this could be a problem for you. For most of us, it matters little if at all. If you are trading options or commodities, it can be critical.

Here are some advantages in dealing with smaller houses: They make their reputation on close personal service and responsible handling of every portfolio and order. To get new business they have to impress their clients enough that they'll recommend them to new investors, dissatisfied investors elsewhere who are seeking their brand of service, or someone new to the area. Service is what let's them compete, what makes them valuable to customers who are willing to pay a little extra.

Discount brokers, who charge very low commissions, are becoming increasingly popular, but are best left to those who make all their own buying, selling, and planning decisions. So, as you can see, you must usually consider the type of brokerage company you want to deal with before you select a broker. Whatever kind or size or quality of company you go with, however, you can still get a dud or incompetent.

To avoid that, take your reduced list of brokerage houses and begin telephoning the office managers. Outline your financial position and then ask them to describe their companies. If you remain mutually interested, make an appointment to meet each manager personally.

It is the manager's job, whether he's half the firm or is in charge of fifty brokers, to ascertain what your needs are, and then to direct you to a broker who can live with your personality and also is experienced with your type of portfolio. If you are the gambling type interested in doubling your money every year, for instance, the manager will steer you away from a broker who studies utilities and mutual funds to the exclusion of all else.

Here's a warning echoed by the manager of every major brokerage house: Don't try to hide anything from the office manager when you review your situation, because it can only lead him or her to erroneous conclusions about your status and your needs. The manager's job is to help you, so don't be embarrassed to tell all. Concealing anything can sink your chances from the start by putting you together with a broker who doesn't relate to you or understand you at all.

When a manager introduces you to a broker, remember that *you* are doing the interviewing. Discuss your entire financial situation with him to acquaint him with your goals and needs. Ask for his philosophy about business—does he share your concerns? Ask how much work he does with accounts the size of yours and with your general objectives. Does he or she share, or at least sympathize with, your investment philosophies? (You can't find this out unless you lay your cards on the table and ask for his or her comments.) Does he inspire confidence in you, or suspicion? After all, personality is a legitimate consideration when you are choosing someone who will be advising you on how to handle your money!

Watch the broker carefully throughout the interview. If he seems insulted by the size of your investment or disdainful of your goals, forget about him. Keep shopping until you find someone you feel you can trust. Go ahead and tell the manager you'd like to speak to a different broker— you have a right to, and they'll probably both understand.

Most people don't take anywhere near full advantage of the services available from brokers and their companies, but would often benefit significantly if they would. Be sure to ask a prospective broker how he or she intends to keep you up to date on your account. (The desired answer is, "If I don't hear from you every month or so or oftener, then I will review your account and give you a call with suggestions or just to keep in touch.") A good broker will do whatever it takes to make you comfortable, within reason. A broker who tries to dissuade a client from taking advantage of services that help his position or help him learn more about the investment or tax situations is doing his client and himself a disservice and should be avoided.

If you find a broker you like but feel uncertain about his or her reliability, you can call your local regional office of the SEC, your state consumer affairs office, or even your state's attorney general's office for information about his or her record of complaints and the firm's legal standing. You can also check with any stock exchanges with whom he is a member or any organizations he belongs to for evidence of his competence and ethics. Basically, though, the office manager will know as much about each broker as anybody.

Just as a competent broker will diversify a client's portfolio by spreading the risk among different investments, it is becoming increasingly popular for investors to diversify themselves by having more than one broker. The idea is to entrust a portion of one's capital to a specialist in income stocks while devoting a calculated percentage to a broker with a track record in, say, go-go funds or options trading. (As you can imagine, this topic is just plain dirt among most brokers.)

The most popular split now is to have a regular full-service broker to handle products he has promoted or which require service and to retain access to the company's full services and information storehouse, then to have an account at a discount broker's where it's possible to trade those items you dream up yourself at a much lower commission rate. If you are a diversified trader, that is, trading in several markets, you must pick a discounter carefully, for many are second tier, meaning they do not have direct access to traders on the exchange floors, but must clear all transactions through another house. In wildly active trading or when volume is very high, rumor has it that the second-tier transactions get shunted aside until the main house's business is taken care of. This is one of those rumors that is so frequently heard and so pervasive in the industry that you tend to take it seriously, even though the practice is technically not proper. Also, many of the small discounters disappeared when the doldrums hit the market, and their clients were in a legal limbo for a matter of days or weeks. So, the history of the firm is as important as the commission rate.

Every brokerage house retains a general counsel who is a lawyer specializing in investment-related taxes. His services are offered to brokers and their clients, but only the very largest accounts traditionally get his department's attention. Ask a broker if he will help you out with tax advice, and he may get you the direct or indirect help of the house specialist. The specialists working for a brokerage house often know more about IRS regulations pertaining to investments than almost any CPA and possibly even the IRS auditors.

INTERVIEWING YOUR BROKER

I don't advocate that you ask every question noted here or that you limit yourself to this list when talking to your prospective brokers. Obviously if you are contemplating using a full-service broker your concerns will be different than if you are thinking of using a discount broker, etc. Just make sure you find out what *you* need to know to feel safe and to know how to interact with your broker to your best advantage.

- How long have you been a broker?
- Do you have another career? How long do you plan to continue?
- Describe your approach to your customers.
- What kinds of investments do you personally follow closely?
- How many customers do you have who share my general goals and are in my general financial condition?
- Have you ever been charged by the SEC or prohibited from trading by any governing body?
- How much time can you give me when I call with a problem or questions?
- How do you normally keep in touch with your clients? Do you have a system for touching base?
- How important is it for us to keep in close communication?
- May I briefly speak privately with your office manager about his recommendations and his experiences with you?
- What kinds of services are available through you and the office, and which ones do you recommend that I pursue?
- What other kinds of products and services do you sell and how are you compensated?
- Do I strike you as the kind of person who would be a good client for you? Be honest.
- May I speak to a couple of your present clients? I promise not to be a pest, to ask embarrassing questions, or to invade their privacy—I only want their honest evaluaton.
- Here are my present goals and ideas, briefly stated. Can you please give me a brief idea of what you think and what your general recommendations would be? Am I the kind of customer you would honestly give proper attention and service to?

Remember, you not only want to clarify and perhaps unearth the broker's background, attitude, and intentions, you also want him or her to feel good about you *after* the interview!

GETTING STARTED

When you establish an account, you want to discuss with the broker how the two of you will communicate. For instance, do you want to keep your securities at home in the fireproof box (you *do* have a fireproof box, right?), or in a safety deposit box, or do you want the brokerage company to hold them for you? You will want to review the ways in which you plan to place your orders, and confirm that you have a mutual understanding of the definition of each type of order placement. These are the more common ways to order stocks, for instance:

- At-the-market order—whatever the price happens to be when the sale goes through
- Good-till-canceled (GTC) order—try to get the specified price until further notice
- Immediate order—effect the sale as quickly as possible
- Contingent order—put the order through only if a specified event occurs
- Scale order—multiple orders on a single issue
- Limit order—specifies a ceiling or minimum price *or better*
- Stop-loss order (good today or standing)—sell when the low price specified is reached

(By the way, if your brokerage house offers to "keep" your stock certificates, be sure you are getting the service you desire. Very often the certificates are not held, but instead the company merely adds your name to a list of part owners of a large account it operates. In this case, you are an investor in the stock when it comes to paying capital gains, etc., but you may lose out on other tax advantages. Check with your broker and your accountant before making this decision.)

Your broker may want written confirmation of telephone orders, and you may want telephone confirmation of executed orders. Life is ever so much easier if these things are spelled out, and understood by everybody, in advance. This is part of getting to know your broker. You want to discuss with your full-service broker what kind of information you are interested in seeing. If you intend to give the broker a commission every week and intend to weigh the fundamentalist, technical, and chartist recommendations on every move of the market, you can reasonably expect to receive a good deal of information in addition to the company newsletter. If you are going to trade only once every other month, it may behoove you to ask the broker what data he can give you, as in most offices the broker has to assemble or at least write directions in order for you to get additional literature. He may not feel it worth his time.

You want to know how your broker deals with the other brokers in his company and how he clears trades to and from the exchanges. As I mentioned, if it is a small firm, he probably goes through another, larger company, and you want to know who that is, how long it takes, what the added fees are (odd-lot trade commissions can add up when you have two pipers to pay). And you want to know the relationship between the various types of brokers.

Your personal broker is usually called an "account executive" these days, and he may himself be a "commission broker." He gives the buy, sell, and trade orders to the company's brokers who are actually at the exchanges, who may variously be "commission brokers" themselves. Or they may be "floor brokers," meaning they actually trade on the floor of the exchange; "specialists," meaning they handle specific kinds of trades or industries, or even certain stocks; "odd-lot brokers," who may be called "specialists" and who concentrate on putting odd-lot buys and sales together so that they can be disposed of properly on the exchange floor. They may be "registered traders," who may be any or all of the above or may supervise them. To compound the confusion, the titles vary from company to company and from exchange to exchange. Get a general description at some point, and then later when the broker casually refers to another broker, you'll have an idea of what is going on. Ignorance is not bliss if you are trying to find out why there was an error in placing your order or if you are emotionally overwrought and want to know why an order couldn't go through or some other problem arises.

SETTING UP YOUR SECURITIES-TRADING LIBRARY

As a writer and researcher, and therefore a regular visitor to the public library, I let that wonderful resource be part of my information bank. But I also subscribe to a local major daily paper, *The Wall Street Journal*, a weekly business magazine (I go for just one at a time, but rotate among several), and a monthly business magazine (which I also rotate). I also subscribe to investment-advisory services, which again I rotate. My plan is to get a variety of points of view—some are politically conservative, some not; some are strategically conservative, some adventurous. You may wish to do the same, but do look around before you settle on any one publication or service.

Among the books you'll find useful, I recommend at least one be of the "How to Make Money on Wall Street" variety. (Louis Rukeyser wrote one with precisely that title, but there are many, including some nice ones in three-ring binders from Forbes, WSJ, McGraw-Hill, and other financial publishers.) What you want is an introductory course in investing along with a glossary of terms and standard jargon and the basic concepts used in the investing world. If you are a more seasoned investor, you want a reference work to which you can turn when that stray word that escapes your lexicon pops up or when you want to refresh your memory about the mechanics of a particular market or are considering trying out a new market and want a good explanation.

You'll also need a book of interest tables and standardized financial calculations. They are available at most bookstores and big office-supply houses. They transform all that arithmetic, algebra, and calculus into simple charts. Want to figure that compounded interest for 256 days? Just look it up! Then, if you have even a simple calculator, you can perform all the math you need to understand your investments, make projections, and generally take masterful control of the numbers that are inevitably a big part of financial planning and wrangling. The nice ones even tell you how to set up your problems to solve them in a few seconds.

Then you'll want some of the more narrowly aimed financial-advice books. If you are planning your retirement, definitely get a good book on the topic and get some pertinent peridocial, such as *Modern Maturity*, the monthly from AIM, the preretiree branch of the American Association of Retired Persons. The journal and the association can guide you to useful literature of all types that will enable you to get on top of your financial planning. The same goes for other special financial goals: There are excellent books on financial planning for college, for buying insurance, for sorting out family legal affairs, for planning a living estate, for tax planning, for sorting out tax shelters, for monitoring your business.

Even if you go out and get one from every category, your financial bookshelf is going to be less than two feet long, and if you were to actually read them all cover to cover, you would be well educated indeed. But as long as you plan to be active in doing your own financial planning, you will do well to have the reference books to fall back on. From there you can branch out into specialty books. Remember, too, that despite the new tax laws, these books are tax deductible, for they are a direct expense of managing your finances, and therefore your taxes.

Finally, a distinction that bears defining. The word "speculate" derives from the Latin "speculari," *to observe*. A speculator is someone who observes what is going on around him and makes decisions based on his understanding. An "investor" is someone who puts money into a venture with not only the expectation of profitable return, but an understanding that the return *will be* profitable, barring unusual circumstances. So, if you put money into a venture without a nearly certain guarantee of profitable return, or without an understanding of your own that leads you to believe, based on your well-considered observation, that you will receive a profitable return, then you are neither investing, nor speculating, you are *gambling*. That is your prerogative, but remember that the smart money on Wall Street is from true investors and speculators. They and the brokers make big money off the rest of the customers, who are really just gambling their money away.

Self-Evaluation Checklist

Answer all questions and evaluate yourself objectively, with the help of someone who knows you if you wish.

1. How interested are you in becoming a much better educated and successful investor? Rate yourself on a scale from 1 (hardly) to 10 (extremely) _____

2. How much time do you realistically expect you will spend *each day* studying market trends and monitoring your investments? _____

3. How much time do you realistically have to spend studying business news, market trends, economic indicators, changes in monetary policy, prospectuses, financial statements, business news, and your investments
   each week? _____
   each month? _____

4. Do you have education or work experience in
   finance
   economics
   psychology
   marketing
   banking
   accounting
   business management? _____

5. Do you realistically believe this knowledge will give you an edge in selecting and managing investments? _____

6. When you make decisions about money, do you tend to follow logic or your emotions? _____

7. When you are faced with decisions about money, are you able to act responsibility and decisively or do you agonize or put off decisions until a crisis arises? _____

8. When you make decisions about money, do you usually make a plan and stick to it? _____

Review your answers and evaluate yourself as an investor.

   • If you qualify as a conscientious, motivated investor, go on to the Basic Investor Self-Profile to help decide where you need to begin or expand.
   • If you see some potential problems, consider hiring a personal financial

planner, a financial counselor, or begin conservatively with low-risk, easy-to-manage investments such as bank certificates, government bonds, pass-through certificates, and major money-market funds.

• If your prospects of becoming a successful investor seem slim based on your answers above, you may do best to forget about trying to manage a complicated investment program. Instead try to set up "foolproof" savings plans such as bank Christmas Club accounts, automatic savings plans, automatic drafts into long-term investments (available through many mutual funds, for instance), or consider having someone else in your household or family make investment decisions for you—someone who has a better chance of succeeding in money management.

Five Rules for Investors

1. Set your goals
2. Invest according to your objectives
3. Buy *and* sell according to plans and opportunity
4. Diversify
5. Review your goals, plans, and investments frequently

Investment Goals

Rank
__ Long-term growth
__ Conservation of capital with income
__ Medium-term growth (one to three years)
__ Medium-term growth with income
__ Conservative growth with highest possible income
__ Rapid capital growth
__ Tax shelter
__ (Define your own) _____

Estimate If You Haven't Set These Already

_____ Percentage assets should appreciate each year
_____ How much annual income should your investments generate?
_____ Based on your current investment nest egg, what average yield is required to provide that amount?
_____ By how much do your present investments fail to meet your objectives, or by how much do they exceed your needs?

• How have your investment objectives changed compared with last year?
• If they are different, how will your investment strategy change compared to last year?
• Which current investments are inappropriate to your new needs?
• Which investments will you want to change first to better meet your new objectives?
• Which investments will you want to reexamine to see if they still meet your objectives?

There Are Five Basic Investment Goals, and Each Person's Is a Mix of These:

1. Return (or yield).
2. Safety. This may be difficult to judge, but prudence here is a matter of knowledge and experience, both of which you can accumulate.
3. Hedge value. This is a double function, for some investments are hedges against inflation while others are hedges against excessive taxation.
4. Liquidity. Your need for liquidity will change, and the mix of investments you have and the mix of liquidity can be an important part of your investment strategy. Broad economic factors such as high inflation can also influence your need for liquidity.
5. Credit security. Not applicable to all, but many investors require assets that can be used to secure credit for personal or business reasons.

Mail-Order Know-How

For a list of correspondence schools on all subjects, including finance, write to:
The National Home Study Council
1601 18th St. N.W.
Washington, D.C. 20009

SHORT SECURITY WORKSHEETS

Records—

stock	date bought	number shares	price per share	comm.	total cost	date sold	price per share	comm.	total net

BONDS AND OTHER SECURITIES WORKSHEET

security	maturity date/pe	date bought	no. of units	unit price comm.	total comm. paid	date sold	units sold	comm.	total gain/ rec'd loss	short/long term tax	units remaining

Usually stocks, bonds, certificates, and other types of securities are divided into separate listings so they can be dealt with individually at tax time.

DIVIDENDS RECORDS SUMMARY

company	number of shares	date rec'd	rate per share	total divs. rec'd	tax exempt?	total rec'd	dividends this year

DECISION SHEETS—

All Securities–

Security	Current Price	Historical Price	Anticipated Value	Anticipated yield/profit	Risk Factor

STOCKS, SHORT FORM—
ALL OF THE ABOVE PLUS

annual growth rate	return on equity	price/earnings multiple	dividend status/yield	other criteria

COMPLETE STOCK RECORDS FORM

Column 1 security	2 market & symbol	3 date of purchase	4 broker	5 no. of shares	6 unit price	7 commis- sion	8 Total cost	9 Dividends

10 date of sale	11 no. of shares	12 unit price	13 commis- sion	14 total receipt	15 net gain (loss)	16 long or short term	17 shares remaining

Investment Calendar

Entries—
- Dates of purchases, sales, trades
- Dates for review of each security and whether it still fulfills your needs
- Tentative date for sale of selected security, with conditions
- Dates for contacting broker even if you have no trading instructions
- Dates for reviewing tax shelters, other tax-related investment needs
- Deadlines for buying/selling tax-oriented investments
- Other dates that affect your management of your investments, such as when you will have new investment monies available, when new laws or other changes in opportunity take effect, when you need to review your financial calendar!

AAII
American Association of Individual Investors
612 North Michigan Avenue
Chicago, Illinois 60611

NAIC
National Association of Investment Clubs
World Federation of Investment Clubs
1515 East Eleven Mile Road
Royal Oak, Michigan 48607

Both the AAII and NAIC have local chapters. They also offer other benefits, including advice on computerized investing, "how-to-invest" courses, worksheets and guides for doing your own simplified technical market analyses, and much more.

ANALYZING YOUR POSITION

Debt Instrument	Due Date(s)	Interest Rate	Payments		Projected Retirement Date
			Annual	Periodic	
_____	_____	_____	_____	_____	_____
_____	_____	_____	_____	_____	_____
_____	_____	_____	_____	_____	_____

Investment Instrument	Maturity Date	Yield	Appreciation	Marketability	Suitability to Goals
_____	_____	_____	_____	_____	_____

ASSETS SUMMARY

1. $ _____ cash
2. $ _____ liquid investments besides cash
3. $ _____ marketable investments
4. $ _____ hard-to-market or long-term investments

Suitability of each to goals: 1 _____
2 _____
3 _____
4 _____

BASIC INVESTOR SELF-PROFILE

Monthly income, average	_____
Checking account, average	_____
Savings accts., average	_____
New to savings/investments, average	_____
Bank CDs	_____
Government bonds, pass-throughs	_____
Corporate and municipal bonds	_____
Mortgages and other debts carried by you	_____
Life insurance (cash value)	_____
Stock and mutual funds (current value)	_____
Real estate (approx. market value)	_____
Business equity, partnerships	_____
Collectibles	_____
Other major assets	_____
Personal net worth	_____

Look for a breakdown of your wealth and assets as well as your total worth. By looking at where your assets are, you can begin to make plans for balancing your resources according to your needs, current opportunities and the economic environment.

Percentage of income going to savings/investments _____

Percentage of investments in cash reserves _____

(bank accounts and other immediately liquid investments)
    in stocks, bonds _____
    in government securities _____
    in money-market instruments _____
    in real estate _____
    in collectibles _____
    other major assets _____

Percentage investments in tax shelters _____

STOCK-EVALUATION CHECKLIST

Date _____
Company name _____
Market & listing symbol _____
Current price _____
Current dividend _____
Price record five preceding years _____
Dividend record, five years _____
Average price increase + average dividends = expected return _____

Age of company _____
Market area (world, U.S., West Coast, etc.) _____
Market share _____
Diversification (wide, narrow) _____
Primary customers, by type _____
Industry outlook _____
Cyclical industry? _____
Assets ratio (see financial statement) _____
Average assets ratio for industry _____
Competition within industry _____
Company's reputed position within industry _____
Standard & Poor's rating _____
Value Line rating _____
Other ratings, recommendations _____

Sales/revenues, past five years
    (up or down & how much) _____
Earnings per share, past five years (same) _____
Stock price, past five years
    (up, down; erratic, stable) _____
Industry performance, five years _____
Apparent reason for price trend _____

Price/earnings ratio, current _____
P/E past five years _____
P/E ratio of industry _____
Profits (pre-tax) past five years _____
Debt ratio, past five years _____
Price compared to Dow Jones or other index
  (past five years or better) _____
Pre-tax profit, last five years

_____ _____ _____ _____ _____   average _____
                                            trend (up/down) _____

Price/earnings

_____ _____ _____ _____ _____   average _____
                                            trend (up/down) _____

At first this may look like a lot of material to look up and digest, but as you research a few stocks, you will find yourself looking for this data all the time, and it becomes quick and easy to find.

Business week and *Barron's* both have much of the above information, if you save several months' issues. Try the *Federal Reserve Composite Index of Industrial Production* for some statistics. Ask your broker for Standard & Poor's sheets, which have much information, especially five-year records and comparisons with industries, the Dow, etc. Some major brokerage firms provide further information on their own "pink sheets." Write to the company secretary for a prospectus and shareholder news, and for a 10-K (some companies will give it, some will not).

Consider the age and reputation of a company and how well established it is, which relate to risk. Most indicators have fairly obvious connotations:

- New companies suggest higher risk
- Single product/service may be risky
- Type of customer may indicate risk
- Do cyclical stocks match cycle?
- Price competition may limit growth
- Asset ratio may indicate management outlook
- Revenue trend (up, down, steady) may indicate potential problems
- Earnings-per-share trend shows management's attitude (look for analyses by experts)
- Price trend is obviously important and may match or conflict with market trends, business cycles. See Standard & Poor's and *Value Line* charts to match factors. S&P sheets will usually have an elementary analysis.
- Sales/revenues trends are often found in S&P sheets
- Price/earnings ratios usually are a good comparison against how the other investors in the stock market view the company's prospects,

and should be compared against the market as a whole as well as against the industry the stock competes in.

If the stock has been selling at unusually high P/E ratios, you will want to find out whether it is temporarily high priced or whether it has always sold at a high ratio compared to the market or the industry.

A Note On "Diluted" Earnings

When companies distribute earnings to equity holders (stock and bond holders), bond holders and preferred-stock holders receive earnings before common-stock holders. For this reason, when analyzing earnings, the amount of earnings that will go to the preferred-equity holders is subtracted from the total earnings, and the difference is used in the price-earnings ratio. Usually the difference is not significant, but when it is, it can be a signal to investigate the company for problems.

The above are some factors stock analysts consistently use when studying a stock. Clearly, other factors are important. For example, does the company have a popular new product or a new government contract? Has it taken part in a merger or acquisition? Is there reason to expect a boom or collapse in the industry, or is there a likelihood of a takeover? If you haven't heard of any news and you have a full-service broker, ask him.

At some point you must make a decision based on what you know about the stock and your evaluations. Among the most basic are:

- Does the stock seem to have a potential for adequate price gains for the short term (less than one year) and long term (over one year)? Twenty percent is a good guideline. _____
- Does the stock meet your requirements for safety? _____
- If you buy the stock, how long would you expect to hold it before it showed enough gain or loss to get you to sell? If it does not gain or lose, how long will you keep it before selling? _____
- Given the current price of _____, if the price rises, at what price will you sell? _____
- If the price drops, at what price will you sell, given current conditions? _____

WHEN YOU HAVE TROUBLES AND COMPLAINTS

At the state level —

Each state has an agency that regulates business or securities or both. They may be called the Securities Commission or the Department of Finance, or the Department of Business Corrections, etc. To register a complaint or to make an inquiry, you will want to contact the official state office in the state in which the corporation has its headquarters.

At the federal level —

The Securities and Exchange Commission regulates all companies that issue or handle securities. It even has jurisdiction over some securities that are handled within a single state's boundaries. The main office of the SEC is at 450 Fifth Street NW, Washington, D.C. 20549. Better yet, there are regional offices scattered around the country. These are often a better bet because they have local loyalties and are more likely to be familiar with a local corporation.

The Federal Trade Commission is in charge of commodity trading and other selected investment markets, They have a Bureau of Consumer Protection in Washington. Also of use are their eleven regional offices. Check the U.S. Government Information (see page 68) for a list of them or call the library for the number of the one nearest you.

At the company level —

NASD, the National Association of Securities Dealers, is powerless to enforce any codes, but it does operate an information service. Like other responsible trade groups, it shows an interest in keeping its members honest. The main office is 1735 K St. NW, Washington, D.C. 20006.

The Over-the-Counter Information Bureau provides a similar service for investors in their market. HQ is at 120 Broadway, New York, NY 10271.

The New York Stock and Bond Exchanges are out to serve members, not traders, but the American Stock Exchange does have an informal information service. They are at 86 Trinity Place, New York City. Most other exchanges have no interest in non-revenue-producing services, especially those that might irritate their members.

Occasionally problems are merely mundane office mixups that can be cured by registered letters to the corporate secretary or president. This can be a cheap solution if your problem is minor. Don't forget that you also have a right to attend, speak at, and vote at stockholders' meetings of most publicly held corporations. If you've the inclination, this is one way for small fish to make big waves.

12

Hiring Your Financial Expertise

TOM ARMSTRONG, a veteran financial planner who handles the monetary affairs of many well-known business moguls, movie stars, and entertainers, guarantees his clients complete financial services, from allocating pocket money and bill paying to complete accounting to sophisticated investment programs that mix a variety of strategies to ensure moderate growth at all times. "Of course be sure to tell your readers that we do have a policy which narrows the list of who will want our services—we charge a minimum of $15,000 per year," he said, beaming.

At the other end of the scale, Stan Benson, one of the highly professional counselors with Consumer Credit Counsellors, a nationwide non-profit organization that works to help people salvage their financial pride when they become mired in credit straits, gives out free financial advice every day. "If you are up to your ears in debt, can't find a legal workable alternative, and don't know how to handle money except to spend it, we're here to set you back on the track to financial health and responsibility, and, hopefully, steer you in a way that will put you on the road to lifelong control over your personal financial affairs."

In between these two extremes there is a gigantic service industry growing up in this country that didn't even exist as recently as the early 1970s. Recognizing America's growing sophistication about money matters, all kinds of money-management-assistance and financial-education services are appearing on the scene. Many cost far more than they are worth, and more still aren't worth a dime, even if they are free. A great deal of very good and valuable financial assistance is even being made available free as a part of regular business promotion. This trend will doubtlessly fade somewhat, but until it does, we have a tremendous, growing resource in expert cheap financial assistance ready at our beck and call.

The trick of course is to find the best advice that applies to your needs and go get it at a fair price. Do this and you'll be ahead of most well-to-do

Americans, whether your income matches theirs or not. If you don't, you'll be passing up some of the best bargains you'll ever run across in the financial-service marketplace.

The places that will teach you to manage your money for free, such as Consumer Credit Counsellors and others, are largely sponsored by the business community, mostly groups that recognize they will lose less money in the long run if we can lower the number of people in their neighborhoods who cheat billers by abusing credit and persisting in unwise buying practices—the two chief wrongs committed by both the poor and the less well-to-do. That doesn't mean that their advice is less than excellent, however. In many offices across the nation, credit counselors save thousands of people with money problems from their own mistakes, and if you are one of them, and are willing, their advice may well set the foundation for lifelong financial-ladder climbing.

Find such counselors for yourself or others through the Yellow Pages, the local business associations, the chamber of commerce, city-sponsored or other ombudsmen offices, your bank or thrift, a major credit office, or contact Consumer Credit Counsellors in Washington, D.C. And there are probably other ways besides.

Those of us who don't have to resort to credit counseling to get us out of a dangerous pattern, but recognize that we could do better by ourselves if we had more knowledge at our fingertips, can also take advantage of some freebees in the financial-advice market. The catch—doesn't there always seem to be one?—is that we must raise our *caveat emptor* shield higher than ever. The business people who offer financial counseling and other services without a fee (this is different from the nonprofit credit-counseling offices) expect to get business from you in some other form, for clearly if they do not, the service would quickly disappear.

The first innovators to jump into this public relations race were the life insurance companies. They have always faced the uphill task of justifying the expense of their products in the face of financial burdens and the natural reluctance of most people to listen to insurance salesmen.

Most insurance salesmen are provided with a fill-in-the-blanks kit that creates a jiffy analysis of the prospect's family finances. Toss in the annual income here, estimate a few expenses there, plan college for the kiddies, and you have your recommended insurance coverage at the bottom of the form. Presto.

If you examine the courses that insurance people are force-fed on this topic, you will quickly understand that most of them truly believe they are giving the customer a valuable insight into his or her financial-security needs. Occasionally that is probably true, but in most cases the amount of insurance recommended on the basis of such "analyses" is far beyond what a prudent financial planner would recommend. And naturally it is usually sold in a form that is less advantageous to the buyer and more profitable to the insurance company. That's the Old American Way for the agent, but for the consumer it's the wrong way.

To the chagrin of the insurance industry, as was mentioned in the chapter on insurance, the New American Way is to evaluate money instruments (for that is what insurance policies are) in detail and weigh the dollars and sense more heavily than the tears and fears. Nevertheless, if you don't have a comprehensive financial plan, and you know that you need one before you can decide how much insurance you need to buy, your agent may be able to help you draw up a brief analysis of your economic status. He expects, of course, to collect his commission on a sale and to retain you as a future customer. If you plan on a bias in his favor when it comes to the amount of insurance recommended, and if he is honest, friendly, fair, and cooperative, that seems to me like a good exchange. The problem is in finding out if he happens to be a good financial planner and analyst on top of being a good salesman. Usually, if he is, he wears many hats besides that of insurance agent.

Other financial-products industries have followed the lead of the insurance companies with the same sort of sales promotion in order to succeed with today's sophisticated public. You'll find that your bank, your thrift, your stockbroker, your real estate agent, and maybe even the company you work for (someday even your milkman, probably) offer financial-planning services either free or for a minimal charge in the hopes of securing your future business or cooperation. If such opportunity rears its head, take advantage of it, for it can't do you harm as long as you are careful. And it can be a painfree introduction to financial guidance and knowledge building. Realize, however, that such promotions are usually highly biased.

The securities brokerage firms have come to court the small- and medium-size investor as never before, and the competition is fierce. Of course, Merrill Lynch, to cite just one example, doesn't give a damn whether you and I are rich or whether we live in an alley, but they care very much whether we have money we are willing to invest through them in securities of one kind or another. They, like all the big investment firms, offer an ever expanding and changing array of financial services designed to lure you into their web of commission-garnering business. Some services, like the quasi-checking accounts, the sweep accounts, and the cash-management accounts, are merely conveniences for potential clients, and can be as useful—or as dangerous—as a credit card in your daily life. Others are meant to appeal to a limited class of clientele, customers who want to build their sophistication, their flexibility, and their track record in money management. And, the logic goes, these are the types of people who will develop the sophistication to expand their participation in the securities markets for years to come. In the trade they say that these people have "the right profile." Turn your head to the mirror of the financial world and see how you shape up. Translation: Go to your banker, stockbroker, insurance agent, lawyer, and accountant and ask each of them for the official company criteria for identifying who is a preferred customer or client. They'll usually tell you.

Most of these services are not free, and some are even expected to turn a strong profit as subsidiary segments of the parent company, but all share the characteristic of being first and foremost courtesy services to present to upwardly mobile clients and potential customers. Best of all, a good many are terrific bargains.

WHAT'S AVAILABLE

You can start at the bottom of the list of available items with the fill-in-the-blank forms and booklets of the sort Citibank first turned out so beautifully in the 1970s. If you've the notion, this is a very good way to begin, although the information tends to be rather basic, is often crippled by inappropriate jargon, and inevitably stresses the importance of banking services (or whatever industry is giving the materials out) entirely out of proportion with 95 percent of most people's real needs and desires.

You must take all the partisan advice with a grain of salt, but the next level of available material is more impartial. It is the computerized forms, available from a growing number of sources, primarily securities houses, which have designed formula analyses meant to be as good as ones you would get from a personal financial counselor. Well, because you are working through a computer, you know they aren't *that* great, but don't write them off. For the price, many of them are a bargain, especially if you are the do-it-yourself type. They cost from about a hundred dollars up to a thousand or so, with the price depending on how detailed they are, how much input you get from a real live financial-planning consultant, and so on. The basic ones simply give you back a computer readout that may be ten or fifteen pages, and which summarizes what you already know and recommends prudent guidelines for cash reserves, safe investment, gives budgeting suggestions, recommends insurance levels, etc.

The most costly versions come in impressively bound little books, just like an expensive portfolio analysis or commissioned business report. They will describe your financial position step by step according to the latest principles, make recommendations with allowances for your personal contingencies, and instruct you in how to calculate future updates. They're filled full of cross-references and beautiful computer-generated charts and graphs, and have lengthy explanations of all the expected ramifications of your position. Often they are still tilted in favor of recommending a disproportionate investment in some product the company offers, although most now try their best to offer acceptably objective advice and analysis. In the places where objectivity is more or less the accepted rule, they expect to get your other business through goodwill and close proximity.

The last form of financial-analysis service is the in-depth workup and continued consultation provided by an expert financial planner. For most people the best feature provided by the most expensive of these services, aside from the fact that the good ones are designed by experts, is that they draw you, the customer, right into the nuts and bolts activity of setting up and maintaining a solid but flexible financial plan. It is a route that can take you straight to the high road.

That sounds simple, and in a way it is, but in the milieu of money, most people, even those who are successful in their professional lives, fail to observe this guiding tenet. There's something about finances that sets them back and makes them feel powerless when they most need to be in control. To be in control, they have to begin by going through the entire planning and analysis process at least once. To verify this, all you have to do is check in at the nearest computer store or business college. Private professionals buy half of all microcomputers used exclusively for business, and they constitute a growing proportion of the student body at business schools. They are tired of knowing just their job and not knowing how to handle their money. They're going to college, and they're buying computer power, and they are hiring financial consultants to help themselves to all the expertise that can be bought, learned, and programmed.

Following their cue, one great way to set up your financial plan for the first time, or to refine your personal analysis to fit your present circumstances and your dreams for the future, is to set up a financial-planning interview with an expert counselor and hire the expertise you lack. You can't hire a magician or a stock-market wizard, but you can hire a real organizational expert who can set all your assets in line with current conventional wisdom.

Clearly, the best way of all is to do it all yourself, but for most of us this just isn't practical. To master all areas of finance today is tantamount to being a "universal man" back in the centuries when the knowledge of mankind was contained in about 400 books. We've all seen dozens of books come and go which purported to give all the information you needed to properly and successfully plan and operate your own financial empire. Unfortunately, not only will all this information not fit into one book (although I heartily recommend that you begin compiling a small library of personal finance-reference books), but in the vast majority of cases the advice in a given book is not appropriate for the person who is reading it, leaving him with pages of useless material and omitting the very information he actually needs.

Presumably by now you've decided what kind of adviser you can use, and how. The question now is, How do I find the one I need?

THEY CALL THEMSELVES PROFESSIONALS

In recent years the Denver-based College for Financial Planning has sponsored a professional designation in financial planning. Those who successfully complete the college's courses, pass the test, and work for a year as a financial planner earn the title Certified Financial Planner, or CFP. Even more recently, a few of the major universities, such as UCLA, Michigan State, and others have launched their own CFP certification programs. It's about time.

It has been the last of the three requirements—that candidates for the title work for a year as a financial planner—which has both helped and hindered the CFP reputation. It is more or less necessary that a professional designation have professional experience as part of its prerequisites, but it has also led to the use of the title by those whose main interest is peripheral to financial planning and to the balanced approach the job requires. As a result, many if not most of the early CFPs were insurance salesmen, securities brokers, bankers, and other professionals who were using the CFP title as a feather in the cap of their other, primary, profession. It was a way to further their credibility and visibility in their existing businesses.

The conflict of interest is obvious and potentially dangerous. Clearly, if a person's primary source of income is from, say, insurance commissions, it is going to be difficult for him or her to tell a client that he doesn't need any more insurance or any different insurance just because that is what a totally objective CFP would say given the potential customer's aims, needs, and ability to pay. As a result, the title CFP has been besmirched, though the colleges are doing a good job of cleaning up the image. Today an increasing number of CFPs are working exclusively as financial planners, and regard income from sales of financial products such as insurance or securities as a conflict of interest. (Most CFPs will rush to tell you that the abuses I have described are not true, and that conflict of interest is an area of ongoing debate.)

At any rate, the CFP title is bound to be a sign that the financial planner you are interviewing has dedicated him- or herself to the career and specialty of financial counseling and views it as a career, not a stopping post or a lure to unsuspecting prospects. To date, the CFP title is not an absolute requirement for competence, for many of the best planners came up through the ranks before the formal designation was hatched. But in place of it I would insist upon a larger reputation, more references, and further credentials.

The International Association for Financial Planning is a trade organization dedicated to promoting the profession. They can also direct you to their members, but there is no guarantee or promise of qualifications, ability, or integrity, for they do not necessarily demand these of their dues payers. They do offer guidelines for selecting a qualified FP. Among their regular recommendations: Early on, quiz the prospective planner to see how current he or she is on recent tax laws, changes in the money market, and economic conditions. Good FPs have a wide range of contacts in all financial disciplines and can name them readily. A few acquaintances who are insurance agents or accountants is not an acceptable list. But that's just the start of the interview.

Interviewing prospective CFPs is no more or less difficult than interviewing other professionals. You must know what information is essential and relevant, and you must be able to gauge the answers you get back. The first thing to look for, according to planners at the College for FPs, is either a concentrated education, à la one of the aforementioned certification programs, plus general grounding in finances along with moderate experience or better, or a great deal of experience in all areas of finance, including planning, which, with a good reputation, replaces any need for formal education.

Although frequently practiced by younger professionals, truly wise financial planning requires more experience and knowledge than just about any other financial career. The best FPs must be well versed in banking, securities, investment strategy, probate and estate law, a multitude of types of insurance, general economics, plus accounting and counseling skills to boot. Making sure that you have a person with a passable or superior mix of all these requires more careful, but fortunately not too painful, planning.

The FPs I have spoken to express no surprise or concern when I ask about their backgrounds, and most are pleased to have the opportunity to pitch themselves. Like a lawyer who is testing expertise in a witness, you want to get an idea of his or her actual knowledge and ability to advise you. Since you are looking for someone who is more knowledgeable than yourself, this requires some careful thought. A lawyer who is examining an adversary before a questioning will not only check out the person's credentials, but will also devise questions that elicit predicted responses. That way, if you get the wrong answer, you have a reason to dig deeper. If you are especially interested in investment opportunity, you might find out from another investment expert, such as a trusted adviser of a friend, what the investment community considers to be the prudent cash reserves for a person with your income, background, and responsibilities.

In addition to having his own opinion, a good adviser should be able to come close to a standard response. If everyone you talk to says that recommended reserves are going down, and upside potential is improving in the stock market, and the consensus revolves in the 25 to 30 percent area, you expect a close response, with justification. Someone who suggests reserves of 10 percent or 50 percent had better come up with some very convincing arguments, fast, and even then I would be suspicious.

Also, your accountant may have brought some key issue to light that you can use to quiz an FP. My accountant, for example, always explains to me the ways in which my home office can be depreciated and applied against my income taxes, while I ensure that I will be able to avoid capital-gains penalties should I ever sell my home. The rules are quite concise and just complicated enough so that you must understand them well to explain them adequately.

I don't expect an FP to be a tax expert, but one whom I mentioned this to blithely announced that I had nothing to lose in depreciating my office space in normal straight-line fashion. I was glad that this flip, overconfident (and *wrong*) know-it-all wasn't steering my financial ship, for according to the then current laws, he was wrong, and he probably would have landed not on the shores of future prosperity, but up the river on an income tax evasion rap. You can work up your own list of interview questions, but please don't be shy. If you are looking for a superior brain surgeon, you don't want to end up with a third-rate proctologist in a career switch just because you didn't ask a few probing questions.

The professional financial planner needs a staggering amount of specific knowledge and a prophet's judgment. His responsibility is to bring in expertise on your behalf when his ability falls short of the best solution. All good FPs will have lawyers (of various specialties), accountants, bankers, real estate experts, securities brokers, and other financial experts whom they can call on for answers to specific questions. That's why it is entirely appropriate to ask what kind of affiliations a person has, including asking for a list of some of the people he or she consults with so you can call and verify the fact. As with a doctor who is on staff at the city's best hospital and consults with the most prestigious specialists, an FP who works with top-notch advisers is obviously more desirable than someone whose sole references barely know him and deny they give, much less trade, advice. I'm not writing off the beginners, for all great FPs also began somewhere, but consider the principle at work here.

I think most professionals can afford a few moments to answer questions such as," Is this other person well versed in my problem area?" "Is his professionalism up to par with his claims?" "Is he in fact welcome to call you for assistance or consultations?" This is a reasonable approach, and you may find out other things about the FP that will be of use. Best of all, even if you decide that the FP has been pulling your leg or otherwise fails to meet your standards, you have already introduced yourself to a small bevy of experts whom you can approach for other referrals or recommendations. Nothing is more valuable when you have a problem than the name and number of a person who might be able to help solve it for you.

A nearly imperative question by all accounts is, "May I speak to some of your current clients?" This is so standard in the business world that no professional will be riled by the request, if for no other reason than he or she gets to select the list of names for you to contact. This will be no refuge for a flack or a flake in the long run, for even friends will confide on the side of truth, usually, if you guarantee them that journalist's ultimate ally, confidentiality.

So you've interviewed and selected a personal financial-planning consultant, and presumably you've negotiated a fee and working arrangements that are mutually rewarding. Now what do you do? First turn out of the gate, *be honest*. Even if you cheat on certain things, be honest about that. Your FP can't help you make intelligent decisions unless you level with him, no matter how clever he is. He may dump you as a client, but then you probably wouldn't have gotten along anyway. If he doesn't, then he can give you advice and help that suit your real needs, not the imaginary needs of a person you pretend to be.

FPs, like accountants, are aware that over a quarter of all Americans cheat on their income taxes, and they are not going to be shocked to find out where their clients play close to the vest with the law. Just don't expect them to become accomplices in the act. Personally, I advise you to stick with the law, for I believe that there are so many opportunities in the legal spectrum of business and finance that they make forays out of the system unnecessary. But, acknowledging the reality that others do not share that view, I feel it is important you work with professionals with whom you can level and who can live with your personal attitudes.

No one who is scrupulously honest wants an adviser who encourages excursions into illegal shenanigans, nor does someone who feels comfortable walking the fine line on the edge of the law want an adviser who takes money to hound him about it. It's a touchy topic to bring up in person, but please don't fail to do so. It's a bad area to find out later you are in disagreement about.

When you set out to find an FP, don't make fees your main criterion, for as in every area of finance, they are only a part of the real bottom-line cost. For one thing, a good FP spends at least 20 to 30 percent of his or her time learning and keeping abreast of changes in the world of finance. That comes to eight to twelve hours per week *not earning*. I like to look at it in the same light as I would a physician who keeps up with the latest development in techniques and research, or the accountant who spends two months each year learning the new tax laws. I'm glad to pay a high hourly fee if I get good solid advice that will improve *my* bottom line.

If you are desperate or adamant about saving money, there are many better ways than by getting by with a half-baked adviser. You can assemble all the information for your accountant so that all he has to do is transfer the information to the proper forms, and then do the work you really hire him for—to make judgments about the tax and reporting requirements. If you want to pay him or her for doing the paperwork, you are certainly entitled to, but in addition to saving money, the work you do for yourself on your own books brings you that much more intimately in touch with your overall financial status. This is a worthwhile goal no matter how modest or great your wealth. It also enables you to intelligently discuss the entries with the accountant when there is a judgment call that requires your direct participation or an error that needs to be cleared up. Every point that applies to the accountant also applies to your FP. If you retain a lawyer, there is often a good deal of footwork you can do, and as I discussed in Chapter 8, the advantages are not just monetary nor immediate in doing as much of it as you can yourself.

All these ideas hold true with your FP, broker, and other financial advisers. The more you know, the better advantage you can take of their professional expertise. Instead of listening to explanations of the basics at a rate of umpteen dollars per hour, you can be concentrating on the cutting edge of your adviser's expertise where the big money-savings and investment savvy often lie. There is no "laying on of hands" when you hire an FP or any other financial adviser; the relationship requires significant work and input from you to make it work.

Most people who are discontent with their investments share a single problem: Their money works for someone else—for the bank where they collect paltry interest, for the department store that collects interest on credit and moves cash payments into its cash flow before delivering services or products, for professionals who must do the footwork and paperwork that their clients are unwilling to take on themselves, for sellers of investments who hoodwink investors into leaving their assets in high-risk or low-yield deals just because it is a hassle to do anything else, or pile up commissions at the expense of profits.

The encouraging thing is that hard times are driving more and more people to educate themselves, to manage their money instead of just banking it, to develop their sophistication so that they can make their money work for them. Being financially savvy is ever faster becoming a survival skill!

If you investigate all the professional financial planners and counselors you find, and still don't find the one who is right for you, you may have discovered that the best FP for you is yourself. The only caveat is to make sure you educate yourself properly. You'll need a background in insurance, all forms of investing, financial calculation, certain areas of civil law, current banking practices and rates, current tax laws and rates, and a pinch of psychology. If you followed the advice in the preceding chapters, you are likely well on your way to attaining just that broad-based a financial education. A good FP can be a terrific shortcut and timesaver, but not a complete substitute for knowledge on your part.

WHERE TO LOOK

So, you decide to give a financial planner a listening to, and maybe a try. Where to find them? Few are in the phone book, and those may not be in your price range.

As you've probably noticed from reading this chapter and from listening to advertising, most financial planners are found through referrals. Try these:

Your Banker. Most personal bankers can refer you to a variety of planners, from cost-free credit counselors to high-priced money-management firms and personal financial managers. Be sure to discuss your problem or needs with the banker so that you end up with the best referral.

Your Broker. All the large, full-service brokerage firms have financial-planning subsidiaries or departments that can provide you with a variety of services. They usually have several levels of service, perhaps starting with inexpensive computerized analyses, to costly reviews of your financial life by a bevy of experts. Many smaller firms have close contacts with a group of planners with whom they work closely as a service to their customers. Contact your broker to find what he or she can help you with. If you do not find what you are looking for through his company, contact another firm, for many will provide services or referrals even to nonclients.

Government Agencies. Many of these are familiar with nonprofit credit counseling offices and will help you find and select one in your area. If you cannot afford a financial manager, or if you are in serious debt, these counselors may be the best help you can find at any price.

Trade Groups. The College of Certified Financial Planners in Denver, Colorado, will send a list of their graduates in your area, as will other similar organizations. Remember that just because a planner is affiliated with a group does not mean he is competent—you must still ask the important questions and discern that for yourself.

Other Financial Professionals. In addition to your banker, your accountant, your lawyer, finance officer, and others may be able to refer you to a good financial counselor. No FP is the right one for you, however, until you have found what you need to know and have successfully chosen the right professional to meet your needs.

YOU'RE STILL THE BOSS

Whether you use a planner or not, you remain the boss and the hub of your own network of financial-support professionals. If you have a group you are confident in, in many cases it can make sense to make the individuals aware of the other professionals who serve you, and perhaps even introduce them, if feasible. If you are entering into a business investment, for instance, your banker, lawyer, and accountant may have to interact anyway. If they already know each other, or at least are not complete strangers, your project has a better chance of success and of running smoothly. Financial professionals are usually glad to expand their circle of acquaintances in the community, and will be pleased to have contacts and references to back up their commitments or risks with you. Further, your confidence may be appreciated. Should you need a new professional referral or just want to change, knowing whom you work well with may give your acquaintances a better idea of whom to refer to you and whom not to.

Interviewing a Prospective Financial Planner

- What are your credentials?
- How long have you been an FP?
- What do you do to keep yourself up-to-date with the fast-changing details of personal financial decision-making?
- What products do you sell and receive commission for?
- What proportion of your income derives from financial-planning services?
- How many other clients in my income bracket do you serve?
- Who are the other professionals upon whom you call when you need special knowledge or insight in narrow topics such as law, banking, investing, tax planning, etcetera?
- May I call them and ask in a very brief and nonintrusive way for their opinion of your service?
- May I speak with, say, five of your current clients to ask about their experiences with you?
- How often do you expect to meet and talk with me and how often may I contact you?
- How do you charge?

- How can I affect the benefit I get from your services and the size of the bill you submit?
- What service do you expect to give me, and why do you think that will be cost-effective and beneficial to me?

Financial-Planning Alternatives

- Many banks and other financial institutions offer financial-planning guides.
- Contact your state services department or look up your local non-profit credit-counseling office. Most offer very good financial-planning guides for lower- and middle-income families and individuals.
- Several publishers also publish comprehensive planning guides.
- Many colleges, universities, and adult-education programs have a variety of financial-planning classes.
- Ask your company's personnel director for financial-planning services and sources he or she can provide or refer you to.
- Build your own library of financial-planning books and assemble your little black book of advisers.
- Hire a professional financial planner.
- Use the financial-planning services offered by a major financial-service business such as your stockbrokerage company, insurance company, bank, etc.
- Contact your banker, your finance company president, your broker, to locate quality financial-planning services and professionals in your area.

13

Cultivating the
Money Habit

IT'S BEEN SAID that the greatest barrier to the success of mankind is inertia. Surely, from Dale Carnegie to the creator of est, successful people testify that moving from inaction to action is the biggest step any of us can take on our way to achieving our aspirations. Getting into the money habit of thinking about money in a constructive way, of paying attention to the many chores of money management, and of pursuing financial ambitions is mostly a matter of overcoming personal inertia. Time expands to allow you to do what you consider to be important. This chapter presents some ways to make financial planning an interesting, regular, and rewarding part of your daily life. There are many mechanisms you can use, but they all depend upon bringing new routines and other influences into your life. The best part is that it can be a really pleasant addition to your lifestyle.

Incredibly, many of the victims in hundreds of fraud cases each year are tossing $100,000 and $200,000 into the kitty just as fast as government pensioners and other smalltimers are putting in their $5000 and $10,000 life savings. It might seem that fraud brokers must run a pretty sophisticated scam to lure businessmen and other successful people into pouring huge investments into their bottomless carpetbags. The truth is almost always otherwise. Nearly all of the investors who lose 99 percent of their stakes put their money in scams based on newspaper advertisements, a telephone sales pitch originating in some boiler-room operation, or printed literature that quotes nonexistent or misrepresented authorities. Most people who have their money stolen spend almost no time investigating the object of their greed after they have spent years, perhaps their entire working lives, earning the money.

How can this be? It's an American tradition. It's also a tradition we can all learn from. If you ask any of these victims if they hadn't thought it a worthwhile investment of time to investigate the company more closely and to scrutinize the information they were given, they invariably say

271

yes, and if you ask them if they were negligently hasty, you get almost as many positive replies. It's obvious—but people don't adhere to common wisdom even when they know better.

Similarly, lack of planning is the key element in the failure of small and independent investors to make money in the securities markets. The professional and successful investors have a complete strategy worked out every time they buy or sell a security. They know when they plan to sell it, either in terms of chronology or price, and what factors they will look for as oportunities or danger signals. They modify that plan as events come to pass, of course, but they stick generally to their plans and thereby maximize their gains and minimize their losses. Unsophisticated investors, on the other hand, tend to enter into a purchase or investment solely on the basis of one expectation of gain, without a plan for limiting downside risk, selling if there is a downside turn, selling if paper-profit levels are reached, or in other ways ensuring that they operate on the basis of what they know rather than on their emotions. Too often they sell in panics and hand profits on a silver platter to the smart players in the market.

A sample plan for handling a given stock might look like this:

- Stock: XYZ COMPANY
- Purchase date: 4/5
- Purchase price: 44⅝
- Expected price: could reach price of 60 or better if new products are as successful as anticipated. Industry cyclical peak is due by end of year. If products do well, the results should be evident by third quarter (10/15 report). If products fail, excessive debt could send price down fast. Plan to sell at first downtick after reaching price of 55.
- Stop loss: heavy short-term debt is obvious, as is competition in the industry. Give broker stop-loss order at 38, but consider dropping at 40 or below—the market may be ready to dump it.
- Term: expect a major price-change within the next 6 to 10 months.
- Probably not good for a long-term holding, as industry cycle is due for a downturn and may turn shaky, and there is no significant dividend. Look to sell within 6 to 8 months. Keep no longer than 12 months.
- Beta: historically a very volatile issue; price fluctuates further and faster than most in the industry. Watch stop-loss price carefully.

If you don't spend some time investigating your investments, you can't expect to come out the winner. At the same time, no one can pretend that a person can know everything about money. If it were at all possible, there would be at least one economist who would be correct more than half the time! But if you want to protect your money, you must spend a minimum amount of time keeping track of it and keeping up with the latest methods of making it grow. To do so, you must be educated enough to make money through safe investments or you have to be lucky enough to make money in speculative investments.

If you want to succeed in speculative investing, proceed one step at a time from the simplest to the more sophisticated. If you want to try your luck in the stock market, try your luck and skill in the stock-holding mutual funds first. You will need the same skills that made you a success there, plus a few more, when you play the stocks directly. Likewise, if you think you have the wherewithall to balance your portfolio with stock puts and calls and to minimize your losses with listed stock options, make sure you understand the market well enough to have first been successful at conservative, basic straight-line investing. The people who are playing the stock-index futures, for instance, are those who understand that market very well and have specific plans and expectations for every move. If you don't, and unless that is the next logical type of investment for you to investigate, better step back and pause before plunging ahead.

If you are already playing the stock market, don't, however, be intimidated by the newer and related markets. For example, some of the most conservative ways of investing involve buying puts and calls against a stock purchase. (These involve buying a contract to buy or sell the stock later at a given price and thereby minimizing the potential for loss at the expense of the price of the contract.) Some also use stock-index futures, which play against the entire market, to balance out their portfolios. If the market slumps, their collective investments won't suffer so badly, and if it bounds, they can take even greater advantage of the good news. If you have developed the knowledge and skill to master one market, odds are you can do the same at the next level if you are conscientious.

FOLLOWING A GOOD LEAD

For years the one perk that has not been merely offered to, but has been pushed upon executives, has been prepaid, top-notch financial planning. When a company is shelling out a high five-, six-, or even seven-figure salary for some whiz-bang CEO or other officer, the last thing it wants him or her to do is spend ten hours a week managing personal finances. They want 100 percent concentration on the company's past, present, and future. Most of these types can still fake it by reading the financial press "in the interest of the company," but they let the lackeys take care of the details. You can consider seeking your own advisers for some of the same reasons, with some limitations.

If your company hasn't come out and insisted that you partake of the services of their $100,000-per-year portfolio manager and FP, then you don't have any excuse for not following the financial press for your own benefit. Most of us with money to invest are at least sophisticated enough that we can follow the major trends in the financial press. People with only $5000 to invest are moving their money back and forth between money-market funds, T-bill accounts, and even limited partnerships as the financial climate dictates. A few years ago many low- and middle-income Americans didn't feel confident enough to invest outside their local bank or thrift. To imagine that you can remain competitive with the Joneses these days without screening lots of financial information is a dated mistake. An example of this is the coverage of finance in the women's press. Look in any of the "big seven" ladies' periodicals and you'll find regular features on insurance, stock purchases, and financial analysis alongside the recipes for angel food cake and medical advice. The financial recipe is a big priority.

Once you have some money invested in an instrument of some sort or another, most funds spent on investment information become tax-deductible. Thus, newspaper subscriptions, magazines, newsletters, computer services, are all subsidized to you by the government (the rest of us). So get yours and get ahead. It's all because the government wants the American people to participate in the capitalist system and because by the time most people become congressmen, they are usually sophisticated enough to be investors and speculators themselves. They are willing to give themselves and the rest of us a nice break at tax time to help rake in the dough. God bless representative government!

ELECTRONIC FINANCES

Without a doubt, the instrument with the potential for educating more people to the level of financial wizardry than any other since the printing press is the home computer. The array of programs available to help manage personal finances is prodigious, and of course anyone who learns the rudiments of programming can create a program, piece by piece, that suits his or her exact needs. The programs that promise to revolutionize the investment world are the analysis programs, which anyone can buy, and which are becoming cheaper and cheaper. I have seen several good ones that will automatically chart several economic indicators, for instance, and apply the inferences of the latest trend to a given investment possibility. Some provide a continuously updated analysis of the position of any stock or other listed holding, and may even gather their own data if you are a subscriber to one of the market-listing services and you have a program that scans the NYSE or other indexes for the listings you request. These will monitor your holdings or follow the progress of some prospective investments almost automatically, once you instruct them to. It's like having your own private tickertape reader and technical analyst right in your home. Shades of J. D. Rockefeller meeting *Star Wars* robots.

With computerized telecommunications, technical analyses can be at your fingertips as quickly as they are for the president of a bank. And, if you are willing to invest in one of the fast reporting services, you can receive complete stock and bond market listings just fifteen minutes behind the ticker tape! For considerably less you can subscribe to an hour, a twelve-hour, or a twenty-four-hour delay.

For a few dollars per month you can have your own securities-analysis service and your own portfolio-updating service right on your desktop. For a few dollars more you can have practically the instantaneous data-access big traders paid thousands of dollars for just a couple of years ago. All you have to do is activate the programs and dial the telephone, unless of course you have a machine with a clock and automatic dialing, in which case your only burden is to punch the desired information onto the monitor screen.

Up until now, few home investors have been sophisticated enough to take full advantage of computer power for home financial planning. For one thing, computers have been difficult for people to approach, except for games, which are a lot easier at first. For another, it has been hard to shop for the best or the individually most applicable programs. Likewise, it can be a real setback to invest $50 or $500 for a program only to find out it is too time consuming to learn or that there are so many errors in it that it is entirely impractical. The software business is starting to sort itself out now, and you can find reliable reviews of personal-finance programs in several of the top computer magazines, notably *BYTE*, *Softalk*, and a few others, and some of the finance magazines are now doing software reviews. The programs offered by some of the big companies such as Dow Jones Irwin and Source have been carefully screened before they were marketed and are a safer bet. The ultimate guarantee is to take advantage of the thirty-day money-back guarantee that many manufacturers give with their software packages. Also, there are so many new programs being created all the time that we will always have new generations of products available to upgrade our computers' personal-finance capabilities.

A few companies have personal-computer terminals solely designed for financial work. They have built-in programming for accessing various markets via their built-in telephone modems, and come complete with automatic dialing, automatic program activation, and clocks to turn themselves on and off. The larger "micros" have a selection of disc-fed programs that expand their capabilities to perform specialized tasks, such as specific stock callout analysis, "what if?" operations such as are used in accounting programs to find out what happens if a price rises or falls, if a sale is made, if interest rates rise or fall, and so on. They even feature built-in graphics capabilities so that information can be adapted to readily comprehensible formats at a moment's notice. The features will expand and drop in price, enabling the average investor to gather and manipulate more data than he or she can possibly handle, and do it affordably. That's power and sophistication at a bargain price.

Shopping for the program that does what you want can be time consuming and frustrating, but there are guidelines which will help. One is the already mentioned reviews. Another is to contact computer-user groups. Many have public-domain programs that may be useful, and others have computer investing clubs. Most widely advertised programs are written to work only with certain kinds of computers. For instance, the Dow Jones packages originally worked only on Apple or Apple-compatible machines, and so were useless to those who owned any other kind. Similar problems exist with other packages. The International Association of Individual Investors offers a newsletter on computerized investing, and other publications are available.

Yet another alternative is to subscribe to a service that does all the computing for you, leaving you to read the results on your home monitor or cable system television. You may still have to have a computer, or at least a "smart terminal," which costs nearly as much, but when you dial the company on the phone, the company's giant business-size mainframe computer does all the work in a matter of seconds. You are charged for the number of minutes or seconds the call takes, and you can take as much information as the memory banks of your machine will allow.

There are several problems with such systems, chief among them being a serious lack of flexibility. The cost per minute of access is quite high, so you want to have your inquiries carefully planned, and if you forget something it is an expensive call back. Plus, you may be restricted to one call per day with some systems. On the other hand, if you want very specific information on analysis, the big computers do a smash-up job, and the information and programming are going to be correct. Another nice feature upcoming in the AT&T and other systems will be access to huge data banks. In effect, you'll be able to have an enormous financial library available at your fingertips, with the data transferred at today's superfast electronic clip.

As I mentioned earlier, many of the programs available for investment analysis tie into the same company's programs for total financial planning, and perhaps other programs as well. Thus, after you assemble the bottom-line figures for your investments, you can transfer them quickly and easily to your home-accounting program or your financial-management records and then see quickly how your new positions affect your overall position. As you can see, the possibilities are just about endless, and they become easier and easier to handle as time passes, and the excuses for not pursuing the latest capabilities grow feebler and feebler.

If you are among the 30 percent of computer buyers who are planning to use the machines for the express purpose of developing your personal finances, you have the added flexibility of picking the size and type of computer that matches the programs you want. First you decide what you want to do, then you pick the kind of software you think will be appropriate, then you select your machine in light of what you want to spend, naturally, but most importantly, how well its capabilities match the programs you will want to run. The smallest computers, ones that will accept fast-paced games, are generally not powerful enough to handle most complicated finance programs, and the machines that effectively handle the larger programs are poor at games. There are compromises available, with machines that handle both, but neither as well as a fully dedicated machine. So you have to be extremely careful about what you buy and how you evaluate it.

If you want only a home-accounting program that will balance your bank accounts and list your assets in easy-to-read form, then even the smallest of the micro home computers will meet your demands, as long as good programs are available for the model you have. If you can do basic arithmetic, however, these "balance-your-checkbook" programs will be just as much trouble to work through as doing the tasks by hand.

But if you want the option of running more powerful programs that perform "what if" financial-planning exercises, then you must have a larger machine that has the capabilities. As you shop for software you'll find that it is categorized according to the machine capability. For example, they may say just "Apple II compatible," or something like "Requires CP/M, 32K RAM and 2 disk drives of 100K each." If your machine lacks any of these parameters, the software is useless to you.

To summarize: (1) Define what you want to do first, (2) investigate the software, (3) evaluate the mechanical requirements, (4) pick out your machine. You'll be happy you did.

If all this sends you into a panic of future shock, I suggest you catch up as fast as you can. There is speculation that as soon as we arrive at the "full-service financial center" stage, there won't be any need to go out of the house when it comes to managing your money. Through your two-way cable TV channel or telephone you will do all your banking, as indeed you can do now if you live in several experimental neighborhoods. When that day arrives, and your bank has securities brokers, insurance agents, and other financial people on staff, it will be just as easy to communicate with them as it is to linger at the teller's window, the personal banker, or—the computer. You'll be able to do all your financial dealing through your home computer the way you make deposits and withdrawals at the bank's automated teller machine today. More to the point, we all may have to.

To compare computer power to the reality of just a couple of years ago, you can see that you have the same capability that Wall Street Wizards paid a fortune for. I spoke with a certain Wall Street mogul back in the 1970s about why he was willing to spend over $100,000 per year to have the only individually held seat on the New York Stock Exchange. His reasons were clear—instant information and instant access. Today, with the information services, you can get the same trading information fifteen minutes after the traders. With the programs and your computer, you can do a technical analysis as quickly as they, and with your telephone and a reliable broker, you can have an order on the floor of the exchange within ten more minutes. That means that you can be twenty-five minutes behind traders who spend a fortune for access to the financial heartbeat. That's what I call economic democracy through the microchip!

GUARDING THE FAMILY TREASURE

Were Diogenes with his lantern to look today for an honest man, he might just as well cry out, "Where is a man who cannot be cheated?" His search could screen the victims of investment fraud and uncover very few souls who weren't hooked by their own weakness for easy money. Instead, we can all be aware that most kinds of fraud, and most dangerous investments, can be sniffed out *before* the sting or the fall. All it takes is a little time and trouble, and a willingness to set aside greed just long enough to do a prudent screening job.

Sadly, many of us fail to screen investment offers as carefully as we should and easily could. Just as importantly, just as many of us are scared away from promising and legitimate opportunities by the fear of fraud or fluky management—a tragedy for someone who would like to branch out into some high-yielding investments but chooses not to do so just because of fear and ignorance. *It requires time and effort, but the average investor* can *do an adequate job of investigation.* Those of you who live in fear of being taken to the cleaners through bad investments, please tune in to how you can avoid that, and thereby make what appear to be risky investments much safer and reasonable.

Perhaps some people feel that doing financial homework is too much trouble (they certainly don't feel that way after they have lost some money; a small amount of investigative work would seem a small price to pay to set back the clock on an investment gone sour). More likely, most of us just don't know *how* to go about investigating, and don't know how much research is enough for a given situation. Fortunately, the various governmental and business investigators and officers who work to prevent and uncover fraud are generous with advice we can use to protect ourselves. All we have to do is take note of their know-how and put it to use. That'll make us part of a special minority—those who know how to screen prospective investment opportunities in a prudent, self-protective way, and actually do it.

Back in 1981 the SEC alone claimed to have retrieved just over $30 *billion* in ill-gotten funds, and given inflation you can imagine what that figure must be by now. The shocker was, first, that they estimated that figure to be between 1 and 5 percent of the total amount investors were bilked out of in 1981 just in hokey investment schemes! That doesn't include local scams, such as sales of fake securities, or door-to-door fraud. Second, they really didn't know whether it was 1 percent or 5 percent, so all we know is that investment fraud is a multibillion-dollar segment of the underground economy, and a segment that hurts nearly everyone, from the victims to the taxpayers who have to ante up extra on April 15 to compensate for this parasitic, untaxed business.

PLEASE, USE THE GOVERNMENT YOU PAY FOR

The great thing about the various governmental agencies that investigate fraud is that they encourage people to contact them *with* information and *for* information. For example, employees in several agencies are on the phone all day, five days a week, taking complaints from upward of 25,000 victims per year. Those same agents will get on the phone to advise you how to evaluate investment offerings. The SEC will provide you with literature telling how to identify legal disclosures, how to look up a company's past, how to look up the corporate *officers'* pasts, and generally how to respond to proffered investment opportunities in a prudent manner.

If you live in Washington, D.C., New York, Chicago, or Los Angeles, you can go to the public records room of the commission and look through the cumulative lists of companies and individuals that have been involved in scams in the past. Usually it is a matter of matching the names you are wondering about against the alphabetical listing. If you live in a less central area, you can get a courier service to do this for you. The fee is negotiable, but at this time, $5 is about the beginning base rate for simple lists and $50 for special inquiries. Consider, that is just *1 percent* of a

$5000 investment—a terrifically low fee compared to what it would cost to hire an investigator or consider insurance, which you can't get anyway. Look on it as the world's smartest insurance policy. Courier services can be found advertised in *The Wall Street Journal*, your local paper's business section, and often your banker can recommend one.

But suppose the deal is legitimate—how do you find that out? A federal investigator counsels: "I have yet to see a deal that was so good that there wasn't ample time to review all the details and check into the backgrounds of the promoters. Scams, on the contrary, rely on a fast-moving operation, investors who will hand over money with few questions asked, and sales tactics that combine greed with panic to cloud the victim's judgment." If you've ever been taken, that should ring some bells.

Full disclosure of an investment offering is far more than merely meeting legal requirements. Interstate offerings require a prospectus cleared by the SEC and/or FTC, but such requirements pertain only to full disclosure of specified information, and can still allow the omission of the most basic facts. The actual promotion may differ considerably, and if the intent is to defraud, there is no assurance that the company will work within the guidelines of the prospectus. Frequently they do not. Many fraud operators are repeat offenders, and many continue to operate long after they have been served with cease and desist orders by state or federal courts.

It is basic in any financial commitment to find out who is running the operation and what his or her track record is. If this is his first time promoting this kind of venture, what assurance do you have that he has the wherewithall to carry it off successfully in competition with other experts? Even if he has been involved with the same area of expertise for some time, what is his record of success? There are many promoters who spend other people's money in failure after failure, hoping for the big payoff. Also, how is the staff compensated, especially the key group? If their incomes derive from anything other than the ultimate success of the venture, it's time to ask serious questions about whether the true aim is success or merely a front to use other people's money to live on and work with.

The founder of one of the fabulously popular self-improvement fads in the 1970s allegedly had an earlier career as a con artist in which he was involved in tricking the officers of large corporations into making investments in thinly fabricated schemes totaling millions of dollars. His main weapon, he claimed, was that people are more embarrassed to admit a mistake than they are determined to ensure the safety of their money. He purportedly convinced officers of large companies that their competitors within the firm were rushing to make an investment that would prove extremely fruitful. By the time the various officers met in a formal meeting with him, to merely question the safety of the investment would have been the same as admitting that they had not been careful in the first place (which they hadn't been because they had assumed their rivals had done the usual checking).

The hammer, as you anticipated, fell hard and fast as soon as the corporate check could be translated into liquid banknotes or cash. As the businesses were mostly publicly held or were subsidiaries of larger corporations, the cost of full disclosure of the nature of the loss could have been fatal, and certainly would have been for the officers who were on record in the corporate minutes as having advocated the move. *Pride, greed, rushing, insufficient investigation*: all sins committed by smart, successful businessmen.

Avoiding these operations is difficult for the individual, so if you are not willing to go through the appropriate checking process before you take the plunge, be prepared for the loss or else forego the risk. For our purposes, the question is, how can a person check out the oil and gas leasing plan or solar energy firm advertised in the paper, or the real estate deal or business partnership presented by the fast-talking guy at work? What questions do you ask when somebody who sounds very professional and knowledgeable calls you with a suggestion for a limited partnership and your brother-in-law thinks it's a great idea?

Here are the caveats that police and government investigators repeat again and again, the same precautions they avow are rarely taken by fraud victims. Keep in mind, too, that these precautions aren't just for guarding against crooks, they are useful for checking out schemes that are half-baked or have fatal flaws despite good intentions on everyone's part.

—The bigger the money, the more care you must put into the pre-check examination. Sounds logical, but people are constantly putting their life savings or their $100,000 speculation wad into a deal on the basis of a couple of phone calls or a fancy literature package that makes many unsubstantiated claims. Let's say you earn $100,000 per year. If you put two and a half days of solid investigation into your inspection, then you have put up just 1 percent as insurance against $100,000. Who wouldn't pay 1 percent for a solid recommendation? More vital yet, if you have spent a lifetime saving that $100,000, why not spend the time or even as much as $1000 on a financial investigator to analyze the deal and the people behind it before you commit your precious funds? It sounds expensive going in, especially if that $1000 is more like your monthly salary or take-home, but then you are talking big money here. If you get taken even once, as about thirty thousand American are every year, then in hindsight it will seem the cheapest precaution possible.

—If it's such a terrific deal you are being offered, you have to wonder why some stranger, or at least a not-so-close associate, is offering it to you. Legitimate businesspeople will refer such marvels to their own kin or to business contacts who will be likely to return the favor at a later date. Flip the coin over, however, and it's plain that the ways scams are sold to strangers (who will have a hard time tracking down the perpetrators after the fact) is by making the lure ridiculously appealing—one you can't refuse—not by threatening you, but by pandering to your greed and spicing the deal with panic pressure-tactics. A bewitching recipe.

—If you sense the above and you are being pressured to act right away, it should immediately make you think, "Something must be wrong." If the situation is such that you can't wait or you risk missing out on the chance, then be sure to wait. There will be other opportunities tomorrow. The chance you'll likely miss is that of seeing your money disappear for good. From fake bank-investigator bunko jobs that take a few hundred dollars from a retiree eager to help a bogus policeman to offers to sell the Eiffel Tower for scrap, the hallmark of most scams is that they push the victims into making *hasty, fatal decisions*.

—An early-warning signal in many questionable deals is that they have unusually high advertised yield, but they are being advertised in a newspaper or journal or are being promoted through a telephone sales campaign. If the potential return is great or the tax write-off above average, and the safety factor very good, then there are other, better, easier ways for the organizers of a deal to market their offering. The legitimate offerings in this category are the deals that go to top accountants' preferred customers, to a top banker's favored accounts, to a broker's high-ticket, well-connected clients. If you don't find out about the deal from someone whom you trust implicitly and explicitly, you have a lot of worrying to do before you can be sure, or even vaguely confident, that everything is on the up and up. And you still have the deal itself to check out.

Ever notice how the people who set up honest investments offer to tell you everything about themselves? They want you to meet their banker, reassure yourself through credit references, know the names of their partners, and generally bore you with their wonderful background. It is precisely this information that the fast-buck artist can't afford to let people have. Ergo, the fast sell and a bank reference in some remote location. Bore yourself with the honest types, for tedium is the hallmark of many safety checks when it comes to money management. You'll get plenty of excitement when you begin checking into the background of a dubious organizer. Of course the background of an entrepreneur is no guarantee of his honest handling of your money and the current venture, but it's often the best early clue.

I've mentioned the lists of names available through the SEC regional offices, and that is one good place to start. Your banker can suggest others, as can investigators who specialize in financial affairs, as many do. In any large city there are many private investigators who make their living checking up on individuals and companies for businesses and financiers. If you can't afford their full services, do what businesses do when they have a problem requiring expertise outside their realm—hire a good one as a consultant, perhaps even for a one-time-only interview, and do the legwork yourself.

Along with the scoop on the backgrounds of the organizers, most legitimate business offerings have a slew of informative literature ready for you. If there is something you wish to know as a potential investor, they have every reason to let you know, for it's all a part of the sales effort, and if the setup is legitimate, why not? The only reason *not* to give out with reasonable information is when something is awry—and that is what you are trying to find out anyway. Going through these investigations the first time or two can seem bothersome, but you'll find that the better investment organizers have all the data you want on hand. Checking things out with them is usually just a matter of asking them for the information. When *you* actually end up doing the footwork, you begin to wonder.

Some people are naturally endowed with faultless memories and have a third eye glued to the calendar. For the rest of us, financial planners will usually devise a financial calendar to keep the money-management ball rolling smoothly. It's easy to remember to pay the bills each month, but a checklist of your financial housekeeping chores keeps things up to date, and it lasts an entire year! Especially for those annual checkups on insurance, legal papers, accounts, and investments, waiting until tax time may be a poor idea. First, you may be wrapped up in the tax-preparation ordeal, and secondly, you find there is just too much to do all at once and do well. However you do your scheduling, make sure you have a record of your financial tasks, both the done and the upcoming. Not only will you make each aspect of your financial life run better, but when there is an emergency, you will be confident that your financial situation is up to date, and you will have a record to refer back to.

Only you can tell whether or not your financial habits are working for you now. There are scarce few of us who could not stand improvement in some areas of our personal methods of dealing with money and security. Getting into the habits you would like to acquire won't be effort-free, but if you really want to change your habits, it won't be hard. To begin planning for a lifestyle you would like to become accustomed to requires becoming accustomed to the financial habits that will help put you there and keep you there.

14

Up The Financial Ladder

ESCALATING THE LADDER OF SUCCESS may not be the universal aspiration, but I have yet to meet anyone who was truly willing to turn the experience down, unless there was some moral barrier in the way. In the financial world, success can be attained at many levels, from having enough money to eat every day to walking among the billionaires of the world. But in America there seems to be a pervasive idea that as we go through life we should be on the upward path, building wealth as we go. The problem is that most of us seem to miss the "up" elevator, find the escalator broken down from overloading, and the ladder up leaves room for only a few. We're too often stuck in the midst of a crowd, trying to go up the "down" staircase and being carried away in the tide of change.

I don't claim to have any magic formula for financial success, nor do I know of any map telling how to get to the top story of the financial-structure edifice. But having spoken with hundreds of successful people in all areas of the financial world, I can tell you that patterns of success repeat themselves, over and over again. Corporate presidents, top executives, self-made businesspeople, bankers, all manner of accountants, financial planners, personal business managers, financial writers and researchers—and more: Distill their advice and comments and you'll find some themes unmistakably repeated. They stand out and bear close scrutiny. The strongest and most consistent reflect a consensus of financial wisdom against which we can check our own insights and opinions.

You have already heard my favorite piece of advice from Armand Hammer, "I seem to get very lucky when I work a fourteen-hour day, seven days a week." It seems to be a standard saying that among the "Forbes 400" (the 400 richest working people in the country) that the single shared characteristic is that they are compulsive, unrelenting workaholics. The companies must know how vital this is, because for over twenty years the one requirement that has automatically come with the job of a company boss at any large corporation has been *comprehensive*

285

financial management. The board of directors wants the man or woman who directs the ship to have confidence and success in his or her personal finances so that his or her full energy and attention are focused on the tasks at hand each day. Yet there is something else that the financially successful have, something that I call *relentless ambition.* It's the ability to set a goal and have the willingness to traverse any obstacle standing between now and obtaining that goal.

These obstacles aren't always, or even often, what the average person would expect. Family happiness isn't necessarily an obstacle, but time to spend with the family is a common one. Personal free time is a big one. Time spent in nonproductive tasks is another. Time spent at work seldom is. Time spent sleeping seldom is (although psychologists tell us that active people need less sleep). Time spent learning seldom is.

A definite pattern begins to emerge that identifies the financially successful: They have been able to set personal goals, maintain them, and persist in finding ways to approach those goals until they are reached, at which point they promptly set new ones. Time after time, in success story after success story, the pattern is the same. If an action brings them closer to the goal, it is done and embraced with enthusiasm; if it takes them away from their aim it is rejected or completed as quickly as possible.

Another universal trait in the group is the ability to postpone attainment of the goal. Psychologists have used the ability to tolerate deferred gratification as a measure of maturity in children and adults. Adults, they believe, learn to perform unwanted or immediately unrewarding tasks as long as they have the expectation of a later, adequate reward. Achievers are able to follow goals not just until the Friday paycheck, the end-of-the-month salary, or the year-end bonus, but are able to draw plans, or maps, if you will, that stretch into the distant future of their lives. Plans change and daily events are a surprise, but the path to the goal is always being refined and shortened. In contrast, credit counselors, who work regularly with those who are up to their ears in debt and cannot translate their income into next week's goals, much less a life plan, point out that a lack of planning and an unwillingness to adhere to a rational plan are the combination of characteristics that virtually all of *their* clients share. These are also the habits which persons who are able to climb out of their financial difficulties are able to leave behind and rise above.

So, the boards of directors of major corporations, famed career counselors, the body politic of psychology, and the most respected credit counselors all identify the same set of personality traits among financial achievers. The question is not whether a person ought to try to emulate the traits, but rather, can he or she change to adopt them, and if so, how? If you get a sure insight into the "how," please let me know. In the meantime I am hard at work believing in the "whether," and trying my damndest to hurry up the "when." I hope you are too.

Corporations and psychologists have for years been trying to figure out what differentiates the successful manager and career climber from the stymied or dead-end employee. The confirmed answers have been few and far between, but they all agree that a major part of the more successful people's time is spent learning in one way or another. Not just on-the-job experience, but daily and persistent inquiry with a passion. How much time? Many of them say 20 to 30 percent of their time. Twenty to 30 percent! *Fortune* magazine conducted a survey that suggested these are bare minimums for successful managers in high-earning positions, for successful small businessmen and moneymaking entrepreneurs.

If you examine other things about these people, you find that the education priority makes a lot of sense. For example, successful men and women report that they put in a much longer than average workday. At the upper levels of management, twelve- and fourteen-hour days are considered normal fare, and there is no overtime at that level, either. It is considered a necessary part of success in management to work overtime, to take work home, to try to excel beyond the parameters of the job itself. If these behaviors are the norm, then working an eight-hour day and minimizing education must be handicaps. It seems that they are from a purely earnings point of view.

SAMPLE TEST—EMULATE THE BEST

Imagine if we superimposed the values of a successful manager on an average worker, let's say a line operator in an auto-assembly plant. We'll assume he works a forty-hour week. As a goal-oriented person, he has his sights set on a job with much higher salary, and he realized that he must work successfully at his present job to support his family and provide a background for advancement. Because he sees his work as valuable in a different sense, when the five o'clock whistle blows, he is glad, naturally, but unhurried. His priorities make him anxious to be sure that before he leaves, all the details of his job, especially those visible to his superiors, are completed or ready for the next day. He makes sure that others recognize he is putting the job ahead of his personal time—within reason.

If he is to emulate the manager, he will be spending from 20 to 30 percent of his time in reading and education. Since he is going to be "working" a twelve-hour day instead of an eight-hour one, this fits neatly into that extra-time space. Let's say he adds the 30 percent reading about his work and educating himself on how to advance and excel at the job. That comes to eighteen hours per week, or a little under three and one half hours per day. Over the span of a year that is 840 hours of study! Of course this time could be dedicated to other learning methods, such as night school, college, or other training.

At the average college twelve hours per week constitutes better than three average courses. What would an assembly worker with five years of such training be ready for, assuming the training was well planned and truly job oriented? Certainly a better-paying job, certainly a more demanding job, certainly *more income*. But wait—remember we said that the worker was going to emulate the manager who works at least twelve hours per day. We have an eight-hour workday, perhaps an extra half-hour at the end of the shift making sure the job is finished in a visibly superior way, and two and one half hours of study. That still leaves an hour to devote to the job and/or career. But what to do with it?

For possibilities, we can look back at the observations of the career counselors and personnel managers at some of the larger corporations, such as General Telephone, Sun Oil, Exxon, Northwest Mutual Life, and others. They report that people who are successful in a company *as well as in the function of their job* spend a significant part of their time socializing with their peers at work and with their superiors. They are not talking about having a beer or a martini after work, though that may be involved some of the time. They are talking about learning the values and priorities that make possible the step up to the next rung on the ladder. They are listening to the people who are also on the way up or are a help in that direction, and are assimilating the skills that make it possible— such as how one gets advanced at the particular company in the real world, not just the official channels. They are making allies so that when they have a dispute or there is doubt about something, they have supporters who will stand behind them and exchange political support at the job level.

In management they call these cliques the "old-boys network," the "newcomers club," and other names that acknowledge the fact that the employees are not socializing simply to massage their egos or soothe their lonely hearts, but to enlarge the foundation that will support their rise through the ranks. It's making friends in the right places and doing it the right way, and it's different from the "ass-kissing" which is universally despised. Unfortunately, there's no formula for where to draw the line in these social situations; you always have to play it by ear. Many people tend to look down on the practice and have derogatory names for it, but those who eschew it are beaten by it. It's not a terrible thing, it's just a fact of life.

Well, there's no guarantee that an auto worker is going to become plant manager by devoting this much time and effort to building a career, but I would be very surprised if he or she didn't end up with a much better paying job and a career that moves up instead of sideways through life. But I don't advocate the idea to anyone except those to whom it has appeal. The career counselors point out that it takes a very motivated person to live that way and be happy. But it occurs to me that there are surely many people who have never realized that it is in such ways that many financially successful men and women have attained goals, and that it is by this kind of outlook and approach that one moves from one financial stratum to another. It also seems to me to be an attractive alternative to the nearly three hours of television that the average American adult indulges in each day, presumably at night.

At many large corporations it is an assigned responsibility of personnel managers and other supervisors to direct employees to job training and educational assistance. No matter where you work, it cannot hurt to ask around for such help. Even if there is no formal program, you will find more usable advice from those who have made the move you are planning. To recoin the old phrase, "It can't hurt to ask."

Some of the consultants who find the talent to fill the top jobs at large corporations—headhunters at the upper-income levels—have interesting insights into what makes a man or woman a candidate for jobs that pay from five up to seven figures: It is vital that a top person be *perceived* as actually *being* a performer. Some of the top executives actually hire consultants who "groom" them to have the appearance that will affect the right people. And I'm not talking only about the "dress for success" fad. It is also promoting the name and image through various communication networks, depending upon the level being addressed.

In other words, if they don't know you are a great performer, they can't reward you for it. The corporate personnel managers also note that there is a rise in the use of awards ceremonies, employee prizes for production, and other means of publicly recognizing behavior that benefits the company and encourages similar behavior on the part of other workers. Visibility of performance is valued by the top management as well as by the individuals. Two industries that have risen steadily through the last twenty-five years, even when the economy has been sluggish, are the sales-incentives business and the performance-premium business. Both the multibillion-dollar industries whose sole function is to help management reward workers with the idea of promoting more and better production.

A secretary produces more reports and receives a nice gift, say a watch or a small appliance. A salesman sells an extra quota of televisions and wins a trip for two to Hawaii. (Since 1980, these kinds of trips have made up over a billion dollars annually of air travel.) It proves that recognition is a two-way street, that it is vitally important, and that it is worth working for. It may not be attainable for you today, but at least it is there for you to pick up on whenever you choose.

The popular perception of career climbing used to be Horatio Alger stories, in which a young man of mysterious qualities overcomes long odds to succeed. Lately it has also spawned a growing consulting industry. The higher you go in business, the more often you will find the successful people utilizing professional job finders with proven track records. Career counselors are often more than just social psychologists ready to spout textbook wisdom. The better ones also have heavy experience in personnel management and can give the individual client a job-market overview that would be almost impossible to develop alone. They can quickly assemble statistics and social and psychological studies that show how, when, and where work is available, how people move from one specific job to another, which skills are needed for which kind of work, and so on. They provide individual counseling to advise how personal behavior can be a roadblock or a help in getting a job or in advancement, and may be able to advise what education, training, and social graces are needed to get to the next plateau on your personal mountain.

Shopping for a career-guidance counselor can be difficult, because there are not many to be found and it is difficult for the average person to discern which are the best and most appropriate ones for them. Shop for them as you would for any professional—through referrals, professional organizations, and by conducting interviews and background checks. For many, it can be the investment of a lifetime. There are counseling agencies for every economic level, from minimum-wage specialists who work for government social agencies or nonprofit groups to executive-grooming counselors who may charge a portion of salaries high enough to generate five-figure fees. Again, in most cases, the expense can be tax-deductible as a legitimate part of job search and professional education.

I do not mean to suggest that long hours and hard work are the only paths to success, for many people devote their lives to both and live in disappointing, if not destitute, conditions. What I want to point out is that there are sound reasons behind the common advice that experts give to those who aspire to success in whatever they are doing. So many people are like TV's Charlie the Tuna—always trying to exude the quality that doesn't count. Half the battle is finding out which quality does count.

THE MONEY MENTALITY

Having a well-paying job and increasing your takehome pay, we know, are not the only paths to riches. We'll always wonder about the janitor who died earning his lifetime top salary of $15,000, and whose will donated over $1,000,000 to charity. It turns out that he was adept in the stock market. I suppose he liked his job. . . .

Whatever his personal foibles, he must have had good "money sense," for he saved all that money in the days before the magic of tax-free accounts for the small saver. His money mentality was keen enough to keep him on the winning side when we know that over time, most investors, especially small investors, end up in the losing side except during bull markets.

How do people develop a smart money mentality? That is the question. I've asked dozens, maybe hundreds, of financial people and almost all the answers I received were vague or differed in the extreme. But I did get a good deal of hedging and detouring which repeated itself over and over. Apparently these brokers and bankers and counselors, consultants and agents, recognized some patterns we should all be aware of.

Starting with the brokers, all experts in securities trading agreed that smart traders always go into an investment with *a plan of action laid out*. It may be scored on paper or in their heads, but it is well defined and specific. For instance, when a stock is bought, there is a plan to sell it or otherwise deal with it if the price drops to a certain level or if it rises to a certain level. There is a method, not a madness, to their actions. As a result, even when circumstances wreak changes which in turn cause them to alter their plans, they at least have a structure to work from and an analytical framework in which to solve their problems. Their decisions are better and more productive, so are their investments, and so are their returns.

In addition to planning investments more carefully before plunking down their money, these types impress the brokers another way—they seem to be well informed and to have a solid understanding of where their knowledge stops. In other words, knowing the technical reasons for buying or selling a security is not good enough—these people either have to feel savvy or they minimize their risk. This is different from being a "non-risk-taker," for that is a person who shuns reasonable risk, even when he recognizes it. A winning risk-taker not only recognizes the size of the risk, but is realistic about his or her abilities to judge what is going on. Gamblers often call these people the "numbers players"; they play the game with their minds, not their hearts. Any broker will tell you that most small investors lose money by selling and buying on emotion rather than with analysis and evidence.

Managing money is often referred to as an art, but the more I find out about it, the more it seems to me to be a science, too, or at least a discipline. There is a certain amount of guessing and intuition—that is true—but there is much more problem solving, number crunching, and statistical figuring that most neophytes realize. The math that a real estate agent should have in order to calculate interest, payment schedules, credit, multiple financing, and whatever else they come up with is quite imposing, and the same can be said for all the other financial specialists. The quality agent may not be able to guess the real estate market six months from now, but he or she can tell you whether you have a good buy or not. The numbers, familiarity with the prices in various areas, and a knowledge of financing procedures and prevailing rates give him that knowledge. It is fact rather than intuition that makes his decisions and recommendations worthwhile, and so it is with individual finance.

What many math-shy people don't realize is that you don't actually have to do many calculations, for the information services and references do that for you. The newspaper not only reports the price of an investment, but also the effective yield; the banks report their investment payments in APR (annual percentage rate); and for complicated mathematics, pick up a book of interest-rate tables and simplified calculations. In other words, you can get all that techincal knowledge without the bother and pain of most of the figuring.

I once interviewed an international banker who conducts billions of dollars in exchanges aboard his fifty-foot sailing cutter, which is also his home. I expressed amazement at the surroundings and the very idea that corporate treasurers, banking consultants, State Department and other federal officers, and representatives of foreign governments should agree to negotiate on a rolling platform at the end of a pier. "Nonsense!" he laughed. "Banking is a matter of judgments and reality. If I have the connections while the banker downtown surrounded by oak and leather panels behind brick and marble walls does not, I will get the business, and therefore I do. Money does not see the trappings, only men do, and only men can be deceived." Not breathtaking wisdom, but we often forget we are dealing with human beings.

It is easy to see a bank or a company as a financial edifice, a structure which embodies the power to deal with us, but except in the case of computerized communication, that is almost never so. People make the decisions that affect us, and even when we are stymied by faulty computers, inflexible policies, inept employees or irascible officials, the solution to our problem lies on the other side of a personal contact. Our task is to identify the person and find the key to unlocking his or her understanding and willingness to help, and generating some action in our behalf. In such ways bank loans and all other business and financial deals are made easier and better.

To find out whether or not you meet the criteria for being an accepted or even preferred customer, or if you plan to mold your presentation in the best possible light, you can usually get the breakdowns merely by asking. Ask the new-accounts officer at the bank what factors make a person a preferred account. Are there other ways to fit into that category? If the answer is difficult to understand, you may have to take the initiative yourself by asking leading questions such as: Would it help if I have a relative who is also a preferred customer? Can the branch manager make discretionary exceptions if he or she chooses? Could a letter of referral from a previously used bank or other contact help?

You must feel around for the combination that works with the people and institution you are confronted with. Too, you must rely on your instincts about what to investigate.

The same principles hold true for brokerage accounts, loan applications, or any other financial dealings. You simply cannot afford to assume that filling out the forms you are handed will give you the best possible introduction, or even that there is only one acceptable way to fill in the blanks. You must be flexible and look for flexibility when it will do you good. Do not mistake this for dishonesty, for there is nothing immoral about presenting your best side as long as you do not hide anything that is legally required.

Financial officers in business make their living by knowing how to approach bankers, financiers, and others. The financial-service person who is used to being taken out to lunch or invited to posh offices for other discussions is likely to be understanding when an individual shows an interest in presenting his or her best financial portrait. In all likelihood it will be taken as an indication of your earnestness, determination, and willingness to conform to the rules of the money game.

I think it would be a great help for most of us if all computer communications had written or spoken at the end, "This was devised by an intelligent person with sincere intentions. Please understand if there has been an error or oversight." Until they install such a standing notice, it remains incumbent upon us to remember it for ourselves. Meanwhile, it is enlightening to know some of the things that make a bank consider a person a preferred customer, beyond a magnificent bankroll.

The manager at our local bank laid it out perfectly one day, almost as if by accident. She was trying to explain why the bank offered services to some customers and not others and said, "It is not just the size of your current accounts, but also the history of your average deposits, whether they have risen or fallen, what kind of business we have done with you in the past, your credit history and our internal reports on you and, well, it's all according to our perception of you." Ah yes, the perception by the bank officers of the customer. There is a way to form those images besides banking large sums, and it is to act in ways the bank considers responsible and which also suggest you will be a loyal customer and one who uses the services (read that "renders income") at the bank. If perceptions lead to better service and access to more help, then courting the bank can be a financial decision. When you have behavior to trade, but not much money, that may be a good concept to keep in mind.

No matter where you are, gathering the financial acumen to improve your finances can be done. The high school graduate can learn to balance checkbooks, bank statements, and calculate a household budget. Beginning families and career climbers can budget growing expenses, credit, and long-term debt. Mature family heads can squeeze budgets to fit hard times, reset their financial goals, establish workable investment plans, and evaluate investments to meet the goals of that plan. Older Americans can get down to the nitty gritty of welding together a retirement plan that works and developing a financial-care system that will maximize their enjoyment of life. And they don't have to be extra smart or spend all their time analyzing numbers. They just have to devote the required time and effort. If old dogs can't, old people certainly *can* learn new tricks—they do every day. If they can, you and I can, and that is worth knowing.

The ultimate solution to money-management problems is to hire it done, and that is a tactic more and more people are choosing. In this age of incredible sophistication among consumers, each of us has to compete against fellow citizens who know more and more about finances with each passing year. Hiring the expertise can be a shortcut to educating ourselves, for we have the subjects spoon-fed to us by the knowledgeable adviser and thus our need for general knowledge is reduced. But this can be taken too far, for it gives you a spotty knowledge of very complicated situations and probably does not give you the really valuable insight that comes from having an overview of the alternatives in a given subject. But that is a matter of personal preference.

"FINANCE-A-PHOBIA"

I believe that our society has encouraged a kind of phobia about finances which many people accept as their own, and the comments I hear from financial planners, credit counselors, and others who daily deal with the general public on personal-finance problems seem to corroborate this. The institutions work to foster this in many ways. For example, it was not until the Morris Plan in the first decade of this century that workaday people were considered eligible for bank loans. A businessman or a landed farmer was considered a worthy investment and a potential source of revenue, but the average salaried fellow was thought to be too ignorant and irresponsible to depend upon. Lenders figured a home improvement loan would end up as a liability as the borrower repeatedly failed to manage his monthly income well enough to regularly pay off the debt. It's rather along the same line as the widespread reluctance to become proficient at mathematics. About two-thirds of us report that attitude (I've long been one of that coterie), but psychologists and educators insist that for 95 percent of us there is no basis in fact for our feelings. If we are taught to feel good about our abilities with numbers as children and students, they tell us, we will grow up to be comfortable with and good at math all of our lives. But most of us don't, and I suspect there is a similar phobia going around relating to financial affairs.

As evidence, I cite the case of two dear friends who are both practicing physicists. They gaily toss around equations as long as your arm as if they were the ABCs. Yet, as they bemoan, they lack the same firm grasp of their finances, and when it comes to investing or handling debt, they feel unsure. Frankly, it boggles my mind, for I have always seen my clumsiness with numbers as a major stumblingblock to evaluating investment options, and here these two geniuses have this wonderful knowledge and capability at their fingertips and it is not enough. Most people have similar contradictions going in their own lives.

"Learning to invest" is one of the most voodoo-laden concepts to come along. Last year there were over a hundred books published purporting to assist the reader in becoming better if not expert at investing, and I have seen tomes that date back to the 1920s in our neighborhood library. Advisory newsletters are the latest fad shortcut to investing wisdom, but the financial analysts say that selecting a service that pays off can be as hard if not harder than choosing investments themselves. What is it aobut the winners in the stock market, in real estate, in debt securities, that makes them consistent winners? Certainly if I could pin it down, distill it and bottle it, *I'd* be a big success myself. But seriously, winning investors appear to have a few characteristics the brokers, agents, and bankers who deal with them seem to be able to identify.

First, everyone I've ever talked to agrees that winners are *knowledgeable* where it counts. A winner on the stock market isn't necessarily a whiz at understanding every element of the market, but he is very well versed in the elements that affect his particular investment strategy and purchase, sale, or trade decisions. His information and analysis make his decisions better than those of most other investors, and because of that, he wins more often. No big revelation, but it may be enough to give a beginning investor, or a losing investor, pause.

The second quality the experts mention most is *flexibility*. In this age when future shock just about gives way to *now* shock, being flexible goes hand in hand with being knowledgeable. In the 1960s, long-term investments in the bond market were classified as those being thirty and forty years in maturity. By the mid '70s, twenty-year bonds were regularly being called "long term," and were being treated and traded as such. Today, many veteran bond traders are calling anything over *ten* years a long-term instrument. They anticipate that fluctuations in the economy will make bonds with that maturity seem like stable reference points, and when they diversify their portfolios, some of them are using the ten-year bonds as their long-term hedge. In Argentina during the last decade, a one-year loan or debt instrument has been considered long term because of the rampant inflation and instability of the currency and banking structure. To be inflexible in Argentina is to be broke, and to be inflexible in the competitive world of investments is to lose out in the long haul. As the pace of change hastens, too, the ability to adapt to investment opportunities quickly is becoming more a standard operating fare. The investment strategy that works brilliantly this year may be as dated as the advice of the dying millionaire in 1910: "Never sell the stock in the buggywhip factory; people will always need horses to get where they're going."

The following idea has been thrown at me so many times by so many people in the financial world that it can't be ignored. They always talk about people with a *winning attitude*. I suppose it relates to the old salesman's pep-talk saw, which goes: *If you want to double your success rate, then be willing to fail four times as much as you do now*. It's a famous line used by a lot of people. It goes well with, *If you want to succeed, don't just give it a try, set it up that way and carry it through*.

I think that is a good message on which to end a book about personal finance. I hope you will find the time and enthusiasm it takes to set up your own success, that you'll build up your personal-finance reference library, your assemblage of experts, counselors and advisers, and that you'll carry through to reach your own personal financial goals. The many people I have spoken to in the world of finance (some of whose opinions I have shared with you) have constantly impressed me with their enthusiasm for playing the money game, their willingness to share their insights, and their nearly universal confidence that anyone who really wants to *can* take his or her financial future by the horns and wrest it in the direction they choose.

Someday we may find ourselves presented with just what we all need—a personal-finance encyclopedia that is continually updated. My personal fantasy is a financial Rumplestiltskin who spins golden words of investment advice from the straw chaff of the financial press and delivers the magic wisdom just before the nation's trading exchanges open. Above all, however, I hope that I have encouraged you to pursue your goals through financial management and perhaps shared with you the idea that all of us can, if we try, make a better world for ourselves. I'm betting on it.

Appendix
Calculating Interest

THE RULE OF 72

THE RULE OF 72 is a mathematical coincidence that gives us a handy rule of thumb. Simply divide the annual interest rate into 72. The answer is very close to the number of years it will take your money to double (if you are receiving interest) or for it to lose half its value (when you are figuring the ravages of inflation or when you are paying interest).

$$\frac{72}{\text{interest rate}} = \text{no. of years it will take money to double or to lose half its value}$$

(or inflation rate)

Example:

$$\frac{72}{5 \text{ percent}} = 5\overline{)72}^{\,14\frac{1}{2}}$$

years for money to double in 5 percent bank account, or 14½ years for inflation to cut the buying power of your money in half

THE RULE OF 78'S

It so happens that if you add the numbers of the months in the year (12 + 11 + 10 . . . 3 + 2 + 1) the sum equals 78. Thus, the number 78 represents the number of "pieces" involved in calculating interest in an annually amortized loan. The numbers of the months (for one year—start with 12, remember) added together, divided by 78 = the multiplier. Multiply it times the amount of the total interest charge of the loan and you have the amount of interest still charged.

297

What good is it? For one, you can figure your tax-deduction allowance. For another, if you are able to retire the loan ahead of schedule, it gives you the amount of interest rebate you are entitled to, disregarding any penalties. For loans longer than one year, multiply the number of years (1.5 = 18 months, 5= 60 months, etc.) times 78 to get the multiplier. Each month is numbered consecutively through the term of the loan (the last month of a three-year loan is month number 36, etc.) This is most easily done with a calculator that will repeat functions or with a computer that will accept the entire equation, but it is a shortcut even when done on paper.

INTEREST-RATE FORMULAE

It is possible to figure interest rates through mathematical calculations, but is usually not worth the effort. The labor-saving alternative is to invest $5 in an interest-rate book, available at most bookstores and business supply stores. They come in specialty versions, such as for real estate, add-on interest only, or in generalized versions.

The figures are given in tables so that you need only find the correct table and multiply the entries in the tables times the amount of your monies. The good ones even have the actual calculations either in an appendix or accompanying each table. This way you can use the calculation to program your calculator or computer and have it give you answers almost as easily as would the book. Make it a part of your personal finance library. Computer owners can simply buy programs that will do the math for them. If you only need a few interest calculations, you can get some tables through banks and finance companies, and of course you can always borrow a financial-calculations book at the library.

EFFECTS OF ANNUAL COMPOUND INTEREST
Multiply by number of dollars to find your total

RATE

YEARS	5%	6%	7%	8%	9%	10%	11%	12%	13%	14%
1	1.05	1.06	1.07	1.08	1.09	1.10	1.11	1.12	1.13	1.14
2	1.10	1.12	1.14	1.17	1.19	1.21	1.23	1.25	1.28	1.30
3	1.16	1.19	1.23	1.26	1.30	1.33	1.37	1.40	1.44	1.48
4	1.22	1.26	1.31	1.36	1.41	1.46	1.52	1.57	1.63	1.69
5	1.28	1.34	1.40	1.47	1.54	1.61	1.69	1.76	1.84	1.93
6	1.34	1.42	1.50	1.59	1.68	1.77	1.87	1.97	2.08	2.19
7	1.41	1.50	1.61	1.71	1.83	1.95	2.08	2.21	2.35	2.50
8	1.48	1.59	1.72	1.85	1.99	2.14	2.30	2.48	2.66	2.85
9	1.55	1.69	1.84	2.00	2.17	2.36	2.56	2.77	3.00	3.25
10	1.63	1.79	1.97	2.16	2.37	2.59	2.84	3.11	3.39	3.71
11	1.71	1.90	2.10	2.33	2.58	2.85	3.15	3.48	3.84	4.23
12	1.80	2.01	2.25	2.52	2.81	3.14	3.50	3.90	4.33	4.82
13	1.89	2.13	2.41	2.72	3.07	3.45	3.88	4.36	4.90	5.49
14	1.98	2.26	2.58	2.94	3.34	3.80	4.31	4.89	5.53	6.26
15	2.08	2.40	2.76	3.17	3.64	4.18	4.78	5.47	6.25	7.14
16	2.18	2.54	2.95	3.43	3.97	4.59	5.31	6.13	7.07	8.14
17	2.29	2.69	3.16	3.70	4.33	5.05	5.90	6.87	7.99	9.28
18	2.41	2.85	3.38	4.00	4.72	5.56	6.54	7.69	9.02	10.58
19	2.53	3.03	3.62	4.32	5.14	6.12	7.26	8.61	10.20	12.06
20	2.65	3.21	3.87	4.66	5.60	6.73	8.06	9.65	11.52	13.74

SHORTCUTS TO COMPUTING INTEREST

interest rate	Multiply the principal by the number of days and divide by this number:
2%	180
4%	90
5%	72
6%	60
7%	52
8%	45
9%	40
10%	36
12%	30
15%	24
18%	20
20%	18

Index